UNCLE

RACE, NOSTALGIA, *and the* POLITICS OF LOYALTY

CHERYL THOMPSON

COACH HOUSE BOOKS, TORONTO

Canada Council   Conseil des Arts
for the Arts   du Canada

 ONTARIO ARTS COUNCIL
CONSEIL DES ARTS DE L'ONTARIO
an Ontario government agency
un organisme du gouvernement de l'Ontario

Canadä

Published with the generous assistance of the Canada Council for the Arts and
the Ontario Arts Council. Coach House Books also acknowledges the support of
the Government of Canada through the Canada Book Fund and the Government
of Ontario through the Ontario Book Publishing Tax Credit.

LIBRARY AND ARCHIVES CANADA CATALOGUING IN PUBLICATION

Title: Uncle : race, nostalgia, and the politics of loyalty / by Cheryl Thompson.
Names: Thompson, Cheryl, 1977- author.
Identifiers: Canadiana (print) 20200155393 | Canadiana (ebook) 20200155407 |
ISBN 9781552454107 (softcover) | ISBN 9781770566316 (EPUB) | ISBN 9781770566408
(PDF)
Subjects: LCSH: Uncle Tom (Fictitious character) | LCSH: Stowe, Harriet Beecher,
1811-1896. *Uncle Tom's Cabin.* | LCSH: African Americans in popular culture. | LCSH:
African Americans in mass media. | LCSH: African Americans—Social conditions.
| LCSH: Stereotypes (Social psychology)
Classification: LCC PS2954.U6 T46 2021 | DDC 813/.3—dc23

Uncle: Race, Nostalgia, and the Politics of Loyalty is available as an ebook: ISBN 978 1
77056 631 6 (EPUB), ISBN 978 1 77056 640 8 (PDF)

Purchase of the print version of this book entitles you to a free digital copy. To
claim your ebook of this title, please email sales@chbooks.com with proof of
purchase. (Coach House Books reserves the right to terminate the free digital
download offer at any time.)

TABLE OF CONTENTS

INTRODUCTION

I love old movies and I love watching Turner Classic Movies in particular. One Saturday evening a few years ago, I stumbled upon *The Great White Hope*. Released in 1970, it stars James Earl Jones as boxer 'Jack Jefferson.' The film is a biopic based on the life of boxer Jack Johnson (1878–1946), who, at the height of the Jim Crow era, became the first African American world heavyweight champion; he held the title from 1908 to 1915. I have been a huge boxing fan since I was a little kid. I first discovered Johnson when I was a teenager, but learned more about his life only when I was teaching a Black Studies course at the University of Toronto. I devoted an entire lecture to the history of Black people in sports. Johnson was truly the first African American sports hero. Yet he was also a controversial figure because he crossed racial and class lines in both his professional and personal life, even marrying a white woman, Etta Terry Duryea (played in the film by Jane Alexander), at a time when interracial relations were not only frowned upon but could result in death by lynching.

At one point in the film, Jefferson is in Budapest shortly before the start of World War I, but not to box. Instead, he is there to take the stage in a cabaret performance of *Uncle Tom's Cabin*. It was an unexpected reference in a film about a boxer, and one I knew something about. Because I have been obsessed with *Uncle Tom's Cabin* ever since I started studying the phenomenon of the nineteenth-century novel and its subsequent spinoffs. When several characters from *Uncle Tom's Cabin* appeared as part of the film's storyline, I had an 'aha' moment.

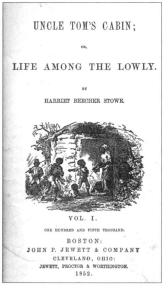

UNCLE TOM'S CABIN;

OR,

LIFE AMONG THE LOWLY.

BY

HARRIET BEECHER STOWE.

VOL. I.

ONE HUNDRED AND FIFTH THOUSAND.

BOSTON:
JOHN P. JEWETT & COMPANY
CLEVELAND, OHIO:
JEWETT, PROCTOR & WORTHINGTON.
1852.

Title-page illustration by Hammatt Billings for Uncle Tom's Cabin *[First Edition: Boston: John P. Jewett and Company, 1852].*

My fascination with the novel, first published in 1852 by Harriet Beecher Stowe, began in my twenties, when I read the book for the first time. I was working then as an insurance claims adjuster, living in a suburb northwest of Toronto. I had heard about the book since I was a little kid. But after someone I knew was called an 'Uncle Tom,' I decided I needed to know where this term came from. Out of sheer curiosity, I began reading the 391-page novel on the commuter train into the city. It took me almost a year to get through it, because nineteenth-century novels are pretty dense. But after I finished, I felt like I had just hit the tip of the iceberg in terms of understanding why, of all the character names in fiction, Uncle Tom's has lingered on in popular culture and politics.

Uncle Tom's Cabin interweaves three narratives. The first is the story of Eliza, an enslaved woman who becomes a fugitive when she flees with her young son over ice floes on the Ohio River to Cincinnati. With the help of Northerners, and in defiance of the 1850 Fugitive Slave Act – a federal law that mandated the capture and return of African Americans into slavery, whether they were enslaved or free – Eliza heads to Canada to reunite with her husband, George, who had run away earlier, refusing to endure his master's cruelty any longer.

The other two storylines involve Uncle Tom and Little Eva. Tom, whom Stowe depicted as a dignified Christian man in his thirties or forties, is born a slave on a Kentucky plantation owned by Mr. Shelby. After falling into financial trouble, Shelby is forced to sell two of his slaves, one of whom is Tom. Even though Tom has a wife and children, he is sold to a slave dealer named Mr. Haley, who takes him to New Orleans. While being transported by boat to the plantation, Tom rescues another passenger, Little Eva St. Clare, a six-year-old who has fallen into the river. Her grateful father, Augustine St. Clare, agrees to purchase Tom at auction.

Once on St. Clare's plantation, Tom and Eva become friends. Tom takes on the role of Eva's surrogate father, but also her plaything. He comforts and consoles Little Eva but does not scold or discipline her. In the early illustrated editions of the novel, Tom and Eva are depicted sitting together in an arbour on the plantation, reading the Bible. In other images, Eva sits on Tom's lap and helps him get dressed.

Eva is a sickly child. She falls ill and, on her deathbed, asks her father to free all his slaves, especially Tom – who is depicted in illustrations as a dutiful friend at Eva's deathbed.

Topsy, the young, enslaved girl in the novel, is a dehumanized depiction of Black girlhood. She is the extreme opposite of Little Eva, the novel's child-angel. Topsy has unkempt hair, she lies, and is frequently in need of discipline. The juxtaposition between Topsy and Little Eva sets the stage for two racial stereotypes that still linger today around white childhood innocence and the far less innocent depictions of Black childhood.

While St. Clare is preparing to free his slaves, he is unexpectedly killed in a fight. Simon Legree, who owns a plantation in a remote area of Louisiana, purchases Tom and St. Clare's other slaves from the estate. Legree is a brutal figure. He beats Tom for refusing to abuse the other enslaved men and women. Finally, Legree whips Tom to death after he refuses to reveal the whereabouts of others who have run away. Uncle Tom is the novel's heroic figure because he chooses not to escape. Instead, he accepts his suffering and becomes Stowe's martyr – a simple, God-fearing Christian whose strong faith does not allow him the apparently selfish luxury of escape. Tom ultimately becomes a symbol for a pious Black masculinity that is non-violent, loyal, and even accepting of the status quo for enslaved people.

Stowe's story profoundly influenced public attitudes about slave-holding and the Fugitive Slave Act, as well as the events leading up to the Civil War. President Abraham Lincoln is reported to have said that Stowe and her book helped precipitate the Civil War. Early readers could not have known that *Uncle Tom's Cabin* was not merely a piece of abolitionist fiction penned by a writer fervently convinced that slavery was patently immoral. Rather, its publication marked the beginning of a cultural, commercial, ideological, and theatrical phenomenon that would endure for generations.

Harriet Beecher Stowe. From the original painting by Alonzo Chappel (c. 1872).

❦

During my first reading of *Uncle Tom's Cabin*, J. K. Rowling's *Harry Potter and the Philosopher's Stone* was released. I had not (and still have not) read her novels or seen any of the films. But I started to see parallels between the early-twenty-first-century frenzy around Rowling's Harry and our long-standing obsession with Stowe's Uncle Tom.

In some ways, Uncle Tom, as a publishing phenomenon, is the nineteenth-century version of *Harry Potter*. After *Uncle Tom's Cabin* was released as a novel, Stowe's original publisher, John Jewett, sold merchandise, such as mementos, card games and puzzles, porcelain figures, needlework, and items of clothing. These items became cross-marketing tie-ins with the novel (though they would not have been called that at the time). Similarly, there have been countless product tie-ins with *Harry Potter* that extend the story well beyond the printed page. There has never been a time when *Uncle Tom's Cabin* has existed only as a novel. Like *Harry Potter*, its multiple and associated images have always coexisted with the book. Rowling, however, managed to achieve what Stowe, given her era, never had the opportunity to do: she became a media mogul, not just a literary icon. Stowe herself is less remembered than her novel, even though she went on to become an editor and a suffragist, in addition to her abolitionist work. *Uncle Tom's Cabin* was a phenomenon bigger than its author. In some ways, it is more synonymous with abolitionism today than actual abolitionists are!

I am most interested in the period after the novel's initial success, when Uncle Tom, as a literary character, morphs into a theatrical Uncle Tom, and then an advertising Tom, followed by a Hollywood Tom. Eventually, he mutates into a racial insult. While some people know that Uncle Tom derives from Stowe's novel, few understand why calling a Black man 'an Uncle Tom' is to accuse him of selling out. In colloquial terms, he is a brotha who just does not act 'Black.' This sense of not 'acting Black' usually means the man who is the target of the insult speaks standard English, identifies as a conservative, dates only white women, and seems to have a hyper-affinity with white culture. In a contemporary sense, an 'Uncle Tom' might listen to country or rock music, wear khakis, and be politically conservative. After reading *Uncle Tom's Cabin*, I needed to connect the dots between the martyr in the novel and the epithet hurled at Black conservatives today.

As I watched *The Great White Hope*, the boxer biopic, the echoes of Stowe's novel were immediately evident. In the film, the character Jefferson appears onstage playing Uncle Tom alongside Eleanor, a white woman who is Jefferson's love interest, and cast in the role of Little Eva. Eventually, they are joined by an African American actor performing the role of Topsy. In front of a Hungarian audience, Jefferson portrays an aged Uncle Tom with grey hair, while Eleanor's Eva mirrors the novel's depiction of a white child with blond hair in ringlets. Topsy is depicted as a motherless 'pickaninny' – a stereotype of an illiterate, derelict, and deprived Black child. The film shows Uncle Tom and Little Eva sitting together under a tree. Eva gazes at the beautiful sky, while Tom professes his wonder at Eva's beauty. Tom seems upset, so Eva asks him what's wrong. 'You and the massa so good to old Tom,' he replies. 'He just got to cry about it now and then.' This scene is strikingly nuanced for a biopic about a boxer. Here is a loosely fictionalized athlete in a Hollywood film playing an actual fictionalized character from a nineteenth-century novel appearing onstage in early-twentieth-century Hungary. I was struck by the serendipity of stumbling upon this reworking of *Uncle Tom's Cabin* depicting both the nineteenth and twentieth centuries while in the midst of writing a book about Uncle Tom's legacy in the twenty-first century.

In this book, I refer to three Toms: Stowe's Uncle Tom, the theatrical version of Uncle Tom, and Uncle Tom as a servile trope and racial epithet denoting Black men who sell out. My aim is to explore Uncle Tom as a literary character, a 'real person,' a theatrical character, and, eventually, as an insult. What are the associations between Uncle Tom's literary, visual, theatrical, and cultural incarnations? How can we understand the life, death, and rebirth of Uncle Tom as produced and reproduced through the novel, minstrel shows, memorabilia, and public performances? Uncle Tom lives on, but he is not the same Uncle Tom created by Stowe, and his name is used pejoratively. At what point did Uncle Tom, the character, change into *Uncle Tom*, the caricature? The origins of this shift can be traced to the theatre.

Blackface minstrelsy, which first arose as a national theatrical sensation in the 1830s and 1840s, was performed by white, mostly male Northern performers who crossed racial and gender boundaries by mimicking African Americans (e.g., they would wear bright red lipstick, darken their faces with coal-black makeup, exaggerate their facial expressions, and cross-dress) to entertain audiences with the 'authentic' music, humour, and dance ostensibly common on Southern plantations. The wearing of blackface shielded white performers from direct identification with the materials they were performing, and yet, as the minstrel show travelled North America and eventually the Western world, audiences began to interpret the performances as 'authentic' glimpses into Black life in America. It has been argued that without blackface minstrelsy, the phenomenon of *Uncle Tom's Cabin* would not have existed, and without *Uncle Tom's Cabin*, minstrelsy would not have continued to flourish.

I came of age over a century later, in the 1990s, a frenetic time that featured Y2K fears, the global access of the internet, and a deluge of historical dramas: *JFK* (1991), *Schindler's List* (1993), *Malcolm X* (1992), and *Titanic* (1997), to name a few. The last decade of the twentieth century was all about nostalgia for individuals and events that had left an indelible mark – visual, cultural, or cinematic – on the century. Similarly, the 1890s were dominated by sojourns into the past via novels, images, and live theatre. These forms not only produced nostalgia; they transformed it into consumable products that mass audiences could take with them into the new century. *Uncle Tom's Cabin* was one of few nineteenth-century works that not only survived but thrived in twentieth-century popular culture.

Uncle Tom travelled into the twentieth century through books, live productions, and even advertising, which boomed in the 1920s and 1930s. Advertising represented a modern form of storytelling that became commonplace in newspapers, magazines, and, later, television. At the end of the nineteenth century, advertisers had turned to nostalgia to soothe distress about moral and ethical upheaval by speaking to, and about, memories of the past. This kind of advertising substituted the solace of simpler and quieter times for the social and cultural crises and disintegration of the present. It is within this context that we can begin to understand how Uncle Tom migrated from the pages of Stowe's novel and minstrel stages onto the commodity packaging and advertising of the twentieth century.

By probing the mutation of Uncle Tom as a literary character in Stowe's novel into his depiction on stage, in advertising, and in film, the chapters that follow explore how a fictional figure became 'real' and has continued to leave an indelible mark on Black masculinity for over 170 years. Every Black man in the public spotlight since 1852 has been either referred to and/or referenced against Uncle Tom. Even in our own era, prominent Black leaders are accused of Uncle Tomism, such as when Jesse Jackson hurled the epithet at President Barack Obama.

Much of this book is based on experiences I have personally had, encountering the various incarnations of Uncle Tom, as well as caricatures of Black people in general. I vividly remember the impact Mammy Two Shoes, a character in *Tom and Jerry* cartoons, had on me as a child. Two Shoes is a heavy-set, middle-aged, apron-wearing maid who takes care of the house where Tom and Jerry carry out their antics. What struck me most about this character is that she is always partially hidden. We never see her face because her head is off-screen. She is a loud, aggressive Black woman without an identity. As a child, I thought Two Shoes was funny. The processes of signification – i.e., the fat Black woman's body as a sign of servitude and inferiority – did not register then. But as I got older, I started to think back to cartoons like *Tom and Jerry*, which also latently reproduce racist tropes about Blackness. That is when it dawned on me how powerful these childhood messages were. My adult disdain for mice and cats undoubtedly stems from watching a figuratively decapitated Black woman become foil to Tom and Jerry's antics.

Similarly, every holiday season, television stations air *It's a Wonderful Life*, the 1946 classic starring Jimmy Stewart and Donna Reed. The main story is centred on George Bailey (Stewart) and his quest to make sure his family business stays out of the hands of the evil Mr. Potter (Lionel Barrymore). When I watch this film, I am always struck by the appearance of the sleeping car train porter – porters were Black men who had to perform the servile role of an Uncle Tom in their jobs. When George Bailey's younger brother Harry (Todd Karns) returns to Bedford Falls via train, a porter is there just to smile and show an interest in the lives of George, his brother, and his wife, while gingerly carrying their bulky baggage from the train.

What's more, during Hollywood's classic period (1930–45), movies with Black characters almost always had some sort of sentimentalized musical interlude performed by slaves on a plantation, or by servants during the postbellum years. Black women were pigeonholed as maids and Mammies, and Black men were stuck playing buffoons or Uncle Toms. When the 1960s arrived, the civil rights era created a new public image of Black masculinity that was, on the one hand, passive, Christian, and docile, and on the other hand, increasingly militant and outwardly deviant. Dr. Martin Luther King Jr., for example, was sometimes dismissed by a younger generation as an Uncle Tom, versus the heavyweight boxer Muhammad Ali.

My own forgetting underpins why I wrote this book. It is shocking to me to reflect on all the racist images I consumed as a child, images that went unnoticed, unexplained, and unexamined until I was well into adulthood. As a Black person, I have the social and cultural tools and experiences to look back on my own life and reflect, unpack, and then reframe these tropes. But how do non-Black people do this work, if at all? Do other people similarly recognize the scenes and themes from their past that reproduced racist tropes? In the 1970s and 1980s, I remember that Russian characters in films like *Rambo, Air Force One,* and *Rocky IV* were always cast as evil villains determined to destroy America and American 'heroes.' Similarly, Hollywood images of South Asian men in film and on television in the 1990s depicted them as asexual, passive, unattractive, and/or socially awkward. These depictions, of course, are not real, but they do shape how we see the Other and vice versa.

As a Black woman, I must admit that it is difficult to know what it truly feels like to have someone hurl the Uncle Tom insult in my direction; I have never experienced it the way Black men have. The killing of George Floyd, coupled with the deaths of other unarmed Black men and women in the middle of the COVID-19 pandemic, brought issues of race and anti-Black racism into clear focus. The global protests that followed shed light on the fact that, while Black people have come a long way since the days of *Uncle Tom's Cabin* and even the civil rights movement, racial issues still feel as salient as they did two centuries ago. This moment confirmed to me that being Black is not just about one's racial identification. There is an unspoken agreement among most Black people that we stick together, no matter what the circumstances. I have seen first-hand how Black people who side with institutions, corporations, and white authority, or who actively hinder Black progress, are either deemed race traitors or have their loyalty called into question. To call someone an Uncle Tom today is to accuse that individual of racial disloyalty. Black men who participate in white institutions are often left with an untenable choice: do they 'keep it real' (i.e., outwardly show their loyalty to Black people and Black culture), or do they perform the jobs they are there to do, irrespective of the community's expectations of how they should or should not act?

Stowe's Uncle Tom is a starting point. In the chapters that follow, I will trace Uncle Tom's tumultuous journey from literary character to minstrel caricature, advertising icon, film, and television stereotype, and, eventually, to his final incarnation as a colloquial insult firmly embedded within Western culture. This book is not a literary critique of *Uncle Tom's Cabin*, nor does it aim to be a comprehensive study of all things Uncle Tom. There are many examples not included in this volume, and these omissions are not oversights. My aim, rather, is to examine the historical trajectory of this indelible literary character and the multiple spinoffs that followed over time. Each has a role to play in articulating how and why Uncle Tom has never left the public's imagination.

After reading *Uncle Tom's Cabin*, I sought out other contemporary Uncle Toms and found one in Spike Lee's *Bamboozled* (2000). The film is centred on Pierre Delacroix (his real name is Peerless Dothan), who is depicted as an Uncle Tom for his apparent lack of Black cultural cachet, such as knowledge of hip-hop, sports (boxing and basketball), and Black art.

Bamboozled got me thinking: Why is Uncle Tom still here? And how has the persistence of Uncle Tom affected the way we think about Black masculinity? *Uncle*, ultimately, is an exploration of cultural production, but one that opens a window on the ways in which American consumer society has produced race for over 150 years.

1

UNCLE TOM'S CABIN

Published nearly 170 years ago, *Uncle Tom's Cabin* is still known to people of different ages, classes, locations, and even languages. It first appeared in the U.S. as a serialized work of fiction, a chapter at a time, starting June 5, 1851, in the *National Era*, a weekly abolitionist newspaper edited by Gamaliel Bailey. Stowe's book not only had a profound impact on American slavery; it also went on to become the bestselling novel of the nineteenth century, and the second bestselling book of that century (after the Bible).

Today, we do not necessarily think of novels as shaping national identity. However, in nineteenth-century America, the experience of reading fiction helped form the way people saw themselves in relation to their nation. Throughout the first half of the nineteenth century, most of the books Americans read were British, while only a small number of American writers were published in Britain.

Uncle Tom's Cabin was one of the first American examples of the sentimental novel, which is characterized by its intention to elicit emotional reactions from readers by putting characters in pitiable situations. Early sentimental novels were brought to the U.S. in the eighteenth century from Britain. Initially, critics felt such novels would corrupt and delude readers with extravagant fancies. As a result, they often included a preface that asserted its pages contained 'useful knowledge' and a 'truthful' record of life.[1] The sentimental novelist conscientiously took on the role of moralist and purported to be a truth teller. Consequently, this genre, more so than an earlier generation's novels, captured the public's imagination, especially with respect to social issues such as slavery, abolition, gender, and class.

With characters who crossed racial and class boundaries, *Uncle Tom's Cabin* would have been seen by American readers as both a sentimental novel and an anti-slavery text, one that appealed to men and women alike. Using romantic literary devices, such as its focus on morality and religion, Stowe encouraged white readers to identify with the Black characters in her book. For the first time in an American novel, she portrayed slaves as moral human beings who suffered inhumane indignities and felt the same pain and anguish that whites would have felt.

Sentimental novels like *Uncle Tom's Cabin* may have galvanized the abolitionist cause, but they did not refute widely held beliefs about the supposed inferiority of Black people. In the early nineteenth century, biological racialists – including phrenologists, craniologists, physiognomists, anthropometrists, ethnologists, polygenesists, and Egyptologists – sought to establish innate biological differences between whites and Blacks. Contrary to eighteenth-century race theorists, who generally attributed racial distinctions to environmental conditions, this new breed of scientist was eager to not only document differences between the races but also to 'prove' the moral and intellectual superiority of the Anglo-Saxon race. Some nineteenth-century scientists such as British ethnologist James Cowles Prichard even sought to show that Black people's heads were covered with wool rather than hair.

Armed with these ideas, many antebellum readers would have closely followed Stowe's sentimental instructions on how to 'feel' for the enslaved figures depicted in her novel. Yet while they may have sympathized with the 'poor slaves' in the text and used her story to renew their Christian faith, most white American readers at the time would have also maintained their sense of superiority.

For sentimentalism to function as a public instrument capable of stirring an audience to social action, it must evoke an *emotional* response, which *Uncle Tom's Cabin* did by depicting the brutality of slavery. But as Barbara Hochman, author of *Uncle Tom's Cabin and the*

Reading Revolution, writes, some white readers related to the book to a degree that Stowe probably would not have approved of, 'temporarily collapsing the imaginative distance between themselves' and the novel's enslaved characters.[2] While some readers lost all sense of self and reality while reading *Uncle Tom's Cabin,* the novel also served as an education for many people about slavery. Along the way, it triggered a lot of anxiety about Black literacy and self-emancipation.

Full-page illustration of Eliza and Tom by Hammatt Billings for the first edition of Uncle Tom's Cabin *(1852).*

Two of *Uncle Tom Cabin*'s most important Black characters knew how to read. When George Harris, a highly inventive figure, runs away from his resentful master and is prepared to kill for his freedom, his masculinity seems untameable. Uncle Tom himself is also literate, the Bible being his primary text of choice, yet he has no desire to run. The duality between loyal Tom and disloyal George undoubtedly signalled to white readers that while slave literacy could lead to faith and self-control, it also posed a dangerous risk.

By the time Stowe published the novel, numerous slave narratives had already established a link between literacy and escape or rebellion. Her earliest readers may have remembered the slave rebellions of the 1830s, when Nat Turner, a highly literate enslaved preacher, set off a two-day uprising by both enslaved and free Black people in Southampton County, Virginia, in 1831. Virginian authorities responded with a brutal crackdown, and the event left many Southerners with a fear of the literate enslaved man.

In sum, *Uncle Tom's Cabin* not only satisfied the public's desire to understand the institution of slavery from the fictionalized slave's point of view, it also tapped into the South's desire to defend slavery. In so doing, Stowe's novel may have contributed to some of the fears around African American freedom. Namely, the idea of African American escape was tantamount to Southern planters losing their livelihoods, which were dependent on free labour.

❧

While the novel dealt directly with the prevailing issue of the times – slavery and its horrors – it also spoke to America's North-South divide. Northerners had increasingly become anti-slavery abolitionists by the 1850s, even as white Southerners remained economically, socially, culturally, and psychologically wedded to an institution that was, by this time, both unprofitable and increasingly unsustainable.

As Sven Beckert, a Harvard University historian and author of *The Empire of Cotton*, explains, 'American slavery had begun to threaten the very prosperity it produced, as the distinctive political economy of the cotton South collided with the incipient political economy of free labor and domestic industrialization of the North.'[3] Since the world was invested in the U.S. production of cotton, it is not surprising that a novel about the lives of the enslaved resonated around the world, and especially in Britain, where the abolitionist movement was strongest outside of the United States.

In May 1852, *Uncle Tom's Cabin* was published in London; within a year, there were twenty-three different editions. According to Michael Pickering's history of minstrelsy in Britain, the novel was available at every book stall in Britain, and by the end of that year, 1.5 million copies had been sold across the country and its colonies. Soon there were a dozen dramatizations of the book, as well as four different *Uncle Tom* pantomimes on the London stage.[4]

Thanks to the novel's runaway popularity, millions of people encountered relationships and characterizations of American slavery unfamiliar to them. With the characters of the enslaved Topsy and the privileged Eva, *Uncle Tom's Cabin* established what historian Robin Bernstein calls a 'black-white logic' in the American vision of childhood.[5] When Topsy, a dark-skinned 'pickaninny,'

Discovery of Nat Turner, *wood engraving by William Henry Shelton, 1831.*

is purchased by Augustine St. Clare at auction, she becomes Eva St. Clare's playmate. After Topsy is caught stealing, Eva is determined to help her become a moral little girl. Eva encourages Topsy to be honest with her, and thus begins the St. Clare family's quest to teach Topsy how to love – because they believe she has never been able to do so. Eva's innocence engulfs Topsy. Yet the polarization between these two versions of childhood pits them against one another. While both *were* innocent children, the violence of slavery, Stowe suggests, is an attack on Topsy's natural innocence, which can be partially restored through the loving touch of a white child, Eva.

Stowe's vision of Uncle Tom constructed a form of Black manhood that similarly required service to whites. Black men were often denied the rights of manhood; for example, enslaved Black men were regularly referred to as 'boy' – regardless of their age – a practice that continued through the Jim Crow era. As such, it was typical of literary uncles before the Civil War to be deferential to white authority. This kind of characterization ultimately suggested that Black manhood could be achieved only by staying in one's place – i.e., through servitude. Despite being ripped from his wife and children, chained, and sent off in a coffle with other miserable chattel, let down by even a good master, and beaten, finally to death, Uncle Tom does not ever speak ill of anyone. Stowe also depicts him as a man in the prime of life: dark haired and broad shouldered, which was a typical depiction of Black men before the Civil War. As Jo-Ann Morgan, author of *Uncle Tom's Cabin as Visual Culture*, writes, 'Before emancipation, a few other dark-haired, broad-shouldered adult Black men had appeared in print. Images of one escaped slave, holding a rifle and standing tall, was inspiring propaganda to justify the war for Northern readers of *Harper's Weekly*.'[6] Antebellum readers would have recognized Uncle Tom as a noble and self-sacrificing figure, traits that were seen as 'good' to white abolitionists.

Captive Uncle Tom, then, was a hero – a devout and pious Christian who will not be swayed from his faith, even at the peril of bodily harm and death. In fact, Stowe presented Uncle Tom as a Christ-like figure. Like Jesus, he suffers agonies inflicted by malicious secular people. And like Jesus, Uncle Tom sacrifices his life for the sins of humankind, to save his oppressors as well as his own people. However, his martyrdom goes hand in hand with his symbolic emasculation. By

Simon Legree beating Uncle Tom, illustration, c. 1885.

turning Uncle Tom into Eva's patron-friend, Stowe intellectually and sexually castrates him. Uncle Tom might have been a hero to most white readers, but for many Black readers, he was an anti-hero. His passivity disavowed Black agency and discouraged Black aggression. If Uncle Tom chooses to acquiesce to his own subordination and yet remains the novel's hero, where did that leave Black men who resisted their oppression?

However, within the context of the novel, both whites and Blacks look up to Uncle Tom. Yet his literary stature did not last. When profit-minded entrepreneurs and theatre producers lifted the character of

Uncle Tom from the pages of Stowe's novel and situated him on memorabilia, consumer goods, and eventually the minstrel theatrical stage, his character began its precipitous decline from hero to pejorative stereotype.

⁊⤳

Uncle Tom's Cabin was not just a work of abolitionist fiction penned by a writer fervently convinced that slavery was patently immoral. It also marked the beginning of a cultural, commercial, ideological, and theatrical phenomenon that would last long after the book dropped off the bestseller lists.

Shortly after the book was published, related merchandise flooded the market, including Uncle Tom soap, Uncle Tom almanacs and songbooks, Uncle Tom wallpaper with panels representing key scenes in the story, and cute Topsy dolls for little English and American Evas to comfort and cherish.

Uncle Tom also influenced nineteenth-century fashions. In New York, gentlemen began sporting the 'St. Clare hat' – a reference to Eva's father, the Southern plantation owner who buys Tom early in the story. Meanwhile, fashionable ladies bought 'Uncle Tom tippets' and scarves printed with scenes from the novel. According to accounts in the *New York Illustrated News*, 'Eliza' dresses were reported as the rage in Paris.[7]

At mid-nineteenth century, *Uncle Tom's Cabin* existed only as a novel, but in the decades that followed, the novel morphed into a global sensation affecting consumer, visual, and literary cultures. The 'Tom mania' that would dominate the 1860s was driven by a combination of increasingly sophisticated consumer manufacturing technologies but also images. With technological advancements in lithographic printing, the circulation of images of Uncle Tom became just as important as his literary character.

2

UNCLE TOM AND EVA

Between 1851 and the centenary of Stowe's birth in 1911, *Uncle Tom's Cabin* was adapted in diverse ways by editors, publishers, marketers, and even readers. And the novel's illustrations proved as enduring – and influential – as the text itself, if not more so.

Uncle Tom's Cabin appeared at a defining moment in the expansion of Western visual culture, a time when cheap forms of pictorial illustration, from wood engraving to the most elaborate colour printing, began to circulate widely. Advancements in printmaking in the mid-nineteenth century gave birth to a culture of images. Lithographs, in particular, were created to be enjoyed, framed, and hung on the walls of homes. They functioned as a 'low' and 'common' form of visual culture, purely for aesthetic enjoyment but also wide circulation.

For the first time, printmakers and photographers were able to offer relatively inexpensive pictures of people and places, which consumers could then proudly display on living-room walls or store privately in cases or folios. Lithographic illustrations, which flourished from the mid-nineteenth century onward, became a faster, and ultimately inexpensive, method of reproduction as compared to engravings and etchings, which were often finished with watercolours.

Marcus Wood, a professor of English and Diaspora Studies at the University of Sussex, argues that illustrators of *Uncle Tom's Cabin* entered a graphic world well accustomed to images of Black bodies. Images of enslaved bodies had circulated in Western visual culture for centuries, such as prints of 'Saartjie' or Sarah Baartman, the 'Hottentot Venus,' who was exhibited in Europe, first in London and then Paris, from 1810 to 1815, as a curiosity because of her breasts, buttocks, and hypertrophied labia. The Black body as 'Other' became a site of fascination for whites; images functioned as 'proof' of a supposed Black inferiority. Wood suggests that the choice of illustrators for Stowe's text highlights the tensions and contradictions between anti-slavery sentiment and the rapidly evolving forms of scientific racism. The latter relied heavily on representations that equated racial inferiority with bodily difference (e.g., skin colour, hair texture, head shape, lip size, and sexual organs), and had impacted much of the Western world's assimilation of the book via images and texts.[1]

In the U.S., the Boston-based publisher John P. Jewett hired Hammatt Billings (1818–74) to do six full-page illustrations for the first printing of the novel in 1852. Given the success of *Uncle Tom's Cabin*, Jewett then commissioned Billings for more than one hundred additional illustrations to go along with new versions of the first six for an 1852 Christmas gift book.[2] His most famous illustration, 'Little Eva reading the Bible to Uncle Tom in the arbor,' appeared on page sixty-three of the first edition. In this image, Tom and Eva sit together on a bench surrounded by flowers. Eva holds Tom's hand while reading

LITTLE EVA READING THE BIBLE TO UNCLE TOM IN THE ARBOR.

'Little Eva reading the Bible to Uncle Tom in the arbor.' Illustration by Hammatt Billings (1818–1874) from Uncle Tom's Cabin *by Harriet Beecher Stowe.*

the Bible to him. In some Western art, flowers are symbolic of virginity and the Virgin Mary; this illustration would have affirmed Eva's purity to American readers. By his proximity to Eva, Tom would have *become* virtuous in their eyes.

Meanwhile, George Cruikshank (1792–1878) – best known for illustrating the work of Charles Dickens – was hired by U.K. publisher John Cassell to create twenty-seven whole-page wood engravings for the British edition of the novel. In Cruikshank's illustration,

Illustration of Tom and Eva by Hammatt Billings for the 1853 deluxe edition of Uncle Tom's Cabin.

'Tom and Eva in the Arbor,' on page 233 of the British edition, he increased the distance between Eva and Tom ever so slightly and removed Eva's hand from Tom's knee. Rather than being seated immediately next to Tom, Eva is perched on a bench next to him, a Bible on her lap and her feet supported by a little stool. While Eva gazes at Tom, his eyes are cast outward toward the arbour, which, in Cruikshank's English garden setting, with tiled floor and peaked roof, was less wild than Billings's nature backdrop. In this scene, the figure of Tom, in relation to Eva, is presented with feminine, not masculine, characteristics. Victorian readers would have registered Tom as an 'ideal Victorian heroine.'[3]

Representations of Tom with his Bible and runaway George Harris reading challenged the notion that African Americans were capable only of being enslaved. Images were pivotal to Tom-mania; it simply would not have happened without the illustrations, which circulated as evidence of racial difference. Just as the novel appeared at a defining moment of the nineteenth century, so too did the illustrations.

Significantly, Billings's images did not neatly reflect the story. As with theatre, there were no copyright protections for authors prior to

1865. Publishers could amend, abridge, and bowdlerize Stowe's text. While Cassell kept the written version intact, the illustrations for the new editions reflected popular beliefs in the desexualized and idealized Black male body. In many editions, the drawings of Tom and Eva in the arbour further emasculated Tom as inferior and exalted Eva as superior. While Tom is Eva's senior, he appears as her equal in each illustration, seated beside her or, in some cases, looking down at her as though he has as much to learn from her as she does from him.

The popularity of this scene endured for decades and, in the hands of Hollywood filmmakers, became a powerful trope for Black male passivity. In the 1930s, more than eighty years after Stowe's novel was published, Shirley Temple's blond ringlets paired with Bill 'Bojangles' Robinson's soft-shoe routine in their 'buddy' films could be seen as a cinematic repackaging of Uncle Tom and his child-patron, Little Eva.

Similar visual evocations of Tom and Eva circulated throughout much of the world during the early twentieth century. The enormous popularity of *Uncle Tom's Cabin* and its related merchandise meant that, as historian Stephen Hirsch writes, Uncle Tom became 'the most frequently sold slave in American history.'[4] One widely circulated advertising card depicted 'Uncle Tom & Little Eva' with a photograph of two stage performers from a travelling Tom Show, Stetson's '*Uncle Tom's Cabin* Company,' one of the largest and longest-lived of the travelling Tom shows (operating from 1886 to 1931). In the image, Uncle Tom and Eva sit together on a bench. Eva, dressed in all white, holds an open book while gazing up at Uncle Tom, who is depicted as an old man with a greying beard, dressed in a black suit. Tom has one hand on Eva's book, but his gaze and his other hand are beatifically directed upward and away from Eva.

The image of Uncle Tom with Eva on his lap or with their legs touching could have been understood as dangerous and sinister, a courting of the unmentionable. Yet these anodyne images unequivocally dismissed Tom's embodiment as a man. Rather, Tom *became* Eva's Tom, a subordinate companion to a child. In the mid-nineteenth century, Black men were often stripped of their sexual identity, symbolically neutered to appease white readers' fears of Black masculinity. While white masculinity was equated with colonial conquest, power, control, and domination, Black masculinity was castrated in popular culture through images that were used to contain the threat of Black sexuality. The passive, emasculated, and childlike persona neutered Black masculinity into safety. In images of Tom and Eva, both Billings and Cruikshank constructed an archetype of Black masculinity as happily contented but always inferior.

The paradox of Uncle Tom's desexualization is that Tom is at once elevated and diminished. In the nineteenth century, many believed that white children's innocence was in some way transferable to the people and things they encountered. This metaphorical transmission is evident, for example, when Little Eva and Uncle Tom are shown cuddling ecstatically in illustrations, as well as in dramatic stagings of *Uncle Tom's Cabin*, games, advertisements, and household items, such as handkerchiefs.[5] Eva and Uncle Tom's embrace made Uncle Tom – and by extension abolition itself – seem righteous. Yet an inverse political interpretation was equally possible: in the eyes of some audiences, the white child's embrace may have been conferring innocence upon not abolition but the institution of slavery.

Ultimately, though, the repeated pairing of Uncle Tom and Eva in text and image would have signalled to readers the potential for a post-slavery America where Blacks were happy in their inferiority, and whites – even children – held authority over them. Each illustration of the two characters together gave readers a small glimpse into how things could be once the social institution that visibly defined them – slavery – was abolished. Uncle Tom with Eva, then, became a vitally important visual trope to remind white viewers of what an idealized Black masculinity could look like: namely, compliant, elderly, asexual, and childlike. This version of Tom became the most idealized image of Black masculinity circulated in the visual culture from the 1850s onward.

3

MINSTREL SHOW TOM

As a form of musical theatre, blackface minstrelsy traces back to the 1830s. It originated with rapid population growth in industrial Northern cities and an emergent working-class culture that desired mass forms of entertainment. At the same time, the question of what to do with increased Black presence in American cities lingered. Blackface performance, as Eric Lott argues in *Love and Theft: Blackface Minstrelsy and the American Working Class*, became one of the arenas in which to make sense of the tumult. 'The rise of American minstrelsy,' he writes, '[as] organized around the quite explicit "borrowing" of black cultural materials for white dissemination, [was] a borrowing that ultimately depended on the material relations of slavery.' Still, Lott adds, 'the minstrel show obscured these relations by pretending that slavery was amusing, right, and natural.'[1] If slavery was seen as entertainment, then the plight of African Americans could be minimized and even erased from the consciousness of white Americans – especially anti-abolitionists, of whom there were many. (In 1834, for example, an anti-abolitionist riot in New York City lasted for nearly one week before it was stopped by authorities.)

Thomas Dartmouth 'Daddy' Rice (1808–60), a New York–born performer and playwright, was one of the first actors to don blackface when he danced and sang 'Jump Jim Crow' on the stage in 1832. His blackface portrayal was based on a dance Rice claimed to have seen an old, disabled Black stable hand perform in the 1820s somewhere in the South. In his dance, Rice would hop around, his arms flying up and down in a silly manner that was amusing to the young and middle-aged working-class men who made up the majority of minstrelsy's audiences during the period. By the time 'Daddy' Rice arrived at New York's Bowery Theatre in 1832, with his caricatured song-and-dance routine, he had attracted an enthusiastic following.

Class fears were coupled with the narrative of Black escape largely in response to the influx of African Americans who had steadily migrated north from the 1820s onward. Like Stowe's novel, the minstrel show spoke directly to America's growing North-South divide. Rather than ask audiences to empathize with the enslaved, however, minstrelsy's derision of Blacks incited audiences to sympathize with Northern whites. The genre exposed the longings, fears, hopes, and prejudices of the white, urban working class by creating a new sense of Blackness and a new sense of whiteness all at the same time. The minstrel stage became a place where whites could make appeals to 'keep Blacks in their place' while helping to solidify working-class bonds among whites and attracting newly arrived immigrants to this popular form of entertainment. By adopting the dominant cultural ethos of anti-Blackness, those newcomers could better assimilate into the mainstream of America. The performance of a white/Black dyad presented slaves and ex-slaves on the plantation and out of place in an urban milieu. As these shows took hold in the North, where slavery was (for the most part) no longer practised, they revealed something unique about the how Northerners constructed and understood themselves, according to Rutgers University professor Douglas Jones. The minstrel show had become an 'aesthetic surrogate for the loss of slavery in the North.'[2]

Minstrel-mania, a precursor to Tom-mania, began in the 1840s as multiple white minstrel troupes in blackface appeared in theatres in New York and London. In 1843, four performers – Billy Whitlock, Dan Emmett, Frank Brower, and Dick Pelham – banded together to form the Virginia Minstrels for a series of New York appearances.[3] The following year, the Ethiopian Serenaders, a blackface minstrel troupe from Britain, played at the White House.[4]

The Virginia Minstrels are often cited as establishing minstrelsy as a national obsession because of the details they put into constructing their personas as 'real' delineators, as they were often called, of African American music and culture. Blackface and its white performers depended on the claim that they had learned their music from African Americans, attracting audiences by marketing their performances as though they were 'interpreters,' delivering the 'authentic' Black music of the plantation in an enjoyable and engaging form. In order to give the impression that they were playing genuine plantation music, the Virginia Minstrels would note on their playbills that their 'instruments were manufactured by themselves,' which was likely true, observes early minstrelsy author Hans Nathan.[5] The Virginia Minstrels also toured Britain in 1843, thereby situating blackface minstrelsy, a distinctly American phenomenon, as part of transatlantic Anglophone culture. The transnationalism of the genre undoubtedly primed British audiences for the reception of Stowe's *Uncle Tom's Cabin*.

In the next few years, minstrel shows featured comic parodies of Italian opera arias, caricatures of the 'Ethiopians' on Southern plantations, and mimicry of African Americans living in Northern urban centres. The Southern character, joyfully at home on the plantation, became known as Jim Crow, while the Northern character, an uppity Northern dandy, was called Zip Coon. While Jim Crow was a comic foil, Zip Coon signified something quite different. By donning the clothing of elite whites, this character implied there was a desire on the part of African Americans in the North not only for social mobility but also for other rights, such as integration and interracial sex. At the same time, the Black dandy caricature struck at the American distaste for pretentiousness and enhanced the pleasure derived from ridiculing those who claimed to be what they truly were not.[6]

Through the 1850s, minstrelsy's second phase, the genre began to establish itself as a definable part of America's national culture. In the turbulent years leading up to the Civil War, minstrelsy opened a window onto the complex culture developing in America's urban centres: it served as both the bearer and conveyer of vital cultural thoughts, feelings, and images. In Northern cities like Philadelphia,

New York, and Boston, and also Canadian cities like Montreal and Toronto, minstrel shows were part of an emergent theatre scene in which blackface rendered permissible topics like sexuality, women's rights, and crude jokes that were otherwise taboo on more legitimate stages, such as opera.

These shows are comparable to the stand-up comedians of the turbulent 1960s, comics like George Carlin, Lenny Bruce, and Mort Sahl, who used social and political humour to provoke and challenge their times. Similarly, by the late 1850s, a time when the political climate in the U.S. was increasingly divided and a civil war seemed inevitable, audiences viewed the minstrel show as entertainment, but its depictions of African Americans had lasting resonance.

Just prior to the Civil War, the minstrel show began to change: some theatre managers sought to capitalize on audience nostalgia for early minstrelsy, while others developed minstrelsy into a variety show – the precursor to late-nineteenth-century vaudeville. During this phase, minstrelsy companies begin to recognize the commercial power of nostalgia. On the eve of the Civil War, in fact, blackface minstrelsy became one of the first popular culture forms to double back on its own repertories, with audiences invited to revisit their first experiences with blackface comedy decades earlier.

❧

This history provides the context for early stage versions of *Uncle Tom's Cabin*. Part of the key to its commercial success lay in its debt to black-face minstrelsy. By 1852, the minstrel show had found a way to take the ambivalent and contradictory racial politics of the times and transform them into entertainment. *Uncle Tom's Cabin*'s representations of Black inferiority spoke to audiences in ways that mirrored the minstrel show. It also aided in turning fiction into reality; people began to relate to Stowe's interpretation of slavery and its horrors as a primary source to such an extent that, for instance, newspapers widely quoted Abraham Lincoln who, upon meeting Stowe, purportedly said, 'So you're the little lady who started this great war.'[7]

Harriet Beecher Stowe never attended a minstrel show and she also reportedly spent little time on Southern plantations. Though Stowe made up much of the story, she based the plot on interactions with formerly enslaved Black men, especially Rev. Josiah Henson (1789–1883), who founded the Dawn Settlement in Dresden, Ontario, for fugitives. After Uncle Tom came out, enterprising theatre producers quickly gravitated to the novel, but chose to reproduce, mimic, and change the story as they saw fit. The minstrel show adaptations took liberties with the 'reality' of Stowe's depiction of slavery and Uncle Tom himself because they could. There was no legal apparatus – e.g., copyright laws – in place to stop them.

For twenty years after the publication of the novel, Henson made a career out of the claim that he had been the 'original Uncle Tom.' He even travelled to England, where he was presented by his escort and biographer John Lobb as Uncle Tom. By then an old man himself, Henson was paraded around the country as the living embodiment of the 'good' Christian ex-slave, his celebrity reaching its climax with a royal audience.

Josiah Henson, c. 1883, Uncle Tom's Cabin Historic Site.

A poster of a Henson public appearance on display at the *Uncle Tom's Cabin* Historic Site in Dresden reads: 'Rev. Josiah Henson resident of Dresden, Canada, The Original Uncle Tom of Mrs. Stowe's Wonderful Story, will give an ACCOUNT of his Slave Life! At the Presbyterian Church at Lake Forest, Thursday Evening, Feb. 3rd, 1881, at 8 'o clock.' 'This entertainment is given FREE to all,' the subheading reads, 'and all are invited to come and learn from the lips of this remarkable man (now 92 years old) what American Slavery has been to him.' It is material evidence showing how Uncle Tom was transformed into a 'real' person via public appearances by Henson, a surrogate Uncle Tom.

Henson's was not the first theatrical version of Uncle Tom. Boston-born writer George Aiken and Nova Scotia–born producer George Howard are often credited as creating the first and most influential stage adaptation of Stowe's novel. When Aiken's script for Howard's production of *Uncle Tom's Cabin* appeared, shortly after the book's 1852 debut, circus magnate P. T. Barnum also commissioned a version, written by Henry J. Conway, which ran at his American Museum in New York. On January 16, 1854, the Bowery Theatre announced yet another stage version, with the minstrel star Daddy Rice in the role of Uncle Tom.[8] Rice, who was nearing the end of both his career and his life (he died in 1860), authenticated the show as representing the 'best' in minstrelsy. As the originator of 'Jump Jim Crow,' and as one of the self-described 'fathers of American minstrelsy,' Rice was no longer a star of the genre, but he represented its origins as a national entertainment.

Cover to an early edition of 'Jump Jim Crow' sheet music (c. 1832).

Small-scale minstrel show productions, which toured in New England and New York State, also came across the border to perform in Canada. These so-called 'Tom shows' attracted a large segment of the population that otherwise would never have exposed themselves to the theatre. Shortly after Stowe's novel appeared as a serial in the *National Era*, two panoramas of *Uncle Tom's Cabin* were presented at Toronto's St. Lawrence Hall, where patrons could view large images of Stowe's novel projected onto the wall. Dozens more performances took place at Toronto's Royal Lyceum from 1853 to 1860, attesting to the fact that Canadian audiences were as captivated by the sentimental abolitionist melodrama as other Northerners.[9]

Uncle Tom's Cabin onstage reflected a change in Stowe's original narrative. Nearly all the Uncle Tom minstrel shows turned the novel's slave auction scene into a kind of variety act, with each 'slave' required to show off his musical and comic talents to the buyers. Minstrel songs were then slotted into other theatrical adaptations, such as Uncle Tom singing Stephen Foster's 'Old Folks at Home' on slave master Legree's plantation.[10] This change is significant because it shifted the original intent of Stowe's novel from a commentary on the horrors of slavery into a form that was meant to be received as fun and frolic. By removing the politics of the time and adding in satirical and comic elements, *Uncle Tom's Cabin* increasingly ceased to reflect socio-political tensions in the nation. Instead, it became low-brow entertainment.

The primary white innovator of minstrel music, Foster used songs like 'Old Folks at Home' and 'My Old Kentucky Home' to evoke a mythologized Southern lifestyle, which was presented as fixed and unmoving, home-based, and passive; Uncle Tom's nostalgic yearning for his life on the Shelby and St. Clare plantations in the novel was effectively reproduced on the minstrel stage. Foster's songs were employed so consistently in theatrical productions of *Uncle Tom's Cabin* that they could be described as a central pillar of Tom-mania. As with *Uncle Tom's Cabin*, Foster's music was used equally 'for abolitionist and pro-slavery purposes,' writes Sarah Meer, author of *Uncle Tom Mania: Slavery, Minstrelsy & Transatlantic Culture in the 1850s*.[11]

For example, Foster wrote songs like 'Camptown Races' and 'Swanee River' for the Christy Minstrels in the early 1850s. Led by Edwin P. Christy, these two songs were the personal favourite of many Democratic politicians in New York City.[12]

1844 sheet music cover for a collection of songs by the Christy Minstrels.

Both spoke to the unifying ethos of the South. Additionally, 'My Old Kentucky Home' constructed two separate worlds: a world of innocence (the plantation South) and the outside world (the industrialized North and elsewhere).[13]

By the late nineteenth century, the songs of early minstrelsy still evoked for white audiences the world of the plantation South. Early minstrelsy had often paralleled white abolitionist paternalism by expressing pity toward slaves, as can be seen in Foster songs like 'Old Uncle Ned'[14]: 'Dere was an old N—, dey call'd him uncle Ned / He's dead long ago, long ago! / He had no wool on de top ob his head / De place whar de wool ought to grow.' While the song established Ned as a victim, the plantation owner becomes the subject of our sympathies: 'when Old Ned die Massa take it mighty hard.' These sentimental songs, which spoke of longing for the antebellum past, proliferated after the Civil War and commingled with ideologies of Southern redemption and the 'lost cause' justification, which referred to the belief among white Southerners that their fight in the Civil War had been a 'noble' one. Foster's plantation melodies also became a sobriquet for old Black men. Names like 'poor old Ned,' for instance, were still thriving in 1893 when Henry Ossawa Tanner's *The Banjo Lesson* – a Norman Rockwellesque painting of an older Black man showing a young boy on his knee how to play – was first displayed in Philadelphia.[15]

Most noticeably, the minstrel shows that featured Uncle Tom re-imagined Stowe's character as an elderly man. The moment Uncle Tom became elderly was the moment when the name Uncle Tom came to connote the lowest rung in the Black social hierarchy. It is when Black people started to conclude that being like Uncle Tom might be one of the worst crimes anyone might commit against the race.

そ

Significantly, Henson onstage as Uncle Tom fits within a continuum of Black performance in nineteenth-century theatre. Interestingly, when African Americans first performed on theatrical stages, they did so, with few exceptions, in blackface. Black minstrel troupes appeared on the scene as early as the 1850s, but it was not until after the Civil War that minstrel managers made serious attempts to exploit the talents of Black entertainers by putting them on the commercial stage. By the mid-1870s, there were many popular Black minstrel troupes acting out the stereotyped themes of 'Negroes' on the Southern plantation.

Among the first of the Black troupes to excite public interest was a group of fifteen ex-slaves, originally from Macon, Georgia, called the Georgia Slave Troupe Minstrels. Organized in April 1865 by a white man, W. H. Lee, they toured widely during the 1865–66 season, and eventually came under the management and proprietorship of Sam Hague, a white minstrel,who changed the troupe's name to Sam Hague's Slave Troupe of Georgia Minstrels.[16] Charles Hicks, however, is commonly viewed as the father of Black minstrelsy (African Americans in blackface performing as *Black* people). He managed the Original Georgia Minstrels, which formed in 1865 and was sometimes also billed as the Only Simon Pure Negro Troupe in the World.[17] Hicks was the first to manage an all-Black minstrelsy troupe, and thereafter the Georgia Minstrels became synonymous with Black or 'coloured minstrels.'[18]

Scene in William A. Brady's 1901 revival of Uncle Tom's Cabin *at the Academy of Music, New York City.*

Blackface minstrelsy ultimately transformed Uncle Tom. The genre twisted, mutated, and deviated from Stowe's novel just enough to keep audiences wanting more, while simultaneously staying true to audiences' expectations for what a 'real' Uncle Tom would look and act like. It is through performance that the fiction of Uncle Tom's servility becomes a reality.

Advertisement for a Black minstrel troupe, c. 1860s–70s.

4

VAUDEVILLE TOM

By the 1880s, the minstrel show had evolved into vaudeville, a reinvention of theatre into the variety show. Unlike mainstream theatre, vaudeville acts drew from all ethnic groups and genders, in all shapes and sizes, and ranged from 'respectable' thespians to circus 'freaks,' and from opera singers to chorus performers.

Vaudeville brought new meaning to Uncle Tom. With bills that combined humour, singing, and dancing, as well as an abundance of ethnic stereotypes presented in sketches and comedy routines, vaudeville transformed Stowe's novel and its theatrical renditions into spectacles of racial mimicry and buffoonery. Consequently, there was a democratized feel to vaudeville that did not exist in earlier minstrel shows. It truly reflected the world of the turn-of-the-century North American city, with its wide variety of classes, tastes, people, and talents.

On December 12, 1893, an advertisement in the *Hamilton Spectator* announced a weekly engagement of an American vaudeville show at the Star Theatre. 'The best ever seen, bar none,' the ad declared, noting that matinee shows would be held on Saturday afternoons for 'ladies and children' at five and ten cents per ticket.[1] Half a year later, in late July 1893, Toronto's the *Globe* reported that Cleveland's Minstrels and European Vaudeville Company would give two performances on one day – a matinee at 2:00 p.m. and an evening performance – at the Grand Opera House.[2] Importantly, vaudeville was not the end of the minstrel show; instead, the genre became one part of a larger theatrical revue that would include burlesque, jugglers, and comedy acts.

Vaudeville shows dominated live theatre in the early decades of the twentieth century, until it was displaced by cinema. Vaudeville's rise coincided with the influx of immigrants from Eastern Europe, and with corresponding debates about the place of racial and ethnic minorities in North American society. Even though vaudeville grew out of the same low-class theatre that had spawned minstrelsy, its variety-show format did not singularly appeal to a majority white working-class audience, but to the general public. As it gained popularity, vaudeville challenged and eventually replaced the giant minstrel show industry as the dominant form of American mass entertainment. Still, as the popularity of vaudeville and minstrel shows intersected, white and Black actors were performing in both venues, which meant vaudeville not only kept blackface minstrelsy alive; it also returned it to its novelty roots, but on a variety stage.

During vaudeville, access to the theatre drastically changed from the earliest minstrel shows. First, when white women performers adopted racial masquerades in vaudeville, it democratized the stage. Women had been largely excluded from minstrel shows. When they took to the stage in vaudeville acts, white women, often in blackface, performed exactly as white men before them had done: they sang popular 'coon songs' in blackface. The term 'coon' referred to raccoons, whose thievery and guile were associated with Black people. The white markings on the minstrels' faces evoked this reference and alluded to the long-standing association of Black people with animals.[3] Coon sheet music often included illustrations that depicted Black people as careless, lazy, watermelon-eating tricksters or buffoons.

The vaudeville stage was highly eclectic. Not only did it include white women for the first time, but there were also Black women, men, and children, as dancers, jugglers, and just about anything that resonated with audiences who would have been familiar with burlesque and circus sideshows, which featured both Black bands and Black minstrel troupes. Additionally, mixed minstrel shows begin to appear onstage, featuring Black performers in one part and white performers in another, or sometimes together. But whereas white performers could turn to new material when interest in minstrel themes declined, Black performers could not escape their stereotypes.

In *Darkest America: Black Minstrelsy from Slavery to Hip-Hop*, Yuval Taylor and Jake Austen explain that Black actors wore blackface, either literally or metaphorically, and performed minstrel stereotypes that emphasized qualities such as laziness, thievery, and dishonesty.[4] These actors took on these personas not because they wanted to, but because it was the only way they could perform onstage in the nineteenth century. While white minstrel entertainers claimed to be pupils, or even kin, of the Black people they mocked, they just as passionately made it clear they were white. But because Black minstrel shows were presented and marketed as authentic representations of Black life, there was little opportunity for audiences to make the distinction between what was real and what was performative.

The third unique feature of vaudeville theatre was that it was intricately linked to the expansion of transnational capitalism across North America. For example, New York theatrical magnate Marcus Loew went to Toronto in 1913 to open Loew's first theatre in Canada, the newest addition to his fast-growing chain of vaudeville and movie houses.[5] This expansion north of the border created a larger theatre circuit and more opportunities for white and Black troupes.

As touring companies, including vaudeville acts, moved across the continent, trying to always end one engagement within a day or two's travel of the next, they were constantly on the move between cities like Detroit, Chicago, Buffalo, Montreal, and Toronto, among other places.

As vaudeville grew, it absorbed nineteenth-century minstrel stage stereotypes and traditions. According to Susan Glenn's study of theatrical feminism and the proliferation and popularity of racial and ethnic humour, 'the commercial music industry and the popular theatre absorbed and reconstituted nineteenth-century minstrel stage stereotypes and traditions.'[6]

White minstrels, caught between their 'authentic' Black competitors and the versatility of variety and musical shows, prolonged the life of their form by shifting to more lavish productions with urban themes;

some even abandoned blackface altogether. By stepping in and out of blackface, vaudeville standardized the genre's other performative aspects – slapstick, buffoonery, comedy, and satire – which became standard theatrical repertoire in the early twentieth century.

⚜

By the time *Uncle Tom's Cabin* was reborn as a vaudeville show in the 1890s, the pastoral plantation myth had created an idealized view of Southern society, as well as of slavery, uncles, and mammies. The impact of this idealized view was significant; three decades after the Civil War, the horrors of slavery had been long forgotten.

As a vaudeville act, *Uncle Tom's Cabin* no longer commented on slavery and emancipation. Instead, this new version of Uncle Tom was emblematic of the dominant culture's desire to keep Black men not only in the past but also perpetually old and desexualized. The figure of Tom, in other words, had undergone a visual death as he moved from Stowe's novel to vaudeville's theatrical bills. At the same time, the opening of the stage during vaudeville to Black actors, both in and out of blackface, marks the moment when Black entertainment became popular among both Blacks and whites. For the former, they could finally *see* themselves onstage, albeit still through a refracted lens, since the vast majority of playwrights and theatre managers at this time would have been white men.

Of the many Black performances that graced the stage in the 1890s, the most popular was a theatrical extravaganza entitled *Darkest America*. The show premiered in 1894, and together with 1895's *Black America*, it came to be seen as the most 'authentic' minstrel show in history. It marked a fundamental change in direction. *Darkest America* was a conventional minstrel show in that the performers, even though they were Black, wore blackface.

Darkest America is important to the evolution of the figure of Uncle Tom because it speaks to the ways in which the stage authenticated cultural tropes about Black Americans. Whites could feel good after seeing Black minstrelsy, just as white readers of *Uncle Tom's Cabin* felt good about the docility and passivity of seemingly authentic characters like Uncle Tom. This newer form of Black minstrelsy reinforced white ideas about the inferior nature of African Americans and the merits of their continuing degradation by staging elaborate plantation fantasies in which Blacks were happy and foolish while the whites, by implication at least, were benevolent and protective.[7]

By 1897, *Darkest America* had become a true sensation. It was one of the first shows to feature many of the major Black entertainers of the time, including Sam Lucas (1848–1916), who went on to play Uncle Tom in one of the first film adaptations of the novel. The show's scenes include vignettes plucked from the pages of Stowe's book. For example, there is a cotton field with a fully operating cotton gin, and the infamous Louisiana sugar plantation that figured in *Uncle Tom's Cabin* – the place where slave owner Simon Legree has Tom whipped to death.[8]

The appeal of the Black minstrelsy in *Darkest America* lay in its supposed authenticity. Although Black minstrels regularly portrayed these typical themes, they also significantly modified them. In the plantation material they themselves wrote, the Black minstrels depicted the 'Old Darky' nostalgically recalling the happy days of his youth, the frolicking children, the tasty possum, the bright cotton fields, the perfume of magnolia blossoms, the lively banjo music, and the comforting warmth of his family.[9] In this sense, Black performers from the 1890s onward acted out the 'feeling' of longing that Black people supposedly held for their Southern roots.

One of the best-known Black performers, Billy Kersands (1842–1915), whose long career began in the 1860s, played heavily caricatured roles that emphasized Black men's supposedly large lips and mouth. Black audiences must have laughed at these characters for some of the same reasons whites did: the physical humour used in the 'mouth routines' and the literalism of these 'ignorant' characters were comic devices with general appeal. Not coincidentally, Kersands was famous for 'Old Aunt Jemima,' a song that became one of the signatures of his stage career.[10] Black actors performing as plantation stereotypes like Aunt Jemima, a prototypical Mammy, set the stage for further uses of this stereotype beyond the theatre. When Black people saw

Black actors like Kersands, they probably laughed at these characters. Laughing at these stereotypes might have softened their negative impact or it might have helped Black people forget the harsh realities of life.

While Kersands's contributions to the stage are mostly forgotten, his Aunt Jemima rendition would have lasting impact on not only blackface performers but the American consumer-products industry that emerged in the 1890s.

5

AUNT JEMIMA IN CHICAGO

Vaudeville was not the only major institution using nostalgia to shape popular notions of race and gender in the late nineteenth century. At the World's Columbian Exposition in Chicago in 1893, American audiences became increasingly obsessed with nostalgia for the antebellum South. Human displays as entertainment enticed late-nineteenth-century white middle-class audiences and continued until the mid-1960s. These 'world's fairs,' 'expositions,' and 'exhibitions' – interchangeable terms – were celebrations of cultural, industrial, scientific, and imperial achievements to promote national pride and economic growth.

The exposition shone a new light on Uncle Tom. The multiple American editions of *Uncle Tom's Cabin* – the first published by John P. Jewett in 1852, and the most recent released by Houghton Mifflin in 1891 – were on display in a section of the Woman's Building Library dedicated to Harriet Beecher Stowe. As in many other contexts at the time, the expo's organizers employed *Uncle Tom's Cabin* to support an optimistic narrative of America's recent past and triumphant present.[1] In the promotion of a 'White City,' as the site was called because of its large white buildings, this electrically lit space presented non-European bodies and the lower classes as exoticized and commodified Others in the disorder of the exposition's midway. The 'White City' in relation to the Other also appeared in newspapers and was made real through advertising copy. Images and cultural events at these world's fairs created a hierarchical universe in which whiteness was positioned as progressive, modern, and wondrous. Meanwhile, racialized bodies were presented as unchanging, strange, and pre-modern. They served one purpose: entertaining white audiences.

Uncle Tom's Cabin became an example of 'classic' American literature. While it was canonized during slavery and post-emancipation as a book written to humanize African Americans, throughout the 1890s, *Uncle Tom's Cabin* helped to reiterate a national narrative of moral and social progress. Stowe's novel had created a mass market for American literature, and as an agent of history, it had contributed to the nation's social progress. At the Chicago expo, however, *Uncle Tom's Cabin* came to represent more than a symbol of the past and proof of America's literary coming of age. It was also presented as evidence of America's moral, political, and cultural coming of age, which worked in tandem to support the ideology of the exposition.

By the 1890s, the public was also primed to view *Uncle Tom's Cabin* as part of the spectacle of modern culture, taking its place alongside the minstrel show characterizations of Uncle Tom. Performances of Tom were not just theatrical extensions of Stowe's character; Tom had become a cultural celebrity independent of Stowe's novel. The exposition's various displays brought Tom into a panorama of modern culture, reminding visitors of a past far away from the racial tensions of the period, which included court-sanctioned segregation and anti-Black violence that was rampant through the North and the South.

Demonstrations of 'colonized people' at the Chicago expo placed racialized spectacles alongside technological and commercial invention. As 'real' Black men and women appeared in public as fictional characters plucked from the era of slavery for the first time, a new era in racial performance was born: the embodied commodity trademark.

Aunt Jemima would become the first of these trademarks. Just as Uncle Tom migrated from the novel to the stage, Aunt Jemima migrated from the stage to the store shelf. She is an important characterization of Black womanhood in the 1890s who played to the public's longing for a simpler past. By understanding Aunt Jemima's rise to public notoriety, not just as an image but also as a marketing symbol of an emergent consumer culture, we can recognize Uncle

Tom's subsequent transformation into commodity trademarks bearing different names: Uncle Remus and Uncle Ben.

❦

Aunt Jemima was brought to life in the 1890s to speak sweetly of the past, and she, too, was plucked from the pages of plantation literature via tales of Mammy, only to be reborn through the minstrel show.

In 1889, Chris L. Rutt, a St. Joseph, Missouri, newspaper editor and flour-mill operator, produced a ready-mix pancake batter. The product had no name. Not long after launching it, Rutt attended a local vaudeville house, where he witnessed two white men wearing blackface and drag performing a cakewalk called 'Aunt Jemima,'

Aunt Jemima Pancake Flour advertisement, 1923.

which featured one of the actors in an apron and wearing a red bandana. (A cakewalk was a pre–Civil War dance originally performed by slaves on plantation grounds. By the 1870s, it had become a popular feature of minstrel shows. As a uniquely American dance, it was first known as the 'prize walk,' for the 'prize' of an elaborately decorated cake.)

For Rutt, the bandana-wearing Black cook personified 'Southern hospitality,' so he decided to use the name and image to create the Aunt Jemima trademark for his pancake mix.

The trademark was eventually sold to the R. T. Davis Milling Company, a St. Joseph firm, which devised a new marketing, distribution, and promotional strategy that included finding a Black woman to perform as Aunt Jemima. Nancy Green was a fifty-nine-year-old woman living on the south side of Chicago, working as a cook and housekeeper for a prominent judge. After responding to the company's advertisement and going through a series of auditions, Green was hired to cook and serve the new pancake recipe at promotional events. Born into slavery on a Kentucky plantation, she became the first Black woman to appear in public and advertising campaigns as Aunt Jemima.

Green made her debut appearances as Aunt Jemima when the company launched the pancake mix at the Chicago expo. Her image tapped into the public's appetite for nostalgic sojourns at the end of the nineteenth century, a period that saw the emergence of mass consumerism and marked an even broader transformation taking place in North American society. Rapid urbanization and industrialization, accompanied by mass consumption and modern advertising, heralded a new era and forever altered the consuming habits of Americans. Between 1890 and 1920, Americans witnessed for the first time the development of brands and brand names.

American popular culture was also shifting dramatically as the century turned and life sped up. Entertainment entrepreneur P. T. Barnum expanded the traditional circus into a variegated spectacle. Travelling vaudeville and variety acts absorbed minstrel shows and often included whatever performing humans and animals a shrewd manager might lay his hands upon. North American audiences that flocked to these mass-produced spectacles were invited to view the Other through a lens of wonder. These developments effectively set the stage for the presentation of mythic figures from the Old South – Uncle Tom and Mammy – who could serve as reminders of the safety of plantation life in an accelerated world.

In the logic of the product's nostalgic appeal, Jemima had to be an aunt. Like 'uncle,' the terms 'mammy,' 'auntie,' and 'Negro' or 'coloured nurse' all appeared in antebellum fiction, describing both a person and a role within the plantation home. Aunties served as nursemaids, cooks, and all-around domestic helpers. Despite this nod to nostalgia, and like a growing number of Black trademarks, Aunt Jemima was very much a product of American modernism. Her presence on packages on grocery shelves reflected advances in American culture. At the dawn of the twentieth century, advertising celebrated and promoted modernity. Packaging once served only as protection for consumer products. But with the advent of brand identification, packaging delivered new kinds of literal and symbolic messages. Thus, when Green debuted as Aunt Jemima, her sole purpose was to wax nostalgic for the old plantation in ways that evoked antebellum aunties and uncles and the 'simpler times' in which they lived. In telling stories about her own early life in slavery – a life an entire generation of Americans were not familiar with – along with plantation tales written for her by a white Southern sales representative, Green served up a combination of historic and mythic narratives that Kimberly Wallace-Sanders, author of *Mammy: A Century of Race, Gender, and Southern Memory,* describes as being 'designed to perpetuate the historical amnesia necessary for confidence in the American future.'[2]

By cultivating national nostalgia for a common racial past, in which enslaved African Americans were happy and content, the advertising at the Chicago expo (and after) constructed a uniform national memory. For both Northerners and Southerners, Aunt Jemima conjured an imagined past where the plantation kitchen stood for positive, enriching experiences.

During the Columbian Exposition, Green appeared in a booth designed to look like a giant flour barrel. She greeted guests and cooked pancakes, all while singing and telling stories of her life on the plantation.[3] Some of Green's stories were real, but most were apocryphal. The appearance of Aunt Jemima as a slave, and by extension her pancakes as a product of her servitude, appealed to the public's desire to imagine a harmonious relationship between Blacks and whites in America. But the brand also framed the Black narrative as something that belonged to the South and to slavery. The subtext was that if Black people like Aunt Jemima longed for the days of slavery, that sanctioned white nostalgia for a past where African Americans were not only stuck on the plantation but were happy there.

The success of Aunt Jemima as a means of selling ready-mix pancake flour inspired imitators: Cream of Wheat created Rastus, a mimetic Uncle Tom, to promote its hot semolina cereal. Later, Uncle Ben became the face of instant rice products. Each of these iconographic trademarks were folk characters plucked from a mythologized pre-industrial time that starkly contrasted with the progressive modernism of the late nineteenth and early twentieth centuries.

6

RASTUS

In the early twentieth century, some of the first silent films – *How Rastus Gets His Turkey* (1910), *How Rastus Got His Chicken* (1911), and *Rastus' Riotous Ride* (1914) – featured a comic Black character. *How Rastus Gets His Turkey* was a short film directed by Theodore Wharton and released by Pathé Frères, one of the first film production companies. Like all slapstick comedies starring the white silent film actor Billy Quirk in blackface as 'Rastus,' these films depict a 'Black' character in various scenarios in which his body is the butt of the joke. Rastus chases after turkeys or chickens. He gets caught in fences. He becomes confused by simple things. According to a December 3, 1910, review in *Variety*, 'Rastus causes considerable laughter by the manner in which he stole a big turkey gobbler. He even carried part of a fence home with him. The theft is well pictured.'[1] These slapstick comedies continued a historical tradition in American culture that depicted Black characters as caricatures to please white audiences.

The film version of Rastus was childlike and non-threatening – a character who would have reminded audiences of Uncle Tom.

The Rastus character predates the release of those early movies. In 1893, Emery Mapes of North Dakota's Diamond Milling Company set out to find an image to market his breakfast porridge, called Cream of Wheat.[2] He decided an image of a subservient and uneducated Black chef was the best fit.[3] As a former printer, Mapes recalled the numerous stock images of Black chefs among his collection of old printing plates. Mapes would also have been aware of the many other products that were sold by Uncles, such as Dixon's Carburet of Iron Stove Polish. One 1890 lithograph advertisement depicted a figure named 'Uncle Obadiah' – an elderly and frail Black man wearing ragged clothes and a smile.[4]

In ads, the grinning Rastus held up a chalkboard. Just as Aunt Jemima's lack of education symbolized her authenticity as an African American, Rastus's use of non-standard 'Black' English reinforced the stereotype of the semiliterate enslaved servant.

Rastus appearing in an advertisement for Cream of Wheat, c. between 1901 and 1925.

The original chef trademark was replaced in 1925 by a more realistic version that was used for decades on Cream of Wheat products. While dining in a Chicago restaurant called Kohlsaat's, Mapes noticed the broad smile of his Black waiter and instantly wanted this image to replace the antiquated woodcut he'd developed many years earlier.[5] Mapes persuaded the waiter to pose in a chef's cap for a full-face snapshot and paid the man five dollars for his services. Just four years later, the Cream of Wheat company, riding high on its new branding, was listed on the New York Stock Exchange. (While Cream of Wheat was once a division of Nabisco, today it is part of B&G Foods.) Rastus, like Aunt Jemima, became more than just a company trademark – he was marketed as a symbol of wholesomeness and stability, or what Ferris State University professor David Pilgrim describes as 'the toothy, well-dressed Black chef [who] happily serves breakfast to a nation.'[6]

The new Rastus appeared in Cream of Wheat ads in *National Geographic,* the *Saturday Evening Post, Good Housekeeping,* and *McCall's.* In Canada, he often appeared alongside white children in *Chatelaine Magazine,* the country's most popular women's periodical. *Chatelaine* held a pivotal role in Canadian women's culture between the two world wars, serving as an important forum for white, mostly middle-class women's discourse. (*Chatelaine* was one of the only publications at the time geared toward Canadian women.) It was also a premier forum for advertising.

Like Aunt Jemima, Rastus ads stand as examples of how race, class, and gender were constructed in print media, and by extension, how white middle-class society sought to symbolically locate Black bodies in the Old South, where they could serve modern consumers as if they, too, were still on the plantation. This imagery provided comfort and stability amid a socio-cultural milieu of Black migration as tens of thousands of families fled the menial labour and servitude of the South for the cities of the North.

During the Depression, Rastus made countless appearances in popular magazines. Like the comic-strip-style Aunt Jemima advertising during this period, the Rastus campaign made it clear that Cream of Wheat was not just a breakfast cereal; Rastus, the happy-to-please cook/ servant, eased the burden on white women and their children. In February 1938, a full-page ad featured a young white boy seated atop a dogsled with a rifle strapped across his chest and a note that read:

Cream of Wheat Advertisement in Chatelaine, *February 1938.*

Dear Mom,
 I've gone prospectin for gold to make us rich. I ate 2 bowls of swell Cream of Wheat for breakfast and I'm full up with food energy goodbye. I may be gone a long time.
  Jimmy.
P.S. Fix me another bowl of Cream of Wheat for dinner tonight. Rover says goodbye too I don't think he likes prospectin like I do.[7]

With a box of Cream of Wheat positioned in the lower right corner featuring Rastus wearing a white chef's hat and holding a bowl of the breakfast product, the ad also included detailed copy explaining the extensive role that Cream of Wheat – and by extension Rastus, as imagined server – could play in a young boy's life.

The dominant ideology of motherhood – purity, the making of and caring for children within the context of the ideal nuclear and patriarchal family – circulated the Western world in the nineteenth century but, by the 1930s, it permeated all aspects of North American culture. It constructed some bodies as more appropriate for motherhood than others, while also positioning white children as rightfully deserving of both nutritious meals and leisure and fun.

This depiction may seem innocent: ads celebrating the wonderment of childhood and the importance of breakfast, a meal that was becoming more and more significant in the twentieth century as marketers capitalized on the need for quick and easily prepared dishes for an increasingly white-collar workforce. But nothing in the realm of children's advertising can ever be wholly benign.

Generation after generation, white children were socialized to associate their happy childhood breakfasts with demeaning images of Black servitude from Uncle Tom to Rastus, even as 'real' Black bodies were not physically present in their homes. The power of advertising lies in its ability to suggest alternative worlds. It can bring to life the fictive and reframe our memory pathways such that as adults, when we think back to our childhoods, we may, in some instances, be remembering the advertisements of our childhoods, and the feelings they evoke, as opposed to our lived experiences.

From October 1939 to February 1942, a lifelike image of Rastus appeared in a series of comic-strip ads in *Chatelaine*. In them, Rastus wears his white chef's cap and appears at the top of the frame. In each subsequent frame, either the entire nuclear family – Dad, Mom, and son – appear, or sometimes Mom and/or Dad are spokespersons for the entire family. There's always a caption beside Rastus that reads 'Old and young agree: That's the food for me!'[8] or 'Here's the way to start your day!'[9]

Within a few years, the Cream of Wheat promotions were being presented as real comic strips, not just ads. Rastus went on to appear as a tie-in for the cartoon *Li'l Abner*, a comic syndicated in newspapers across North America and Europe from 1934 to 1977. Written and drawn by Al Capp, these cartoons featured a fictional group of rowdy kids living in the poor mountain village of 'Dogpatch, U.S.A.' Most comic strips of that era focused on characters living in the North; what made *Li'l Abner* unique is that it was one of the first to be based in the South. This strip helped influence the views of a whole generation of children in the American South, including their perceptions about the role of Black people. Like *Keeping Up with the Joneses*, a comic strip by Pop Momand that ran from 1913 to 1938 and Tad Dorgan's Tad cartoons (1920s), *Li'l Abner* depicted Black men as dim-witted, lazy, and foolish figures who worked as cooks, waiters, or bellhops and spoke non-standard 'Black' English, with their conversational misunderstandings and dialogue misspellings.

In the 1950s, however, the elaborate Rastus Cream of Wheat magazine ads all but disappeared. As women's magazines turned their attention to telling stories about life in America's emerging suburbs, advertising copy also shifted from breakfast foods and coffee ads to cosmetics, toiletries, and hair-colouring products, as well as cars, home appliances, and washing machines.

To keep Rastus in front of consumers, the company focused on strategically placing the boxed product in contexts where children would see the breakfast dish as an essential part of their lives in the suburbs. In one representative full-page ad in *Chatelaine* that appeared in February 1958, a young white boy outside on a cold winter's day wears a hat, scarf, mitts, and wool coat. He is pulling his hat over his ears while other children stand in the snow behind him. The caption reads 'Cold tomorrow?' With a box of Cream of Wheat positioned in the lower right corner and Rastus's face enlarged to take up nearly half of the box, the copy continues, 'That's "Cream of Wheat" weather. Guard your family with hot "Cream of Wheat."'[10]

Aunt Jemima ads during this period similarly show white middle-class families how to protect their 'good life' in the suburbs. On one hand, the ads celebrated mothers in white nuclear families doing their own cooking without the corporeal presence of a Black domestic. At the same time, Aunt Jemima was still stuck in white kitchens as the symbolic assistant in food preparation. And while Rastus was no longer featured in cartoons and comic strips geared toward children, Cream of Wheat still represented a symbolic connection between Black servitude and white comfort. In other words, Rastus still served white families.

Rastus and Aunt Jemima are interconnected with, and inseparable from, Uncle Tom. During the first half of the twentieth century, figures of Black servility were stock templates for countless consumer brands. For example, in the early 1930s, Maxwell House ads in Canada featured a Black butler. In one ad that appeared in the *Toronto Daily Star* in 1932, a Black butler appears alongside an elegantly dressed white couple. The caption reads, 'Ever since the Southland [Railway] sent famous House Coffee to Canada, it has been right royally welcomed.' At around the same time, Gordon Brown Scheibell created *Uncle Eben Says*, a cartoon depicting an old Southern Black man often sitting on a wooden basket. He wears a straw hat and smokes a pipe or walks at the side of the road using a cane. The strip appeared in daily newspapers. In one installment, Uncle Eben says, 'I may be a pessimist, but I is gwine ter keep right on lookin' bofe ways hefo' I crosses any c'dese one way streets.'[11]

These stock depictions of African American men and women helped keep Uncle Tomism alive and well in the imaginations of twentieth-century children and adults.

THE RECONSTRUCTION OF UNCLE TOM

Just south of Natchez, Mississippi, on Highway 61, sits Mammy's Cupboard, a restaurant that pays homage to the Mammies of the South. Opened in 1940 and still in operation today, the restaurant has as its facade an enormous Black woman whose skirt serves as the entryway to the dining room and gift shop. The restaurant was created by Henry Gaude, an entrepreneur who wanted a roadhouse that would capitalize on the success and popularity of the 1939 film *Gone with the Wind* and Hattie McDaniel's Oscar win for the role of Mammy. While the shade of the exterior wall of Mammy's Cupboard has progressively lightened over the years with each subsequent repainting, the restaurant's website still depicts the original and very popular Black Mammy – dark-skinned with white hair, holding out a tray.[1]

As it happens, *Uncle Tom's Cabin* had the first popular literary representation of a loyal Southern Mammy, a character named Aunt Chloe. Harriet Beecher Stowe described Aunt Chloe as a nurturing Black woman with a round body who is protective of her white family, but less than caring toward her own children. This depiction helped to construct the prototypical Mammy later perpetuated in the Aunt Jemima advertising trademark: self-sacrificing, white-identified, rotund, asexual, good-humoured, and loyal.

In the early twentieth century, the figure was made popular through hit songs like 'Mammy's Little Coal Black Rose' (1916) and 'My Mammy' (sung by Al Jolson in blackface in *The Jazz Singer*, 1927). In *Imitation of Life*, the 1934 film adaptation of the Fanny Hurst novel,

Aunt Delilah, a Black maid played by Louise Beavers, inherits a pancake recipe. With the assistance of her white boss, Bea Pullman (Claudette Colbert), she turns the recipe into a thriving business, although her success comes at the expense of her own family. Aunt Delilah was not only a prototypical Mammy, but also an Aunt Jemima caricature.

Mass-media products like pancake mix kept Mammy alive as a dream in which white America could live in a world where Black folks, content to remain as faithful servants, shrugged off any anger about past (and present) injustices at the hands of whites. Instead, they are depicted as grateful for the 'good white folks' who give them employment – and their sense of self.

The mythologization of the Mammy figure reached its zenith in the early twentieth century when members of the United Daughters of the Confederacy (UDC) lobbied the U.S. government for a monument 'in memory of the faithful slave mammies of the South.' Founded in 1894, the UDC's main goal was to raise funds for memorials to Confederate soldiers. In 1923, however, the UDC, along with the Sons of Confederate Veterans, sought not only to pay tribute to the fallen Confederate soldiers but also promote the idea that slaves were loyal to the system of slavery, and that Blacks, too, longed for a pre–Civil War past.[2] The faithful-slave myth became a vehicle for white Southerners to justify the institution of slavery and its successor, segregation. These heritage groups sought to commemorate loyal slaves and servants – the Uncle Toms and Aunt Chloes – who did not rebel against their masters during the Civil War. The UDC's bronze monuments would forever identify the South's uncles and aunts as martyrs for the 'Lost Cause,' a belief among Southerners that their fight in the Civil War was noble rather than racist.

After the Civil War, both Northerners and Southerners built monuments to commemorate those who died. While Northerners celebrated their victory and paid tribute to their heroes, Southerners used monument building to remember the cause and mourn their losses. As of 2019, there were 718 Confederate monuments and statues across the U.S. in commemoration of the South's 'Lost Cause.' In 2020, however, in response to the Black Lives Matter movement, and the tragic death of George Floyd, dozens of monuments were removed or slated for removal.

For the most part, these monuments were not erected during the Reconstruction era (1863–77); rather, the vast majority went up between the 1890s and 1930s. The statue of Confederate Army commander Robert E. Lee, for example, was commissioned in 1917 by Paul Goodloe McIntire, a white Virginia businessman, and dedicated in 1924 in Market Street Park in Charlottesville. These symbols of slavery made manifest a collective denial of the extreme racial violence that African Americans suffered during enslavement, through Reconstruction and into the period of Jim Crow segregation at the turn of the century. They represent a way of life where race served to create a rigid social hierarchy that white Southerners both welcomed and regarded as necessary. Such monuments and statues make tangible a nostalgia for a past – and a pastoralism of Southern slavery – that did not exist. And, because of groups like the UDC, this white desire to revive the feeling of the antebellum period found expression in the halls of the U.S. Congress.

The UDC emerged from networks of women's hospital associations, sewing societies, and knitting circles across the South. Membership was open to descendants of Confederate soldiers or those 'who gave material aid to the cause.' By World War I, the UDC had a membership of about twenty-five thousand women in seven hundred chapters across thirty-two states.

One of the ways in which the UDC asserted its belief in the contentedness of Black servants was through the curation of pro–Ku Klux Klan propaganda. In 1914, for example, the in-house historian of the UDC Mississippi chapter, Laura Martin Rose, published *The Ku Klux Klan, or Invisible Empire*. In a chapter titled 'Carpet-Baggers, Scalawags, and Negroes' she writes:

> [T]he negroes, many of them proved most faithful. Some followed their masters to the war, others remained with 'ole Mistis and de Chillun,' looking after their wants and protecting them in every means in their power. Even after the war, many Negroes declined to accept their freedom, seeming to regard it

as something thrust upon them which they neither appreciated nor desired, and preferred to remain with 'their white folks.'[3]

When the UDC lobbied Congress to erect a monument to Mammy, one Southern Congressman said, 'The traveller, as he passes by, will recall that epoch of southern civilization [when] fidelity and loyalty' prevailed. 'No class of any race of people held in bondage could be found anywhere who lived more free from care or distress.'[4] The bill passed in the Senate, but was defeated in the House of Representatives.

Almost a century later, in 2017, following riots over the proposed removal of Robert E. Lee's monument in Charlottesville, the UDC issued a rare public statement. In an open letter to the membership, president general Patricia M. Bryson, wrote, 'We are grieved that certain hate groups have taken the Confederate flag and other symbols as their own.' The letter went on to condemn anyone who promotes racial divisiveness or white supremacy.' 'Join us,' she urged, 'in denouncing hate groups and affirming that Confederate memorial statues and monuments are part of our shared American history and should remain in place.'[5] In effect, her statement denied that the intention of such monuments was to keep African Americans mired in a past of enslavement, servitude, and 'loyalty' to whites.

While the UDC 's Faithful Slave Memorial Committee failed to erect a monument to Mammy, it succeeded in memorializing Uncle Tom. In 1931, the UDC dedicated the Heyward Shepherd Monument in Harpers Ferry, Virginia. Heyward Shepherd, a free Black man, was shot and killed during an 1859 attempt by abolitionist John Brown to initiate a slave revolt in the South by taking over a U.S. military arsenal.

A story in the May 29, 1910 issue of the Chicago Tribune *is headlined 'To Build a Monument to "Ol' Black Mammy."'*

As historian Paul Shackel explains, many of the post–Civil War advancements made by African Americans in the South had vanished due to Jim Crow laws and the terrorism orchestrated by the Ku Klux Klan. By the turn of the century, he continues, many Southerners believed that African Americans could play only a subservient role in the segregated South because they had proven themselves to be 'inept in handling their newfound freedom.'[6]

Early twentieth-century popular culture, such as D. W. Griffith's *The Birth of a Nation* (1915), reinforced this belief. The film told the 'story' of the Old South, the Civil War, the Reconstruction period, and the emergence of the Ku Klux Klan. In the film, Griffith created Black archetypes: 'faithful souls' such as Mammies and Uncle Toms, as well as Black 'bucks' – brutal and oversexed men who grew violent and frenzied as they sought out white women. As one of the first feature films in U.S. history, its perceived realism left an indelible mark on audiences. Many were too young to have experienced the events depicted in the film and regarded Griffith's version as factual. Even Virginia-born President Woodrow Wilson, after a White House screening of the film, reportedly remarked, 'It's like writing history with lightning. And my only regret is that it is all terribly true.'[7]

By 1923, Jim Crow laws, rampant lynching, and economic peonage had effectively re-enslaved African Americans in the South; meanwhile, Blacks who migrated north during and after World War I were greeted by the worst race riots in the nation's history. In the capital, in addition to

Scene from The Birth of a Nation. *Director: D. W. Griffith, 1915.*

screening *Birth of a Nation*, Wilson also moved to segregate federal facilities. Encouraged by an overtly racist movie that exalted the Ku

Klux Klan, Klan members throughout the 1920s won control of mayors' offices and state legislatures across the nation.[8] Even though African Americans were not pleased with the erection of the Heyward Shepherd Monument, the sentiment across America was one of white supremacy, from the old plantations of the South to the White House and mansions of the North. America was in the grip of anti-Black racism, even as popular culture continued to exalt a deeply nostalgic view of Black servants and cooks.

꓾

Uncle Tom's Cabin had to be reimagined to fit within this milieu. When the novel first appeared in 1852, tensions over slavery had reached a fever pitch. Under the Compromise of 1850, slavery would not be allowed in new western states like California, New Mexico, and Utah.[9] In the decades following the end of the Civil War, *Uncle Tom's Cabin*, the novel, waned in popularity even while audiences flocked to the minstrel-inspired Tom shows.

Public interest in commemorating the Civil War grew toward the end of the nineteenth century. The Reconstruction era had left many questions unanswered about the future of race relations in the U.S. and sparked a renewed curiosity about life before the war. Against this backdrop, the figure of Uncle Tom was revived not as a symbol of the clash between slavery and abolitionism, but rather as an expression of a renewed desire by many Americans to situate Blacks as loyal, subservient, and the embodiment of a *better* past.

The evolution of popular images of Black men mirrored the shift in the depiction of Uncle Tom. Following the end of the Civil War, some paintings and sculptures depicted enslaved and semi-nude Black men exulting their emancipation by holding up broken manacles and kneeling in gratitude before godlike, formally clad whites.[10] The 1876 Emancipation Memorial in Lincoln Park, Washington, D.C., for instance, depicts an elegant President Abraham Lincoln standing over a kneeling and shirtless Archer Alexander, a formerly enslaved African American, who looks up wearily. Born into slavery around 1810 in

Richmond, Virginia, Alexander, like Josiah Henson, was often hired out to do handyman chores such as bricklaying because he was seen as a 'good worker.' He worked as an overseer of other slaves on plantations in Missouri, and never ran away.

The abolition of slavery only intensified the problem of how to represent Black men in visual culture. Once abolished, slavery retreated to the domain of memory. There, those collective memories had to be reckoned with in one way or another: suppressed, integrated, or romanticized. Emancipation, in effect, moved four million formerly enslaved African Americans, with their history of enslavement, into the national memory.

It is not a coincidence that the Emancipation Memorial mirrors a headpiece illustration by Hammatt Billings, the American illustrator of *Uncle Tom's Cabin*. Appearing on the title page for chapter thirty-eight of the second edition (which had 117 new pictures in addition to the six engravings that appeared in the original edition), it is almost identical to the statue, except that Jesus stands in the place of Lincoln, Uncle Tom in the place of Alexander. There are later photographic images that can be found in archives such as the Library of Congress that evoke the Emancipation statue in style, appearance, and sentiment. Yet in these, a white man in blackface wearing pinstripes replaces Alexander while the Lincoln-like figure wears a suit with the words 'civil rights' printed on his sleeve. Such images conjure up the trope of Blacks 'piggybacking' on the shoulders of whites – a highly popular narrative in the post–Civil War era.

By the end of the nineteenth century, two comforting antebellum figures – Black uncles and aunts – began to reappear in music and theatre. 'Dixie' in turn came to symbolize nostalgia for the character of the eleven Southern states that tried to secede from the Union prior to the Civil War. This was the region where Southerners had fought to maintain a way of life and an economic system built on cotton, tobacco, and free labour.

During Reconstruction, it was very common for a freed man, ragged, miserable, and pining for Dixie, to sing songs like 'The Dear Old Home We Loved so Well.' Other published works of sheet music depict a feeble old Black man groping his way home and singing, 'I'se Gwine Back to Dixie.' This profusion of aging Uncles in popular culture created the impression that they were returning to the South to find happiness and eventually die in peace.

⚜

Against this backdrop, Uncle Tom by the 1890s had been transformed into an 'old folk.' New editions of *Uncle Tom's Cabin*, mostly published in the North, often pointed out that questions of Black freedom were no longer popular. As *Uncle Tom's Cabin* literary historian Barbara Hochman writes, 'these editions ... often acknowledge that "the great emancipation question of a few decades ago" did not sustain "all the old interest" for contemporary readers ... [T]he feeling [was] that Uncle Tom had "outlived his usefulness, his day and generation."'[11] The novel's once popular sentimentalist themes of freedom and escape, evangelicalism and religiosity, now seemed anachronistic and irrelevant to a new generation of readers, audiences, and playwrights.

Nevertheless, by continually restaging the story of Uncle Tom, white actors, producers, and artists found a way to keep slavery viable as an ideology of race and class. By the end of the nineteenth century, an estimated four to five hundred Uncle Tom troupes were actively performing onstage, providing a major source of employment for Black actors.[12] Uncle Tom's further encroachment into the popular imagination via advertising must be understood in terms of how consumer products, by the end of the nineteenth century, had become powerful agents for image making.

First, goods that relied on the Uncle Tom trope were never 'just products.' They were deeply imbued with widely held beliefs about race and the supposed inferiority of Black people. Scholars like Anne McClintock have written extensively about advertising and 'commodity racism' in the late nineteenth and early twentieth centuries. 'In advertising,' she explains, 'the axis of possession is shifted to the axis of spectacle. Advertising's chief contribution to the culture of modernity was the discovery that by manipulating the semiotic space around the commodity, the unconscious as a public space could also be manipulated.'[13] Advertising, then, has always been invested in Black bodies while simultaneously disavowing that investment through ridicule or ambivalence.

Second, nineteenth-century concepts such as 'aura,' or the devaluation of images through mass reproduction, did not fit the narrative of Uncle Tom. The more Uncle Tom was reproduced and reimagined in new visual forms – first lithography, then advertising, and eventually film and television – the more his aura expanded.

Further, the standardization and mass production of Uncle Tom (and derivatives like Rastus) comforted white people because he had become a trusted friend and a loyal companion. We cannot talk about the use of Black bodies in advertising without acknowledging the ways racial difference became part of the process of selling goods geared primarily toward white people. In this sense, capitalism and commodification have bred the conditions of nostalgia, in which evoking memory became a method of socially positioning consumers to view products as inseparable from their lived experiences.

African American literature and history professor Saidiya Hartman writes that Blackness in *Uncle Tom's Cabin* was delineated by 'darky' antics – lying, loafing, stealing, and breakdown dancing – and therefore even saintly Tom's performance was embellished with minstrelsy. The convergence of abolitionism's sentimental structure and pro-slavery discourse was apparent in the stage productions of *Uncle Tom's Cabin*, Hartman argues.[14] The Old South pastoralism in Uncle Tom imagery, productions, and products narrated a distinctive kind of social experience and relationship with the past. From the Reconstruction era onward, advertising engendered feelings that were both social and material.

❧

For over two centuries, nostalgia has been used to soothe distress about moral and ethical upheaval by speaking to, and about, memories of the past. Aunt Jemima took consumers back to a time of the

Southern Mammy and homespun wisdom in the form of a cook/nursemaid. Rastus recalled a time of happy-to-please Black cooks whose joy was derived not only from whites enjoying their cooking, but also from the very job itself.

This kind of memory-making reframes the past as a better, simpler time, as opposed to the present that is dominated by conflict, division, and turmoil. The use of human characters in advertising and on packages marked an important shift in people's understanding of consumer products. It was an indication that manufacturers understood that packaged goods had to establish a relationship with the consumer – a relationship that replaced, or at least supplemented, any relationship the buyer might have had with individual storekeepers.[15]

It is within this context that we can begin to understand how a constantly evolving Uncle Tom migrated from the pages of Stowe's novel and the minstrel stage onto the boxes, packages, and advertising pages of newspapers in the early twentieth century. This context also explains the birth of Uncle Tom's most direct spinoffs: Sambo and Uncle Remus.

8

SAMBO AND UNCLE REMUS

In 1957, Sam Battistone Sr. and Newell Bohnett launched the first of a chain of Sambo's restaurants in Santa Barbara, California. Soon after, another Sambo's popped up; Ronald and Matilda Krieger opened Lil' Black Sambo's in Oceanlake, a community in Lincoln City, Oregon. The brand was very popular; when the National Association for the Advancement of Colored People (NAACP) protested against Sambo's restaurant chain in the early 1960s, it was to little effect. As of the late 1970s, Sambo's was still advertising widely. In 1981, however, the chain was forced to close 447 of its 1,114 restaurants. Within two years, Denny's began acquiring its locations.[1] Today, only the original Santa Barbara restaurant remains.

Sambo's name was ostensibly taken from portions of the names of its co-founders, Sam and Bohnett, but the franchise took its inspiration for the brand from a character by that name from decades earlier. Lil' Black Sambo in Lincoln City, now known as Lil' Sambo's Family Restaurant, admits on its website that its original name was borrowed from the 'hero of a fictional story about an Indian boy, tigers, and pancakes written by Helen Bannerman in 1899.'[2] 'Little Black Sambo' first entered popular culture in 1899, when Helen Bannerman, a Scottish author of children books, wrote a story following a trip to India; at the time, authors were creating recognizable Black characters to take their place alongside the generic Mammies and Uncles already in print. Sambo was one. Though Bannerman wrote several other stories with the prefix 'Little Black' – 'Little Black

Quibba,' 'Little Black Quasha,' and 'Little Black Mingo' – Sambo remains best remembered because of the wider cultural meanings attached to the word 'Sambo.'

The name has West African roots but was an all-purpose pejorative for supposedly inferior Black men. The name amused Portuguese and Spanish enslavers because it sounded like 'zambo,' a word for monkey. Anglophones eventually adopted it as a funny-sounding diminutive of Sam.[3] Then, as now, humour provided manoeuvrability, in that the 'joke' helped to mask, if desired, outright hostility while perpetuating racist images of Black males as fools.[4]

The typical Sambo figure was depicted with an unusually wide mouth filled with large, carnivorous white teeth and encircled by thick, ruby-red protruding lips. The eyes in these depictions – often in advertisements – typically bulge in an expression of ecstatic fright.[5] Sambos fit into a large category of consumer product caricatures; from black rag dolls to cookie jars, cream-and-sugar sets, spice containers, cornmeal and pancake mixes, cigarette lighters, Halloween masks, recipe cards, cookbooks, and syrup pitchers, the Black body has been the literal object of consumption and nostalgia.

Bannerman's Sambo character did not come out of nowhere. There were multiple examples in nineteenth-century British visual culture that primed the public with a vocabulary for derogatory Black characters. For example, the artist Henry James Pidding's 1828 print entitled *Massa Out. 'Sambo Werry Dry,'* which depicted a Black male servant sitting at a table by an open window at night, pouring wine into a glass with a smirk on his face. He looks to be in conversation with the dog seated at his feet and appears to take pleasure in the fact that he has gained access to his master's wine cellar.[6] George Cruikshank, the illustrator for the British *Uncle Tom's Cabin*, also created images of Sambo in books such as *George Cruikshank's Omnibus* (1842). In the illustrations, Frank Heartwell, a white man, is accompanied by his sidekick, Sambo, who is rendered so dark that in the prints, his features are indistinguishable.[7]

Little Black Sambo eventually crossed the Atlantic, becoming part of the visual culture of the United States. In the late 1880s, the N. K.

Fairbanks Company introduced cartoon images of two Black children, the Gold Dust Twins (Goldy and Dusty), to promote its brand of soap. Like Aunt Jemima and Rastus, Goldy and Dusty became embodied caricatures. The inspiration for the twins came from a cartoon in the English humour magazine *Punch* that showed two Black children washing each other in a tub. The caption read, 'Warranted to wash clean and not fade.' The campaign was created by a company executive who thought it was funny and the firm commissioned an artist to draw the twins for the washing powder package in 1887.[8]

A decade or so later, Black children were being hired to play Sambos – casting choices that continued the habit of employing 'real' Black people to perform as fictionalized consumer brands. In 1902, during a trade convention in Chicago, Fairbanks' marketer selected David Henry Snipe and Thomas (last name unknown) to pose as the Gold Dust Twins. Such ads exploited Black children by presenting them as docile, ignorant, and grotesque. Reinforcing the caricature, the company hired these children to hand out product samples and pamphlets at major public exhibitions, such as the 1904 St. Louis World's Fair.[9]

The notion of soap as a product capable of alchemizing change lay at the core of the use of Black children in these trademarks. The ad's selling point, after all, was the apparent transformative power of the product. The unsubtle subtext is that Blackness equated to dirt, while whiteness meant cleanliness.[10]

The Sambo children harkened back to Stowe's Uncle Tom in a few ways. First, they evoked the trope of Black childhood, most prominently depicted in the character of Topsy, a motherless, unkempt, immoral waif. Additionally, just as *Uncle Tom's Cabin* had its knock-offs, so too did Bannerman's story when it was published in the U.S. In 1917, Cupples & Leon Company, a New York firm, published *All About Little Black Sambo* in an edition illustrated by John B. Gruelle, an illustrator best known for creating the Raggedy Ann and Raggedy Andy dolls. The book featured Sambo in a raincoat and 'knickers,' but no shirt, and holding an umbrella. While he is coal-black with a clownish white mouth, he is not at all cute, and is presented more as a trickster.[11]

As a refracted Topsy emptied of innocence, Sambo became another prototype for the 'pickaninny,' the dehumanized Black juvenile that emerged from advertising images (such as the Gold Dust Twins) to become a staple of U.S. popular culture.[12] Importantly, pickaninnies were not only commonplace depictions of Black children in children's literature but also figured in early cinema. For example, Thomas Edison in 1908 created *Ten Pickaninnies*, a series of ten scenes in a short film about anonymous Black children. Each carried a caption: 'snowballs, cherubs, coons, bad chillum, inky kids, smoky kids, black lambs, cute ebonies, and chubbie ebonies.'[13] As Debbie Olson writes in *Black Children in Hollywood Cinema*, 'Shorts like *Ten Pickaninnies* and the numerous versions of *Uncle Tom's Cabin* that followed positioned black children within the narrow confines of old-style racial stereotypes.'[14]

Uncle Tom's Cabin further provides a template for probing how white authors framed Uncles in relation to pickaninnies. In contrast to the angelic (white) Eva, Topsy is a liar and a cheat. She knows no better because slavery has deprived her of both family and a moral compass.[15] In subsequent stage productions, Topsy was portrayed as incorrigible, but for comedic purposes; her childhood difficulties, in other words, were made into a joke. There is a direct line between Stowe's Topsy and the numerous Black children who performed in the role of Sambo on early-twentieth-century soap packages.

❧

Uncle Remus was the titular character in a collection of folk tales adapted and compiled by Joel Chandler Harris (1848–1908). When these stories first appeared in book form, they amplified the association between Uncle Tom as a literary character and public notions of Black servitude and nostalgia for Southern plantation life.

In 1879, Harris, a white American journalist, began producing tales about a figure called Uncle Remus in newspaper installments in the *Atlanta Constitution*. These would become the first literary iterations of Stowe's Uncle Tom. Harris published 'The Story of Mr. Rabbit and Mr. Fox as Told by Uncle Remus,' the first of twenty-four tales that would eventually be published as *Uncle Remus: His Songs and His Sayings* (1880). Harris's illustrated Uncle Remus stories were so-called recollections of an idyllic South, featuring a benign, if cagey, old Black storyteller. Uncle Remus's tales were trickster stories about the exploits of Brer Rabbit, Brer Fox, and other 'creeturs' created by Harris, who presented himself as an amateur folklorist, children's author, and literary comedian.[16]

Uncle Remus: His Songs and His Sayings included folk tales, old plantation songs, and Remus's Atlanta street sketches. After its success, Harris wrote six more volumes of Uncle Remus stories, including an 1895 revised edition of his first book, illustrated by Arthur Burdett Frost. Two more volumes would appear posthumously, followed in 1955 by *The Complete Tales of Uncle Remus*, a collection of all 185 tales, edited by Richard Chase.

The Uncle Remus Museum, located in Eatonton, Georgia, is a memorial to Harris. According to its website, Harris is described as having 'voiced the African American critter tales he heard as a boy working at Turnwold Plantation through Uncle Remus, a composite character drawn from several local slaves who shared the stories with him.' Like Stowe, and minstrelsy's early 'delineators,' Harris is remembered for his first-hand accounts of 'witnessing' enslaved Blacks on Southern plantations singing songs, telling folk tales, and waxing nostalgic for the Old South. Uncle Remus, like Uncle Tom, constructs Black men as non-threatening and childlike.

This depiction of Harris is, of course, a complete denial of the reality of how the trope of Uncle was used to erect a symbolic boundary between whites and Blacks, ensuring that the latter were trapped forever on the plantation. As Harvard scholar Henry Louis Gates Jr. has written, 'Dialect signified both "black difference" and that the figure of the black in literature existed primarily as object, not subject; and even sympathetic characterizations of the black, such as Uncle Remus, by Joel Chandler Harris, were far more related to a racist textual tradition that stemmed from minstrelsy, the plantation novel, and vaudeville than to representations of spoken language.'[17]

The earlier evocations of Little Eva and Uncle Tom were clear: 'When plantation writer Joel Chandler Harris posed an unnamed white "Little Boy" on the knee of the happily enslaved Uncle Remus,' observes historian Robin Bernstein, 'the propinquity between a white child and an African American adult transferred innocence from white childhood to a political endeavour: abolition or post-Reconstruction romanticization of slavery, respectively.'[18] White children's innocence was transferable to surrounding people and things, and that property made it politically useful. This image had great staying power. Decades after the Uncle Remus tales were first published, Hollywood films *The Green Pastures* (1936) and Disney's *Song of the South* (1946) reproduced the pairing of white innocent children and old, childlike uncles. Such depictions also affirmed Uncle Tom's final transformation into an old man with grey hair and beard and, sometimes, reading glasses.

Uncle Remus, like Uncle Tom, began as a literary figure. But similar to the illustrations of Uncle Tom, when the American artist A. B. Frost illustrated Harris's Uncle Remus tales, the figure of the folksy 'Black-talking' old man from the South became more real. Uncle Remus was depicted as playful, harmless, neighbourly, and always happy. As a reinvented Uncle plucked from the blackface minstrel stage and out of the pages of 'Negro-dialect' literature, the familiar figure of Remus was well positioned to push root beer, breakfast cereal, salted peanuts, tobacco, thread, sweets, and numerous other consumer goods.[19]

In fact, the success of commodity products like Aunt Jemima and, later, Uncle Ben, lay in what psychoanalyst Carl Jung described as 'the collective unconscious.' Generations of white children, even those who did not live in the segregated South, were introduced to Black people through such mythic figures as Uncle Remus. Black faces, from Uncle Tom to Sambo, Rastus, and Aunt Jemima, adorned the packaged products that they constantly consumed in their kitchens. Because the fictional Black servant was ubiquitous in the visual and commercial culture of North America, 'real' Black servants were unable to be seen as anything but Uncle Toms or Aunt Jemimas as the twentieth century wore on.

SLEEPING CAR PORTERS AND UNCLE BEN

During the years between the two world wars, a caricature of Uncle Tom emerged not only in images but also in real life. As versions of Uncle Tom appeared on endless postcards and in magazine advertisements, the happy-to-serve stereotype was also required of the Black men who shined shoes or worked as bellhops, house chefs, and porters on the railways' sleeping cars.

As tourism became more common and affordable, rail travel came to be one of the primary modes of transportation for middle-class whites. The combination of expanding railroads and the emerging rapprochement between Northern and Southern whites who shared a nostalgia for the Old South made the postwar South a popular travel destination with Northerners.[1] It was on those railways that Black men were expected to be 'ready-to-serve' Uncles, once George Pullman, the American railway baron, developed the first sleeping car service.

The Pullman Palace Car Company introduced its sleeping car service in the 1860s. These cars were the first to allow passengers to stay overnight on the train in private cabins with fold-out beds. American and Canadian railway companies modelled their sleeping and dining car services on Pullman's plan, favouring Black men for the task of serving affluent white passengers. These jobs afforded Black workers an opportunity to earn a place on the rails – they were excluded from engineering positions – and railway companies eagerly sought Black men who would perform the role of the broad-smiling, white-gloved, crisp-uniformed servant. Because of this hiring policy, the railway companies earned millions while Black porters served wealthy white travellers. These tourists would have been familiar not only with *Uncle Tom's Cabin* but also the ubiquitous images of servile Black men, found in magazines they might have been reading while on the train. What these travellers may not have understood was the link between Stowe's literary Uncle Tom and the porters catering to their every need as they dined, slept, and relaxed.

As paid employees, these porters had very few rights of recourse against mistreatment. Those who fought back against racism were fired. They were also often treated like second-class citizens. The porter was on call 24/7, responding to the needs of passengers without much time to sleep or eat. Once assigned to a car, porters ensured it was clean and fully equipped, buffing, and polishing everything before their white passengers boarded.

On the journey, the sleeping car porters were responsible for remembering passengers' schedules and could be harshly reprimanded when someone missed his or her stop. They were, for all intents and purposes, servants, and could be treated as such. Just as many whites dismissively called Black men 'boy,' passengers condescendingly called the porters 'George,' likely after George Pullman, regardless of their actual names.

The figure of the sleeping car porter became a cultural touchstone, laden with meaning. According to journalist and editor Brando Simeo Starkey, who wrote *In Defense of Uncle Tom*, two kinds of Uncle Toms appeared in the sleeping-car period between 1896 and 1954. The first is what Starkey calls the 'Servile Uncle Tom,' a Black male whose relationship with whites mimics that of servant and boss, or worse, slave and master.[2] The Servile Uncle Tom, in the real world, relents to oppression; rather than striving for a more just society, Starkey says, the Servile Uncle Tom accepts his unequal lot and subordinates himself to whites.

Starkey's second archetype is the 'Sellout Uncle Tom.' He is someone who 'purposefully fashions himself to be useful in the maintenance of white supremacy and appreciates the personal benefit in being co-opted.'[3] Servile Uncle Toms do not necessarily lack socio-cultural awareness of the implications of their roles. But for survival in a racially segregated environment (these were the Jim Crow decades, after all), they were willing to risk reprimand within the Black community if it meant that they had a job. The Pullman sleeping car porters fit into the category of the Servile Uncle Tom.

A 'Pullman porter' making the bed of an upper berth, aboard the Capitol Limited, bound for Chicago, Illinois. Photographer: Jack Delano, 1942.

Black men employed as porters certainly experienced racial discrimination and exploitation on the job. Many were not even provided with sleeping quarters aboard the trains. Also, it is important to remember that being a railway porter was, in many instances, the only work available to Black men at the time. As David Pilgrim reminds us, the Jim Crow system was undergirded by beliefs and rationalizations by whites that they were superior to Black people in all important ways: 'intelligence, mortality, and civilized behavior.'[4] The dominant ideology of the time asserted that to treat Black men as equals would encourage interracial sexual unions and destroy the U.S. as a white nation. Consequently, white individuals and institutions used the threat of violence to keep African Americans at the bottom of the social hierarchy. While some Black men did adopt a servile approach to their jobs, they were keenly aware of the desire among white travellers for them to perform as Uncle Toms. In private, these proud men were socially and politically aware of the world around them.

What's more, because of their highly mobile lifestyles and connections to urban centres, sleeping car porters quickly emerged as agents of political mobilization. These men moved across North America. They carried with them jazz, magazines, culture, and politics wherever they went. Between the two world wars, porters even created institutions such as a railway union, a Black press, and various racial uplift associations that became national organizations almost overnight by enabling rapid dissemination of information.[5]

The sleeping car porter was a product of the times. The passage of the Thirteenth, Fourteenth, and Fifteenth Amendments to the U.S. Constitution (1864–70) granted African Americans the same legal protections as whites. But because whites in Southern and border states felt threatened by Blacks, state legislatures in these regions enacted laws that restricted their liberties.[6] In 1890, Louisiana passed the 'Separate Car Act,' which created 'separate but equal' cars for Blacks and whites. The statute made it illegal for any Black person to sit in coach seats reserved for whites, while whites could not sit in seats reserved for Black people. The law, in effect, created the commercial conditions for rail service to replicate the master/servant relations of pre–Civil War plantation slavery.

The following year, a group of African Americans decided to test Louisiana's law. While Homer A. Plessy was sufficiently light-skinned (seven-eighths white and one-eighth Black) to 'pass' as white, he was nevertheless considered Black according to the 'one-drop rule.' When Plessy sat down in the whites-only coach one day, he was arrested. In the ensuing landmark case, *Plessy v. Ferguson* (1896), the Supreme Court ruled that African Americans access to the legal system, equal to that of whites, but they had to maintain separate institutions to facilitate these rights.[7] The ruling institutionalized a racial hierarchy that placed whites at the top and Black people at the bottom in nearly every facet of public life. After all, the Jim Crow laws demanded Jim Crow behaviour.

In this environment, Black people were forced to acquiesce to the white public's desire to perpetuate the servile relations of slavery. Blacks who violated Jim Crow norms risked their homes, jobs, and lives. As well, the Black community had little political or legal recourse against white violence. As a result, this period saw the highest incidence of lynchings, the most extreme form of Jim Crow violence.

Lynching was a sanctioned violent act that took place across the United States from 1882, when the first reliable data were collected, to 1968, when lynchings finally became rare. To live in this society meant that Black men and women had to choose not only between racial loyalty and disloyalty, but also between life and death. Survival meant performing as Uncles and Mammies in public or on the job.

By examining the railway and the role Black men played in providing 'comfort' for white passengers, we can begin to grasp the structure of feeling that shaped attitudes reinforced by a deluge of nostalgia for the Old South. As North American society modernized, socially and culturally, Black people were forced to remain in a past of white longing for Black servants. The Servile Uncle Tom, though born on the railway, evoked the plantation in terms of power structure. Within this milieu, the nostalgia for the Old South was also vital to an emergent consumer culture populated by Aunt Jemima, Rastus, and, later, Uncle Ben. In other words, sleeping car porters and these Black trademarked Aunts and Uncles, with their 'authentic' personalities, provided white America with a respite from the world of rapid change. Servitude, then, was no longer limited to slavery. In the twentieth century, advertising and sleeping car porters helped to keep Black servants ubiquitous in the panorama of modern life.

❧

In 1998, African American artist Renee Cox's *The Liberation of Aunt Jemima and Uncle Ben* depicted two contemporary Aunt Jemima Pancake Mix and Uncle Ben's Converted Rice products. The image features two Black women and a Black man. Both women and the man are slender and athletic. The women wear swimsuits (one a black bikini, the other a full one-piece in the colours of Pan-Africanism – red, gold, black, and green), and long black boots. Their hairstyles are also highly politicized (one wears an Afro, the other dreadlocks), and each has sharp blades protruding from their fingers. The message of Cox's piece is clear: Black women (and men) must free themselves from the bondage of commodity culture.

Cox's decision to represent Uncle Ben instead of some of his predecessors – Tom, Rastus, Remus, etc. – was not an accident. There were many options. Besides Rastus, for example, the Schulze Baking Company in the 1920s promoted itself with an image of an old banjo-strumming Tom pitching Uncle Wabash Cupcakes. In the 1940s, Lister-ine used a Black porter figure in its magazine ads, while Mil-Kay Vitamin Drinks put smiling Black waiters on its posters and billboards.[8] Most of these, however, are long forgotten. Of all the Uncle Tom deriva-tives in advertising, Uncle Ben remains the most recognizable and best remembered example of these smiling brand mascots.

The original Uncle Ben, from which Uncle Ben's Converted Rice derived its trademark, was a rice farmer in Houston. According to a *New York Times* editorial on Uncle Ben, 'during World War II, Gordon L. Harwell, a Texas food broker, supplied to the armed forces a special kind of white rice, cooked to preserve the nutrients, under the brand name Converted Rice.'[9] In 1946, Harwell had dinner with a friend in Chicago and he decided that a portrait of the restaurant's *maître d'hotel*, Frank Brown, could represent the brand. He named his product Uncle Ben's Converted Rice and reintroduced it to consumers.

Like Rastus, who was 'discovered' in a restaurant, Brown (who died in 1953) was asked to pose for the picture, likely for nominal pay, that would appear on Uncle Ben's boxes. When first introduced in the 1940s, the Uncle Ben portrait appeared over the entire front of the box. In later years, it was reduced to a small oval located on the upper right-hand side, where it remained until 2020 when, following Aunt Jemima's lead, Mars Inc. announced that it would rebrand Uncle Ben. The company said that in 2021, the brand would be known as 'Ben's Original,' and the image of an older Black man would be dropped from the revamped product. While his image is removed, Ben, like his predecessor, still has no last name or honorific.

Why does the image of a smiling, elderly Black man on a package of instant rice still resonate with consumers in the twenty-first century? As Micki McElya's *Clinging to Mammy* (2007) asks, why are we still clinging to Uncle, just as we cannot let go of Mammy, even as much as we remove their images – 'aunt' or 'uncle' – from their titles?

Uncle Tom and his surrogates – Rastus, Remus, Ben – have had a prominent presence in grocery stores for well over a century, yet most people barely notice the trademarked images or register the racial significance of these branded characters. What is so striking about the original Uncle Ben trademark, however, is that he was dressed as a servant. Like the sleeping car porters, whose servant-like outfits included ties and crisp, white-collared shirts, Uncle Ben wore a bow tie and white-collared shirt. While Rastus prepared Cream of Wheat in the uniform of a cook, Uncle Ben, all these years later, could still be found on supermarket shelves in the guise of a Servile Uncle Tom. Even now that Uncle Ben no longer appears on Converted Rice products and in ads, the image of him without a body or the bow tie, his face positioned above the products while his open white collar presented a visual contrast to the product's red packaging, will linger in both our collective memory and online. This disembodied uncle will continue smiling, even as he is no longer presented as a servant. The elderly father-like figure will live on in perpetuity as a surrogate for Uncle Tom.

10

TOPSY-TURVY DOLLS AND SHIRLEY TEMPLE

Uncle Tom might have been the most famous character in *Uncle Tom's Cabin*, but Topsy, the poorly dressed, neglected Black child, became just as famous for being the novel's most prototypical pickaninny. Stowe describes Topsy as 'one of the blackest of her race.' With her 'woolly hair,' she writes, there was 'something odd and goblin-like about her appearance.'[1]

Where Sambo was the dominant caricature of little Black boys, the pickaninny was the best-known racial caricature of little Black girls. These images were then reproduced and circulated on postcards, posters, and other ephemera. They are the origin of the visual stereotype of Blacks eating watermelon or fried chicken.

As a visual residue of Stowe's novel, the pickaninny was not confined to the kitchen, advertising inserts, or the cartoon sections of newspapers. The racially charged image found its way into other corners of daily life, from mass-produced toys to blockbuster films. In the case of Topsy in particular, there were countless minstrel show versions of the character, and later variations showed up in films such as Thomas Edison's *Ten Pickaninnies* (1908) and British mystery writer Agatha Christie's *And Then There Were None* (1939), which became widely associated with the nursery rhyme 'Ten Little Niggers' ('Ten Little Indians' or 'Ten Little Soldiers' in later editions). All these depictions presented Black children as not only impoverished but also wild and animal-like, fending for themselves in a world of Black parental neglect.

In the decades prior to George Cruikshank producing his illustrations for the first British edition of *Uncle Tom's Cabin*, popular representation of Black people had become increasingly aligned with that era's pervasive racism, which projected an inferior status on the Black body. Cruikshank's 1847 work *De Black Dollibus* was inspired by advertising campaigns promoting a Black doll. In the lithograph series, the Black doll is worshipped as being exceptionally capable in the kitchen. A white nurse tends to a Black rag doll, who will be revered in the kitchen; in another version, English cooks kneel before the idol of an enlarged Black doll. In yet another, Black dolls in frilled bonnets mimic a blackface minstrel group. The dolls and accompanying text make an explicit link between these toys and Black Londoners.[2]

Dolls were wildly popular in nineteenth-century America, and they were intended to teach little girls about domesticity.[3] Dolls still perform a similar function today. But, as in the nineteenth century, they can evoke a racial logic that constructs Black childhood as immoral and deprived. Pickaninnies were often shown 'crawling on the ground, climbing trees, straddled over logs, or in other ways assuming animal-like postures.'[4] As recently as 2019, a store in Newark, New Jersey, made international headlines after a photograph went viral showing Black rag dolls for sale with instructions to 'find a wall' and slam them against it. Approximately one thousand dolls were subsequently pulled from the shelves of three One Dollar Zone stores after customers and New Jersey State Assemblywoman Angela McKnight deemed them offensive and racist. Still, what is most telling about this story is that One Dollar Zone president Ricky Shah apologized, but then added, 'This somehow slipped through the cracks.'[5]

Further, in the history of Barbie, the first official African American Barbie did not appear until 1980. In 2016, the Barbie Fashionista collection introduced a diverse number of Barbies to address the historical erasure of Black, Asian, and Latina dolls.

Derogatory Black dolls depicting figures in the mould of the pickaninny, Aunt Jemima, Uncle Tom, and others have never left popular culture, and certainly did not slip through the cracks. Toy makers have been manufacturing and circulating such dolls since before the Civil War.

Where Uncle Tom, Uncle Remus, and Aunt Jemima became commercial icons in part because of the blackface minstrel stage and the pages of 'Negro-dialect' literature, doll culture in the nineteenth century also looked to these icons to bring the pre–Civil War plantation to playrooms and children's bedrooms.[6] Consumers could buy Aunt Jemima rag dolls, kitchenware, and cooking utensils; Uncle Tom dolls, paintings, puzzles, cards, board games, plates, spoons, china figurines, bronze ornaments, dolls, and wallpaper; Uncle Remus dolls, figurines, and other memorabilia.[7] Until the 1960s, Aunt Jemima syrup pitchers were also extremely popular, with more than a million distributed before they were discontinued. The pitcher series included a cookie jar, sugar bowl with a lid, a six-piece spice set, and salt and pepper shakers featuring 'Uncle Mose' – a derivative Uncle Tom who also appeared as a creamer and a cast-iron coin bank.[8]

❧

Of all the characters derived from *Uncle Tom's Cabin*, Topsy had the most enduring impact on nineteenth-century images of Black childhood. Even though most people cannot quite pinpoint when they first heard the phrase 'topsy-turvy' and likely do not know its racial origins, the 'topsy-turvy' doll predates Stowe's novel and the Civil War.

The topsy-turvy doll is two dolls in one. It has two heads – one white, one Black – with the torso of each doll joined at the waist: when a child flips the long skirts of the elegant white girl over the doll's head, she reveals a grinning, wide-eyed pickaninny.[9] These dolls likely originated in plantation nurseries. They are among the oldest handmade rag dolls in North America. Mammy historian Kimberly Wallace-Sanders points out that late-nineteenth-century topsy-turvy dolls had lithographed faces, making them rarer than dolls from the same period with painted faces or hand-stitched features. Later versions, which appeared at the turn of the century and remained popular until the early 1940s, situate a Black Mammy at one end and a white infant at the other.[10] Importantly, their construction positions the Black part of the doll as the 'natural' servant to the white child. But they also project the message that the Black doll is the opposite to the white doll and, by inference, that Black girls are separate from white girls.

White children often staged minstrel performances using Black dolls named Topsy, and white children and adults also 'blacked' up to perform as Black dolls named Topsy (as opposed to costuming themselves as the human character named Topsy). In each situation, childhood historian Robin Bernstein asserts that 'a white child temporarily donned a mask of blackness – cork or doll – and performed according to minstrel conventions.'[11] There were also advertisements that encouraged white children to play with Black dolls. In 1893 and 1894, for example, the Arnold Print Works of Massachusetts advertised Black dolls called 'Topsy' and 'Pickaninny.' 'What child in America does not at some time want a cloth "Nigger" dollie – one that can be petted or thrown about without harm to the doll or anything that it comes in contact with[?] "Pickaninny" fills all the requirements.'[12] The advertisement also claimed the doll could and should be 'thrown about' because it was black and made of cloth. It was desirable because it could be abused, with ads sanctioning violent play with Black dolls. As Bernstein explains, 'many white children performed the violence that black dolls and children's literature co-scripted: they whipped, beat, and hung black dolls with regularity and ritualistic ferocity.'[13]

When one imagines that these dolls were then passed down to little girls and boys, generation after generation, it becomes clear how the pervasive devaluation of Black children and Black bodies is perpetuated, and why the slogan 'Black Lives Matter' does not speak to just the contemporary moment. Over a century of American material and visual culture was rife with anti-Black images, products, and narratives that then became embodied as anti-Black racism.

By the mid-twentieth century, topsy-turvy dolls grew so popular that they were mass-manufactured and widely available in department stores across North America. In Canada, a 1933 Christian edition of a department store catalogue offered a 'Happy Topsy,' the only Black doll among a dozen white dolls described as 'a real lovable pickaninny' with a 'roguish smile.'[14] An ad for a 'Just grown up' Topsy doll also appeared in the September 1937 issue of the Canadian women's magazine *Chatelaine*, with a tagline that read: 'You just can't help liking this happy-go-lucky, fat, coloured baby doll.'[15] Today, topsy-turvy dolls can be found in museums, private collections, and contemporary art galleries. In recent years, the dolls have re-emerged as collectible items available for purchase on the Internet.

Debra Britt, co-founder of National Black Dolls Museum of History and Culture, located in Mansfield, Massachusetts, believes the dolls might have also enabled enslaved children to have something forbidden: a doll that looked like them. 'When the slave master was gone,' she explains, 'the kids would have the black side, but when the slave master was around, they would have the white side.'[16] Additionally, in *Women in Early America*, historian Dorothy A. Mays asserts that enslaved girls on plantations were often paired with the similarly aged daughters of their owners 'to be companion and servant.'[17] Thus, the topsy-turvy dolls reproduced this dynamic between Black girl servants and white girl misses.

The topsy-turvy dolls also reinforced the racial distance between them. While Black girls were tasked with caring for white children, they had to simultaneously perform the role of play companion. In this sense, Stowe's characters of Topsy and Eva provide the most obvious examples of the racial dyad reinforced in the white-Black logic of the topsy-turvy doll.

Uncle Tom's Cabin configured childhood itself as a polarized experience. Topsy, the pickaninny, was a foil to Eva, the angelic white child, indicating the irreconcilable differences between Black and white youth. Yet the physical symbolism of conjoining both figures together in a single doll – with the Black doll stationed figuratively and literally at the end of the white doll – suggests they are somehow connected.

During the vaudeville era, performers Rosetta and Vivian Duncan, also known as 'the Duncan Sisters,' capitalized on the extreme popularity of Topsy and Eva blackface comedy routines. In *Topsy and Eva*, a 1927 silent film directed by Canadian Del Lord, Stowe's *Uncle Tom's Cabin* is remade from the point of view of Topsy. When Topsy (Rosetta) is offered for sale by Simon Legree at a slave auction, she is purchased by Little Eva St. Clare (Vivian), while Uncle Tom and other enslaved characters are turned over to Aunt Ophelia to be cleaned.[18] In the end, after Eva becomes gravely ill, Topsy (like Uncle Tom) prays for her recovery. But whereas Eva dies in Stowe's novel, in *Topsy and Eva*, she recovers. Both Eva and Topsy are reunited as 'friends.' Soon after this film's release, topsy-turvy dolls made a resurgence with consumers, reaffirming the enduring nature of Stowe's characterization of childhood.

In the Duncan Sisters' film, Uncle Tom is played by the African American actor Noble Johnson (1881–1978), who appeared in such films as *Moby Dick* (1930), *The Mummy* (1932), and *King Kong* (1933). Johnson was followed by other African American actors and filmmakers, including Oscar Micheaux, the first African American to produce a feature-length film (*The Homesteader*, 1919) and a sound feature-length film, *The Exile* (1931). Johnson also founded the Lincoln Motion Picture Co. (1916– 22), to produce what would be called 'race films,' movies made for African American audiences and that were ignored by the mainstream film industry.[19] The all-Black company was the first to produce movies portraying African Americans as real people, as opposed to the racial caricatures that dominated late-nineteenth-century theatre and silent films.

In addition to topsy-turvy dolls, 'Beloved Belindy' was another enormously popular doll, created in 1926 by cartoonist John Gruelle. Beloved Belindy was reportedly produced so that Raggedy Ann and her brother Andy, also Gruelle inventions, could have a Mammy.[20] By examining the history of these dolls, we gain insight into the ways in which *Uncle Tom's Cabin* provided a template for reproducing a racial dynamic that implicated not just Black men and women but also Black children.

❧

In the 1930s, the child star Shirley Temple (1928–2014) appeared in a series of films with Bill 'Bojangles' Robinson (1878–1949). The duo recalls Uncle Tom and Eva, as well as the Black-white racial dynamic of *Uncle Tom's Cabin*, with Eva's wavy blond hair refashioned as Shirley Temple's famous ringlets.

The Little Colonel (1935), based on Anne Fellows Johnston's 1895 novel, features tousle-haired Temple as a reluctant young Belle, with Robinson, in an Uncle Tom–inspired role, as her 'servant' pal. *The Littlest Rebel* (1935) was another rendition of Uncle Tom and Eva, where a Southern missy dances around with her best friend, an older male slave named Uncle Billy. Here, Robinson as Uncle Billy portrays a good-natured, well-mannered Uncle Tom to Temple's Virginia Houston Cary, a feisty young daughter of Captain Cary of the Confederate Army. Similarly, in *Old Kentucky* (1935), with Will Rogers, and *Just Around the Corner* (1938), with Temple, Robinson reprises his role as a genial, loyal servant.

Generations of people grew up enjoying the Shirley Temple–Bill Robinson movies. But, stripped of the glow of nostalgia, these films are condescending and belittling. Temple is presented as smarter, wittier, and wiser than Robinson, even though he is at least fifty years her senior. African American film historian Donald Bogle observes that Temple and her Black servants were 'buddies' in the sense that 'the servants' vitality, spontaneity, and childlike qualities equalled her own.'[21] As they danced, sang, and laughed together, Temple and her subservient 'buddies' gave Depression-era audiences the impression that as long as Black people remained smiling, serving, and happy, they could soothe white people's fears in an uncertain time. By eliminating any possibility of interracial sexual relations between Black men and white women, these films subtly offer the upbeat Robinson as a cinematic antidote to the ambient instability of the Depression. While many white audiences might not have had control over their own lives, they could vicariously enjoy a sense of control in the presence of Robinson's docile Black servant. Shirley Temple, like a topsy-turvy doll, also embodied the public's desire to reframe Black-white relations as collegial, uncomplicated, and equal. The logic was simple:

Black people were not discriminated against by whites; rather, they 'liked' serving and working in menial jobs. In reality, they did not. In fact, as *Uncle Tom's Cabin* was repeatedly reimagined on the big screen in those first decades of the twentieth century, this revisionist reframing of the past became ever more grandiose.

﷯

In 2018, *Mary Poppins Returns* hit North American theatres. The film, directed by Rob Marshall with a screenplay by David Magee, stars Emily Blunt as Mary Poppins. The movie is based on the book series by P. L. Travers, and reads as a sequel to the 1964 film, made famous by Julie Andrews. *Mary Poppins Returns* picked up four Oscar nominations, but also ignited a very contemporary debate about the use of blackface and an updated version of the Topsy doll.

In one of the most memorable scenes from the 1964 film, Poppins accompanies the Banks children, Michael and Jane, up their chimney and her face gets covered in soot. Instead of wiping it off, she blackens her face even further by applying more soot to her nose and cheeks. She then leads the children in a dance number across the rooftops in London alongside chimney sweeper Bert (Dick Van Dyke). Her soot-covered figure evokes the Dutch character 'Zwarte Piet' or Black Pete, a companion of 'Sinterklaas' (Saint Nicholas), who appeared for centuries with a soot-blackened face in the Netherlands.

Black Pete is the helper of Sinterklaas, a Roman Catholic prelate who arrives each year in November from Spain, where he purportedly lives, to celebrate his birthday on the fifth of December. Sinterklaas rides on horseback over roofs while his helper, Black Pete, goes down the chimneys to deliver presents to children. When he reappears, his face is covered with chimney soot.[22]

In 2013, the United Nations established a research group to examine whether Black Pete was indeed a racist figure. The question was contentious: while critics complained that the figure in blackface is a hurtful, racist remnant of slavery, others fiercely defended what they saw as an essential element of Dutch culture.[23]

In an article in the *New York Times*, literature professor Daniel Pollack-Pelzner opined that the blacking up in the chimney-sweep scene in *Mary Poppins Returns*, like the 1964 original, continues the legacy of racist caricature. In his review, Pollack-Pelzner draws parallels between the pickaninny and the 'dark-lit grins and unflappable footwork of the lamplighters [who] turn their dangerous labour into comic play.'[24]

But he also traces the historical connections of minstrelsy, which run through Travers's books all the way to Disney musicals. 'Blackface minstrelsy,' he writes, 'could be said to be part of Disney's origin story.'[25] In an early Mickey Mouse short, a 1933 parody of *Uncle Tom's Cabin* called *Mickey's Mellerdrammer*, Mickey puts on blackface to become Topsy, who is portrayed in a similar light to Stowe's Topsy.

Pollack-Pelzner also observes how, in *Mary Poppins Returns*, Meryl Streep plays Topsy, yet another variation on 'Mr. Turvy,' from Travers's 1935 novel *Mary Poppins Comes Back*, whose workshop 'flips upside-down.'[26] In the film, Streep's Topsy similarly owns a shop where she can fix everything, and whose shop flips upside-down every second Wednesday in a dance number called, 'Turning Turtle.' As Pollack-Pelzner brilliantly illustrates, the *Uncle Tom's Cabin* trope of a Black-white dyad is so embedded in our visual culture and historical memory that even after all these iterations, aspects of Stowe's Topsy remain visible. More significantly, the spinoff 'topsy-turvy' entertainments continue to appeal to twenty-first-century audiences that may know nothing about their origins.

In the Netherlands, defenders of Black Pete argue that Sinterklaas is a celebration for children, that he represents the innocence and magic of times past.[27] The idea of white childhood innocence is often intertwined with nostalgia for racist caricatures. In fact, for many adults, it is very difficult to question something that was enjoyable in childhood. While these toys and characters were built on the debasement of Black people, they remain strongly associated with cherished childhood memories, and thus defended.

The argument is simple: '*Mary Poppins* in 1964 cannot be racist because I really liked it as a child and times were different.' Similarly, '*Mary Poppins Returns* is not racist either. It is merely staying true to the original.' Topsy-inspired characters will continue to turn up in popular culture because the imagery, for all its racist antecedents, has become so normalized that most people do not even notice it.

ॐ

In 2019, Alison Saar exhibited *Grow'd* at the L.A. Louver in Venice, California. The single work was inspired by Stowe's Topsy and was in the tradition of her mother, Betye Saar, whose 1972 mixed-media assemblage, *The Liberation of Aunt Jemima,* which sought to reclaim and reimagine who Aunt Jemima was, and who she could be, through multiple Aunt Jemima Pancake Mix trademarked images that serve as backdrop to a very dark, heavy-set, eyes-bulging, wide-grinning Aunt Jemima cookie jar. That piece was an overt critique of white America's love affair with Mammy. In *Grow'd,* Topsy is seated on a bale of cotton, holding a sickle in one hand and cotton in the other. Her hair, resembling the branches of a tree extending into the air, is braided with cotton. The show was in conversation with Saar's earlier work *Topsy Turvy,* which features a similar Topsy figure surrounded by other Topsy children.

In an interview about her work, Saar explained that her portrayal of Topsy is meant to push back against the visual cues of Stowe's depiction of enslaved children to reconfigure the negative depiction into a positive one. 'If you look at early lithographs, they're not super derogatory. Her hair is in pigtails. Later on, the change really came through media – through print and film,' Saar said in an interview with the National Academy of Design.[28]

By reclaiming iconic figures like Topsy, contemporary artists ask us to grapple with the important role images play in our lives, whether we are aware of it or not. Can a negative stereotype be turned into a positive representation? I am not fully convinced that you can ever completely erase the original meaning attached to such loaded imagery, like Topsy, but the courage of artists to attempt to do so gives me hope that it might one day be possible.

UNCLE TOM ON THE BIG SCREEN

As we saw in the last chapter, Uncle Tom was reimagined in count-less ways for the big screen in the early twentieth century. These cinematic portrayals took Uncle Tom even further away from Stowe's original than the nineteenth-century theatrical versions.

At the turn of the twentieth century, film technology was in its infancy. In 1891, inventor Thomas Edison, assisted by William K. L. Dickson, created the first visual technology to display film. Known as a 'kinetoscope,' the device was publicly demonstrated as a cinematic 'miracle' at the 1893 Chicago expo, and became the first commercially viable projection machine.[1] When the kinetoscope business began to decline a few years later, Edison's next cinematic invention, the 'vita-scope,' became a popular attraction.[2] This invention made Edison into one of the most celebrated inventors of his time. It also allowed him to try his hand at producing films.

In 1903, Edison teamed up with Edwin S. Porter, director of *The Great Train Robbery* (1903), a critically acclaimed silent film of that era. That year, they produced *Uncle Tom's Cabin*, a twelve-minute adaptation of the novel. This film is often credited as the first moment when a Black character appeared on the big screen. Uncle Tom, however, was not performed by an African American actor but by an unnamed white actor in blackface. In other words, 1903 marked the moment when blackface minstrelsy migrated off the stage and onto the silver screen.

As a cinematic experience, Edison and Porter's film did not just retell Stowe's story, it reinvented the numerous Tom shows that had appeared on the minstrel stage in the nineteenth century. With each stage adaptation, *Uncle Tom's Cabin* was less and less faithful to Stowe's novel in both letter and spirit, and the transition to film simply magnified the distance between these new versions and the original.

The most significant outcome of Edison and Porter's *Uncle Tom's Cabin* is that it created a stock film character, 'Uncle Tom.' That their Uncle Tom was portrayed by a nameless, slightly overweight white actor in blackface made the mutation of Stowe's Tom even more significant. In his book *Toms, Coons, Mulattoes, Mammies, & Bucks: An Interpretive History of Blacks in American Films*, film historian Donald Bogle argued that Porter's Tom was the first in a long line of socially acceptable 'Good Negro' Tom characters who, despite being 'chased, harassed, hounded, flogged, enslaved, and insulted they keep the faith, n'er turn against their white massas, and remain hearty, submissive, stoic, generous, selfless, and oh-so-very kind. Thus they endear themselves to white audiences and emerge as heroes of sorts.'[3]

The emergence and popularization of cinematic technology had a profound effect on notions of representation. While reproduced images were perceived to be illusions, audiences also believed them to be more accurate than human perception or imagination: when people saw Uncle Tom on the big screen, they believed the character to be more *real* than the fictional Uncle Tom of Stowe's novel. That is to say, they could finally *see* what Uncle Tom *really* looked like, how he spoke, and, most importantly, how a real Uncle Tom behaved. This shift in perception was tied directly to the way Stowe's heroic Uncle Tom morphed into a much more pejorative figure.

The casting of Edison and Porter's film helped to further this transformation. Rather than recruiting an entirely new cast for their film, they hired an existing Uncle Tom minstrel troupe that happened to be in the New York area at the time they were filming. Edison and Porter decided to shoot the stage versions of several scenes, thus blurring the theatrical and cinematic adaptations. According to Uncle Tom historian Brando Simeo Starkey, this first celluloid Uncle Tom bowed and scraped when in the company of his masters and embarrassingly deferred to whites in most scenes – gestures that reimagined Black-white relations during slavery.[4]

The film shows enslaved African Americans as light-hearted people and romanticized the slave auction. There are scenes, for example, where slave characters cannot stop dancing.[5] The movie's subtitle, *Slavery Days*, also authenticates the visual representation as faithful to historical reality. As David Pilgrim observes, 'Porter's Uncle Tom, like the Toms on stage, was a childlike, groveling servant. In the first quarter of the 20th century there were many cinematic adaptations of *Uncle Tom's Cabin* which portrayed slavery as a benevolent institution, Little Eva as an earthly angel, and blacks, especially Tom, as loyal, childlike, unthinking, and happy.'[6]

In the decades after Uncle Tom first enters the modern visual medium of film, he takes on the form of a stock figure who, in some movies, resembles Stowe's Uncle Tom but also evokes Uncle Ben and sleeping car porters.

The obsequious Black movie character may be the most enduring cultural legacy of Uncle Tom. Edison and Porter's 1903 film started the tradition of taking liberties with Stowe's novel and Tom shows, and subsequent *Uncle Tom's Cabin* film adaptations blurred the lines between the novel, theatre, and reality even further.

❦

In 1914, *Uncle Tom's Cabin* was reborn on the big screen, with an African American in the lead role as Uncle Tom. Sam Lucas (1848–1916) was a vaudeville minstrel performer, known for his appearance in *The Creole Show*, produced in 1890 by Sam T. Jack, a prominent white burlesque producer who developed the concept of a chorus line of beautiful Black women.[7]

Sam Lucas and his wife (who also starred in *Darkest America* in 1896) were not new to the character of Uncle Tom. As far back as 1878, Lucas had performed as Uncle Tom onstage. When he appears in the 1914 film, directed by William Robert Daly, he is no longer a young man. At sixty-six, he plays an elderly and enfeebled Uncle

Tom, a depiction that made a lasting impression with American audiences.[8]

In 1927, Universal Pictures made a silent version of *Uncle Tom's Cabin*, produced by Carl Laemmle and directed by Harry A. Pollard. Universal Studios initially pegged the respected stage actor Charles Gilpin (1878–1930) for the role of Uncle Tom. (In 1916, Gilpin had made a memorable appearance in whiteface as Jacob McCloskey, a slave owner and villain in *The Octoroon*, an adaptation of Dion Boucicault's 1859 novel of the same name.) When producers were unable to rid the *Uncle Tom* script of its inflammatory material, particularly Uncle Tom's docility, Gilpin turned down the role and returned to his elevator-operator day job. As Starkey argues, Gilpin's move expressed 'defiance on the part of African Americans determined to devise their own revisions of *Uncle Tom's Cabin*.'[9] Ultimately, Laemmle and Pollard's film features another Black actor, James B. Lowe, in the title role.

Lowe's Uncle Tom evokes Edison and Porter's blackface Uncle Tom. He is genial and passive – a happy servant. In this film, unlike in the novel, Tom dies but returns as a vengeful spirit who confronts Simon Legree before leading the slave owner to his death. Black media outlets at the time praised the film. But the studio, fearful of a backlash from Southern and white film audiences, ended up cutting controversial scenes, including the film's opening at a slave auction.[10]

Ever since the era of the Tom shows, many Southerners had had a contentious relationship with *Uncle Tom's Cabin*. As John W. Frick, author of '*Uncle Tom's Cabin*' on the American Stage and Screen, explains,

> While actual full-scale riots were relatively rare, considering the subject matter of *Uncle Tom's Cabin* and the sectional tensions it reflected, simply to mount the play meant to *risk* a riot each time it went on stage; and the incipient hostility toward the play and the players remained to such an extent that as late as 1900, performing it in some areas of the country was regarded as being dangerous to the peace by local authorities.[11]

Consequently, many later theatrical and cinematic adaptations of Stowe's *Uncle Tom's Cabin* were not shown to Southern audiences.

Instead, they remained largely Northern entertainments. Just as the minstrel show was invented and performed in the North, so too were Hollywood adaptations of Stowe's *Uncle Tom's Cabin*.

In fact, during Hollywood's classic period (1930–1945), films continued the minstrel-show tradition: those that featured Black characters almost always included some sort of sentimental musical interlude performed either by slaves on a plantation or by Black servants if it was set during the post–Civil War decades. Black women were pigeonholed as maids and Mammies. Black men were stuck playing buffoons or servile Uncle Toms.

Black male actors in the 1930s and 1940s were largely restricted to playing 'coon' caricatures, such as Stepin Fetchit (the stage name of Lincoln Perry [1902–1985]), or Tom-like characters, such as Bill 'Bojangles' Robinson. Mantan Moreland's bulging eyes and cackling laugh routines harkened back to blackface theatre while Willie Best's 'Sleep n' Eat' caricatures perpetuated stereotypes of Black laziness and illiteracy. (The characters of Mantan and Sleep n' Eat in Spike Lee's 2000 *Bamboozled* are modelled after these real-life African American actors.)

In the case of Stepin Fetchit, Lincoln Perry depicted a lanky, slow-witted, simple-minded, obtuse, confused humbug, and he was probably the best known and most successful Black actor working in Hollywood during the 1930s. As Bogle writes, 'Stepin Fetchit developed into the arch-coon, and as such he had no equal.'[12] He introduced Depression-era white audiences to the antics and tomfoolery that would be expected of Black comedians thereafter.

At the same time, Depression-era dramatic films featured servile characters with varying degrees of dignity. In the context of the 1930s, this attempt at humanization translated into Black inferiority. Virtually every film that dealt with slavery included an Uncle Tom-like character who was pathetic, stooped, hesitant, and solicitous with white characters. (Other examples are Clarence Muse as a janitor in *Show Boat* [1936], Eddie Anderson as Gros Bat in *Jezebel* [1938], and Oscar Polk as the servant Pork in *Gone with the Wind* [1939]). But white audiences at the time would have interpreted these characterizations as humane because they avoided the buffoonery of Stepin Fetchit types.

In the 1950s and 1960s, Black actors such as Harry Belafonte and Sidney Poitier became civil rights activists. But on the big screen, they were often cast as Uncle Tom figures. Poitier, for example, did not play characters who were submissive or cheerful servants, but many of his roles, as Pilgrim observes, were 'white-identified.' 'In *Edge of the City* Poitier sacrifices his life, and in *The Defiant Ones* he sacrifices his freedom, for white males.'[13] For the mass white audiences, these Black men satisfied expectations. As Bogle asserts, '[Their] characters were tame; never did they act impulsively, nor were they threats to the system. They were amenable and pliant. And finally, they were non-funky, almost sexless and sterile. In short, they were the perfect dream for white liberals anxious to have a coloured man in for lunch or dinner.'[14]

In 1946, MGM considered shooting another original version of *Uncle Tom's Cabin*, but the studio scrapped its plans when the NAACP launched a campaign to stop the remake.[15] The Black community had simply had enough of Uncle Tom, who, by this point, had fully evolved into a pejorative stereotype. There were no other serious attempts to make a full-length feature movie version until 1965, with the release of a German film (*Onkel Toms Hutte*), with dialogue dubbed into English. It would be the last attempt to bring a combination of Stowe's novel, the Tom Show, and early film adaptations to the big screen.

The fact is that Hollywood had moved on from trying to present Stowe's novel. As radio towers began to appear in the 1920s, this new form of mass technology reached audiences across North America, transforming the way people accessed entertainment. Instead of going to the theatre and or sitting in a cinema with strangers, people could enjoy newsreels, plays, or comedies on the radio in the comfort of their homes. The emerging medium of radio became yet another outlet for the perpetuation of Uncle Tom.

12

AMOS 'N' ANDY

Bridging the gap between the blackface minstrelsy of the stage and the Uncle Tom caricatures of Hollywood were the radio shows of the 1920s, and *Amos 'n' Andy* in particular. Radio, like television in the 1950s, created new forms of familiarity with celebrities. As people tuned into their weekly program, radio personalities cultivated a more personal attachment with their fans. People really felt like they knew who radio stars were. While filmic or stage caricatures of Blackness were visible, the depictions on radio were not, so the other elements of performance – voice tone, inflections, and dialect – became more significant markers of racial difference. Listeners knew a character was 'Black' not by how they appeared but by how they spoke.

In 1926, Chicago radio station WGN and its owner, the *Chicago Tribune*, introduced Midwestern listeners to *Sam 'n' Henry*, a show developed by two white performers in blackface, Charles Correll and Freeman Gosden. Two years later, WGN renamed the show *Amos 'n' Andy* and ran it in fifteen-minute segments, five days a week. The show gained popularity at a time when white Americans were watching the films of Bill 'Bojangles' Robinson and Shirley Temple, reading Uncle Remus tales, and stocking their kitchen cabinets with products branded with Aunt Jemima and Uncle Ben – all cultural icons that can trace their roots to Uncle Tom.

Over the years that followed, *Amos 'n' Andy* became the most listened-to radio program of all time.[1] Gosden and Correll's portrayal of two Black men came to dominate America's listening habits, and it even significantly influenced the country's daily routines. When Democratic nominee Gov. Al Smith of New York was running for president in 1928, he scheduled his radio spots so they did not compete with *Amos 'n' Andy*. As Irish playwright George Bernard Shaw once commented, 'There are three things which I shall never forget about America – the Rocky Mountains, Niagara Falls, and *Amos 'n' Andy*.'[2]

Unlike most blackface characters, observes *New York Times* critic Mel Watkins, *Amos 'n' Andy* reflected many values common to lower-middle-class Americans. 'White audiences could empathize with the universal aspects of the experiences of the black people depicted on the program – financial problems, personal relationships, even reactions to contemporary events – while laughing at their supposed ethnic traits,' he wrote.[3] (A generation later, *Good Times* similarly connected white audiences to universal themes of poverty, family, and community.).

The plot was quite simple. Amos and Andy work on a farm near Atlanta, but eventually they relocate to Chicago, where they live in a rooming house and experience difficult financial times. However, they tough it out and eventually launch their own taxi business. The show revolves around the ensuing hijinks and tomfoolery of Amos and Andy. Several other characters pick up that motif, such as George 'Kingfish' Stevens, leader of the Mystic Knights of the Sea Lodge, who often lures the duo into get-rich-quick schemes or tricks them into getting into trouble. Kingfish's catchphrase, 'holy mackerel,' became so popular that it entered the general lexicon.

While Amos came across as dense and naive, he was also honest, dedicated, and hard-working. Andy, on the other hand, was depicted as lazy, conniving, and pretentious, but also good-natured.[4] These characters were relatable, especially during the Depression, when many Americans – both Black and white – struggled to survive. Additionally, the movement of the characters from the South to the North reflected the Great Migration, when hundreds of thousands of African Americans abandoned the Jim Crow South and relocated to the cities of the North and the West in the first decades of the twentieth century.

Illustrator J. J. Gould's 1930 drawing of Amos 'n' Andy for New Movie *magazine.*

For Northern white listeners, it created a milieu similar to what they experienced in their own lives.

Despite its immense popularity, the show also drew criticism for its rendition of Black life. The first organized *Amos 'n' Andy* protest took place in Pittsburgh in December 1930, after members of the African Methodist Episcopal Zion Church wrote an article in the *Pittsburgh Courier*, then the second-largest African American newspaper, denouncing the show for its lower-class stereotypes and 'crude, repetitious, and moronic' dialogue.[5] Their condemnation did little to change popular opinion about the show. Indeed, within the decade, *Amos 'n' Andy* would be syndicated for international audiences, including Canadian listeners.

The same stereotypes that dominated minstrel shows appeared in *Amos 'n' Andy*, albeit on the radio instead of onstage. Minstrel shows, for example, depicted the Southern 'Negro' as lazy and ill-spoken, with a fondness for watermelon and debauchery. When white Depression-era audiences tuned in to listen to the characters developed by Gosden and Correll, they were consuming long-held views about race and region, with the result that any stereotypes they may have had about the South and Southern Blacks were reinforced.[6] The extent of the show's reach, moreover, was enormous. At its peak, the U.S. audience for *Amos 'n' Andy* was an estimated forty million listeners – 53 per cent of the country's radio listenership.

While it is not known how many Canadians listened regularly, a series of advertisements published in *Chatelaine* between April and August 1930 described *Amos 'n' Andy* as 'the most popular radio feature' that aired 'every night except Sunday over NBC network,' from coast to coast.[7] In some of these ads, Gosden and Correll appear in blackface, accompanied by this telling caption: 'You will find yourself awaiting eagerly these incomparable blackface artists.' 'You will enjoy these inimitable blackface artists,' another ad stated. '[T]he children will enjoy them, too.'

Those issues of *Chatelaine* were read by 280,000 predominantly white Canadians. Many doubtless believed that 'real' Black people were like these characters, even though Gosden and Correll were white and the situations in the show fictitious. One of the minstrel show's lasting legacies lay in its ability to convince white people that its portrayals of Black people were accurate.

Amos 'n' Andy as a radio show marks an important transition in the representation of racial stereotypes. Unlike the theatre or film, radio was both a mass-media technology and a form of entertainment that did not require you to leave the house or to purchase a ticket. Just as the stage had looked to literature for content, radio similarly looked to the stage, and in so doing, it created a more intimate and familiar experience for listeners.

For example, in 1932, when *The Jack Benny Program* (1932–65) premiered on what was then a new radio network, the National Broadcasting Company (NBC), some of the first material it featured was *Uncle Tom's Cabin* done in dialect. In the episode, introduced by Benny as an 'immortal classic of the American theatre,' he plays Uncle Tom, Mary Livingstone plays Eliza, and Marie Dressler plays Little Eva. The episode revolves around a resort hotel called *Uncle Tom's Cabin* and the closing song is a chorus of 'Dixie.'[8] As the entertainment medium changed, *Uncle Tom's Cabin* was still being introduced to audiences, just in a slightly different form.

13

SONG OF THE SOUTH
AND UNCLE REMUS'S RETURN

Disney originally acquired the rights to Joel Chandler Harris's Uncle Remus tales in 1939. Shooting for the film began in 1944. Stylistically, *Song of the South* was a great novelty – a live-action spectacle with clever animated sequences interspersed throughout. But its theme, that of the pastoral Old South, was familiar terrain. The film focuses on a young boy, Johnny (Bobby Driscoll), who moves to his mother's family plantation in Georgia when his father leaves the family to fight for some unspecified cause in Atlanta. Alone and depressed, Johnny is comforted by the tall tales of Uncle Remus (James Baskett), an ex-slave living on the property. As Johnny sneaks away from the plantation, the voice of Uncle Remus comforts him by telling tales about a character named Brer Rabbit.

While the setting of *Song of the South* implied that the Black workers are no longer Johnny's family's property, they are still completely subservient, and happily so. James Baskett (1904–48), as Uncle Remus, is a preternaturally jolly companion. Even though a young Black child named Toby is assigned to look after Johnny, the adult African Americans in the film only pay attention to Toby when he neglects his responsibilities as Johnny's minder. When Toby and Johnny are with Uncle Remus, the old grey-haired man directs his attention almost exclusively to Johnny. In nearly every scene, the Black cast in *Song of the South* are seen as happily deferential to the film's white characters while also neglecting their own needs and the needs of their children.

The secondary cartoon figures in *Song of the South* speak in a heavily caricatured dialect and maintain a pleasantly sentimental relationship with the white plantation owners. But in Baskett's role, we can also locate what many critics describe as the 'magical-Negro presence.' As dear old Uncle Remus, Baskett's character glowed with joy. 'In his spare time, Uncle Remus sings as animated bluebirds and butterflies whiz past,' writes film historian Donald Bogle. '[H]is greatest delight is telling wondrous stories to the dear little white massa. Everything's just zip-a-dee-doo-dah.'[1] The film also featured Hattie McDaniel (1893–1952) in the role of 'Aunt Tempy,' the family's Mammy.

The problem with the Uncle Remus tales is not Uncle Remus's 'character' or 'essence.' Rather, their failing has to do with Remus's reactions, and how these can be taken as a paradigm for how people such as himself – racial archetypes – react to their indentured circumstances. More generally, the representation of the plantation in this and other films has had a devastating impact on Black representation in film. Disney's Black characters depend almost exclusively on the whites around them and show no signs of political awareness or resistance.[2] This depiction of Black helplessness and smiling dependence had real-world implications, especially in the 1940s.

ℛ

'I'm trying to find a way to get people to start having conversations about bringing *Song of the South* back, so we can talk about what it was and where it came from and why it came out,' Whoopi Goldberg said in a 2017 interview.[3] Goldberg, like celebrities such as Oprah Winfrey, Stan Lee, Mark Hamill, and Julie Taymor, had just been honoured as 'Disney Legends,' the highest award the studio bestows on performers and creatives. As she talked about the honour and her favourite Disney films, Goldberg's comments about the studio's most controversial title reintroduced the sixty-year-old live-action-and-animated film to contemporary audiences. While *Song of the South* was never released on video or DVD in the U.S., its soundtrack – both the music and the dialogue – had been widely available from the time of the film's debut until the early 1980s. Even after its fortieth-anniversary screening in 1986, Disney limited access to *Song of the South*. As film and media scholar Jason Sperb writes in *Disney's Most Notorious Film: Race, Convergence, and the Hidden Histories of* Song of the South (2012), the film remains 'one of Hollywood's most resiliently offensive racist texts.'[4]

Up to that point, in both its live-action and animated features, Disney's productions featured very few African American characters. When the studio optioned Harris's Uncle Remus tales, Disney was eager to bring the stories to a new generation of American children who had not read the books and who had less knowledge of these early and ubiquitous folk tales about slavery. As Patricia Turner, author of *Ceramic Uncles & Celluloid Mammies*, explains, 'Recasting the stories in the 1940s, Walt Disney was clearly also concerned about reactions of his white audience.' Perhaps for that reason, she continues, 'Disney's twentieth-century re-creation of Harris' frame story is much more heinous than the original.'[5] In *Song of the South*, the story about a Southern plantation is populated with happy-go-lucky African Americans singing songs about their wonderful home as they work in fields shot in Technicolor. There is no attempt to render the musical score in the style of the spirituals and work songs that would have been sung during the era. Instead, Disney's version takes place in an imaginary time when Black people live cheerfully in slave quarters on a plantation, while an old Black man narrates their tale.

I grew up in the 1980s and watched all the Disney classics as they were re-released: *Snow White and the Seven Dwarfs* (1987), *Bambi* (1988), and *Peter Pan* (1987). I have no memory of seeing *Song of the South*. Yet I knew of Uncle Remus and the film's best-known ditty, 'Zip-a-Dee-Doo-Dah,' which won the 1947 Academy Award for Best Original Song. In fact, the song ranked forty-seventh in the American Film Institute's 100 Years … 100 Songs survey.[6]

One of the inexplicable aspects of popular music is that most people cannot pinpoint the exact moment when they became aware of a particular work. Somehow, songs like 'Zip-a-Dee-Doo-Dah' and its lyrics about 'wonderful days' and 'everything going my way' continue to exist outside of a film that few people have seen today. They have passed from generation to generation because the music itself is unconnected to the era depicted in the film. Harris set his Uncle Remus and Brer Rabbit tales in the post-slavery era; they were not about slavery, but its aftermath. However, Disney chose to situate his upbeat, revisionist tales during the period of slavery, thus subtly encouraging 1940s audiences to ignore the context and social history of the original work. The studio's choice stimulates a sense of nostalgia for a past that has been revised in a positive light.

In a 2007 article for the *Guardian*, critic Xan Brooks poses the question 'Is *Song of the South* too racist to screen?' 'In depicting a (literally) fabulous Deep South strung sometime between slavery and Reconstruction,' he writes, 'the film trades in a dubious form of myth-making – implying that African Americans stuck below the Mason-Dixon line were a cheerful bunch who liked nothing better than going fishing, spinning tall tales and looking after white folks' kids.' Brooks goes on to argue that if *Song of the South* were not a kids' film, it would still be screening today. Brooks remembers seeing the film as a child and liking it a lot. 'This is a little worrying,' he recalls. '[I]t suggests that the film's dodgy agenda either sailed clear over my head or has affected me so deeply that I remain unaware of it to this day – blithely going through life in the belief that there was zip wrong with segregation that a little doo-dahing couldn't cure.'[7]

In 2019, Disney launched its own streaming service, Disney Plus. CEO Bob Iger confirmed that every film in the Disney library, including those movies normally locked away in the 'Disney vault,' will be available through Disney Plus, either at launch or shortly thereafter.[8] There was one exception. When Iger was asked in 2010 if fans would ever see a *Song of the South* DVD, he replied by describing the movie as 'antiquated' and 'fairly offensive,' and said there were no plans to make a DVD or Blu-ray. Nine years later, the company remained true to Iger's earlier decision, and *Song of the South* was not released via Disney Plus.[9]

While the film can be found on independent websites and from online retailers, the question of whether *Song of the South* should come out of the Disney vault and be shown to a new generation of young people (and those who remember it) lingers. Is it important to engage with the past, however difficult that past might be? Should all history, no matter how difficult and/or misrepresentative, be made public?

To put *Song of the South* into historical context, and to understand why it has not been re-released, we have to return to Harris's Uncle Remus tales, and to the juxtaposition between slavery and post-slavery depicted in the film at the time of its release in 1940s America. It is through the disjuncture between Uncle Remus's Black America and white America that we can begin to understand why this, of all of Disney's films, continues to evoke the deep-seated racist desire among whites, whether conscious or unconscious, to perpetuate the image of African Americans stuck and apparently content on the Southern plantation.

The social and legal contours of race in America had changed dramatically during the decades between Uncle Remus's first incarnation and Harris's late-nineteenth-century children's books and, finally, his 1946 reappearance in *Song of the South*.

After the 1896 Supreme Court ruling (*Plessy v. Ferguson*) that sanctioned segregation, Black Americans responded by voting with their feet. 'Their Great Migration to the urban North,' historian Evelyn Brooks Higginbotham explains, was 'met with riots as well as discriminatory housing and employment practices. A virtual epidemic of violence pervaded the nation's cities as whites responded to Black urbanization with fear and anger. Random attacks on Black neighborhoods and full-scale rioting ravaged urban communities in both the North and the South.'[10]

Even Black veterans of both world wars remained disfranchised by the Jim Crow laws and often, in the South, faced the very real threat of lynching.[11] In the North, there was de facto (customary) segregation, while in the South, de jure (by law) segregation proved to be unwavering and draconian.

Against this fractured social backdrop, *Song of the South* reassured audiences that Blacks were at peace in slavery. As the conspicuous cheerfulness of its best-known song suggests, this depiction was deeply exaggerated, to the extent that Black characters appeared to be grateful to be held in servitude. *Song of the South* was Walt Disney's first major box-office hit after World War II, the latest instalment in a string of cartoon features that had begun in 1937 with *Snow White and the Seven Dwarfs*, *Pinocchio* (1940), *Fantasia* (1940), *Bambi* (1942), and *Dumbo* (1941).

In 1945, Hollywood's classic period peaked in influence and profit, and the film industry began to decline largely because of postwar changes in Hollywood's audiences. That year, average weekly theatre attendance hit an all-time high of ninety million moviegoers, with box-office receipts of almost $1.7 billion. A year later, there were already eight thousand television sets in American homes. As a result, Hollywood's money-making formula waned due to the fragmentation of its traditional audience. Surveys of postwar audiences revealed that they were younger, more liberal, and more educated. They also increasingly perceived film as an art form rather than escapist entertainment, as was the case before and during the war.[12]

Several years ago, a friend bought me a collector's DVD version of *Betty Boop*, the Max Fleischer animated cartoon created in the 1930s. *Betty Boop* had a bit of a revival in the 1980s, and I remember loving it as a child. But when I rewatched it as an adult, I was appalled at its overt racism. In one 1932 episode, titled 'I'll Be Glad When You're Dead You Rascal You,' jazz trumpeter Louis Armstrong and his orchestra perform the song 'You Rascal You.' After a live-action introduction featuring Armstrong and his musicians, the episode segues to a cartoon jungle, with Betty being carried by her sidekicks, Bimbo and Koko. A horde of African 'savages' begin to chase the trio and run off with Betty. While attempting to find her, Koko and Bimbo find themselves being chased by another 'savage' whose head is slowly superimposed onto Armstrong, a visual cue linking him to the savage.

In a contemporary context, we have language to call out racism. In *The White Racial Frame* (2009), American sociologist Joe Feagin describes racial thinking as so deeply institutionalized that it operates both consciously and unconsciously in highlighting the privileges and virtues of whiteness when evaluating and relating to racialized people, especially Black people. 'Even when whites do racist performances targeting Americans of color,' Feagin writes, 'the old racial frame accents that they, as whites, still should be considered to be "good" and "decent" people. The dominant racial frame not only provides the fodder for whites' racist performances, but also the means of excusing those performances.'[13]

In 1946, however, there was no language for describing *Song of the South* or the cartoons that had come before it. Just as American consumers did not question the visual representations of all the Uncles and Aunties on their food packages, film audiences did not challenge the Uncle Toms and Mammies on the big screen.

⤳

Song of the South was not a huge hit when it was released. The final production tab exceeded $2 million, with the film essentially breaking even when it eventually grossed $3.4 million.[14] The reason for the film's lacklustre commercial performance had to do with the assumptions behind Disney's marketing strategy. As Jason Sperb, author of *Disney's Most Notorious Film*, explains, 'By opening first in the South, and then later distributing it to the East and West Coasts – its own "Southern strategy" – Disney anticipated that favorable Southern press would send *Song of the South* off on a path to huge box office success.'[15] But times had changed. Indeed, clues about the response to the film preceded its release. As the influential African American newspaper the *Chicago Defender* reported, *Song of the South* came under 'considerable panning from the press when Producer Walt Disney first announced his intention to film the whimsical story.'[16]

The backlash against the film started when Disney hired Clarence Muse, an African American performer and writer, as a screenplay consultant. When he quit because of what he felt was the film's negative portrayal of African American characters, he wrote letters to the editors of the Black press about his concerns. These news organizations began to turn the spotlight on Disney and its portrayals of Black people in general.[17]

At the same time, the NAACP had begun to target Hollywood and other American institutions for perpetuating racist stereotypes and disenfranchising African Americans. Most notably, the NAACP during World War II supported what became known as the 'Double V campaign,' a campaign to promote the fight for democracy both overseas and at home for African Americans. Articles about Double V published in the *Pittsburgh Courier*, America's largest-circulation Black newspaper (350,000 copies per issue), the *Chicago Defender*, and the *Amsterdam News* drove home the point that African Americans were no longer going to remain silent about Black Uncles or Mammies on the big screen. As Neil A. Wynn, a professor of twentieth-century American history, writes, 'The black press and civil rights organizations continued to call for an end to segregation throughout the war,' including racially motivated attacks at home.[18] Faced with a rising tide of criticism, Walt Disney changed the film's original name, *Uncle Remus*, to *Song of the South*. He hoped it would be enough to minimize the African American community's response to the film. It was not.

As Disney's pre-release positioning efforts anticipated, the attacks began as soon as *Song of the South* appeared in theatres. In *Multiculturalism and the Mouse* (2005), Douglas Brode notes that 'heated criticism during the initial release was largely levelled by *white* reviewers, over-eager to display their newly acquired heightened awareness.'[19] Emerging from the war years, white critics had become more attuned to racial discrimination.

The post-war shift in racial attitudes was apparent in other domains. American troops were racially segregated during World War II. But in 1946, Jackie Robinson was drafted to play for the Montreal Royals, a Brooklyn Dodgers minor-league team. The next year, he joined the Dodgers, breaking the colour barrier in major league baseball. This cataclysmic shift set the stage for other strides in the integration of America. As mainstream media outlets began to sense the erosion of Jim Crow in the postwar years, they also began to recruit African American journalists, shifting not only the tone of reporting on race in America but also the content.

According to Sperb, *Song of the South* was thought by some to be progressive because Uncle Remus could be understood as subverting the Uncle Tom stereotype at a time when audiences would not have accepted a strong Black lead character.[20] Unlike Uncle Tom or derivatives like the Temple/Robinson duo, Uncle Remus was not merely a sidekick to a white child. He related the Brer Rabbit tales and revealed himself as a character with an endearing, rather than self-effacing, form of wisdom. What's more, until then, no major Hollywood film aiming to attract a largely white audience had relied on an African American narrator. Because voice-overs create an intense bond between characters and audiences, and even signify a film's moral core, Uncle Remus was seen by some to be a positive influence on the child, Johnny.[21]

And like the film versions of Uncle Tom, Disney's Uncle Remus is not solely a revamp of Harris's literary character, who would wax nostalgic for the old plantation. Thanks to the magic of cinema, Disney's Remus is transformed into the arbiter of white safety and security. Whenever Johnny peers back over his shoulder at the plantation house, for example, it appears cold, sterile, and off-putting. By comparison, Remus's cabin is where Johnny can feel completely at home – loved, wanted, respected.[22] And while Uncle Remus was not a remake of Uncle Tom, both characters enticed white audiences to feel like things were going to work out fine. That burden, however, sat on the shoulders of old Black men.

African Americans were outraged by *Song of the South* and they refused to keep quiet about their feelings. When the film was first released, Walter Francis White, the executive secretary of the NAACP, released a statement condemning the film's depiction of Black people. 'In an effort neither to offend audiences in the north or south, the production helps to perpetuate a dangerously glorified picture of slavery,' he wrote. 'Making use of the beautiful Uncle Remus folklore, *Song of the South* unfortunately gives the impression of an idyllic master-slave relationship, which is a distortion of the facts.'[23] His statement sparked further outrage in the African American media and protests in New York City.

꘎

By the late 1940s, Black audiences had also changed. They were no longer willing to censor themselves about the debilitating stereotypes that had figuratively held African Americans captive on stage and in film. In 1948, for example, *Ebony* magazine reprimanded Hollywood and its habit of pigeonholing Black women into Mammy roles. 'For all its self-professed righteous reforms of recent years,' the magazine declared, 'Hollywood is still sticking to the same old stereotypes of moon-faced maids and groveling menials, zoot entertainers and bug-eyed Stepin Fetchits in casting Negroes. The typical month's output of celluloid from the movie capital, as seen on these pages, shows Hollywood slipping back into the prewar rut of Dixie-minded presentations of the Negro.'[24]

The NAACP's Hollywood branch and the Congress of Racial Equality also pressured the film industry to both upgrade the cinematic image of Black people and employ more Black women and men in all capacities. Indeed, on December 14, 1946, less than a month after the *Song of the South*'s premiere, the *New York Times* reported on a picket line outside Manhattan's Palace Theater, where two of the nineteen picketers carried signs that read, 'We fought for Uncle Sam, not Uncle Tom' and 'The *Song of the South* is slightly off-key because Disney says it's wrong to be free.'[25] *Ebony* ran a full-page attack on the film next to a full-page photograph of the smiling face of James Baskett. The article, headlined 'Needed: A Negro Legion of Decency,' stated that the film had 'disrupted peaceful race relations,' was 'lily-white propaganda' in the guise of a Technicolor feature, and would unconsciously promote 'Uncle Tomism as the model of how Negroes should behave in white company.'[26]

By the early 1950s, *Ebony*'s editorials and the NAACP protests had begun to have an impact on Hollywood's outlook. This period saw the emergence of films with distinct Black characters played by actors like Paul Robeson, Ossie Davis, Harold and Fayard Nicholas, Dorothy Dandridge, Lena Horne, Hazel Scott, and Ethel Waters. They all helped to transform the profile of Black men and women in films, from caricatured stereotypes to something more like a star system. By the 1960s, in fact, the Uncle Tom trope had all but vanished from film.

But it did not disappear altogether. Rather, as civil rights gained momentum, Uncle Tom re-emerged in the realm of politics and media, this time as an epithet to be hurled at Black men considered to be disloyal or out of touch with the needs of collective Black progress. Men considered too conservative, too passive, or overly desirous of white approval were disparaged as Uncle Toms – a development that marked the final mutation of Stowe's stoic martyr.

14

UNCLE TOM'S 1960S TRANSFORMATION

S ong of the South's Uncle Remus was the culmination of decades of cinematic Uncle Toms who were disconnected from the realities of the African American experience. While Remus was whistling about his 'wonderful' day in *Song of the South*, it had become impossible to ignore the reality that life for millions of African Americans in the postwar years was anything but cheery and bucolic. Whereas Hollywood was content with Black people as happy-go-lucky servants or violent tricksters, the Black community in the 1950s was increasingly vocal about its discontent with not only movie stereotypes but also the restrictions placed upon Black bodies under Jim Crow.

Writing in the 1950s, essayist and author James Baldwin, who is often remembered as one of the first voices of the civil rights movement, perfectly articulated the contradictions. '[White Americans] are caught in a kind of vacuum between their past and their present – the romanticized, that is, the maligned past, and the denied and dishonored present.' He argued that the collective refusal of white American society to recognize African Americans formed a structure of suppression and denial that 'manifests itself politically, in terms of institutional racism and segregation, and psychologically, in terms of a distorted and destructive national self-image.'[1] This contradiction is most observable today when looking at the expansion of the suburbs and mass consumerism in the postwar years.

The 1950s marked the heyday of the baby boom, a period when about four million babies were born each year during the decade.

Additionally, an economy built on mass consumer products and brick-and-mortar manufacturing also surged. The baby boom precipitated the suburban boom. New American suburbs became homogeneous and affluent places filled with detached homes, cars, washing machines, small appliances, and a host of consumer durables that flooded the market. Tract housing became the hallmark of these communities. The 1944 GI Bill also subsidized low-cost mortgages for World War II veterans, affording them the opportunity to buy cheap suburban homes instead of returning to the rental apartments in the city they left behind during the war years. Millions of white Americans during the 1950s left the downtown cores of cities like New York, Philadelphia, Detroit, Chicago, and Los Angeles. Postwar prosperity allowed white Americans to take advantage of the economic and demographic boom to trade tenancy for ownership.

Systematic racial discrimination in mortgage lending beginning in the 1930s further helped shape the demographic and wealth patterns of America's suburbs. The practice, known as 'redlining,' was enforced by government surveyors who graded neighbourhoods in 239 cities, colour-coding them green for 'best,' blue for 'still desirable,' yellow for 'definitely declining,' and red for 'hazardous.'[2] The 'redlined' yellow and red neighbourhoods were the ones predominantly made up of African American households. In effect, the baby boom combined with systemic racism to create 'white flight' – the exodus of middle-class white city-dwellers from urban industrial pollution and the social problems imagined to be associated with city life. In the white suburbs of America, Black people were not welcome, and moving to suburbia meant white families no longer interacted with African Americans socially.

Instead, white suburbanites' primary images of Black Americans were as domestic servants, sleeping car porters, butlers, or drivers, as well as representations on TV or in movies. The suburbs, in effect, helped to create an America where whites could live 'the American dream' while Black people remained sequestered in decaying neighbourhoods in a nightmare of curtailed rights and freedoms.

At the same time, Black businesses, such as soul-food restaurants, barbershops, garages, hotels, and other establishments listed in *The Negro Motorist Green-Book*, became cornerstones of the community during the 1950s. As Texas A&M historian Julia Blackwelder writes, 'Having little or no access to credit, African American businesses began with small private investments and expanded only as their agents consummated sales based on purchases measured in dollars and cents rather than in hundreds or thousands of dollars.'[3]

But while the Black community enjoyed some commercial successes, it was within the confines of a segregated America. In 1953, for example, the net worth of the typical Black household was just 20 per cent of that of a typical white household, according to a 2018 working paper on the racial gap in household finances prepared by the Federal Reserve Bank of Minneapolis.[4]

The first indication that structural racial discrimination had reached a breaking point occurred in 1954. That year, the U.S. Supreme Court made segregation illegal in public schools in the case of *Brown v. Board of Education*. The decision reversed the 1896 *Plessy v. Ferguson* decision, which had legislated Jim Crow across America. With *Brown*, the civil rights movement gained momentum, and what emerged was not only a new era in Black social consciousness but also a newly visible community of Black activists who rejected the enforced 'yessah' deference imposed by white America. The civil rights leaders who emerged in these years challenged the images of Uncle Toms and Stepin Fetchits that had graced Hollywood's big screen for decades. As a result, *Brown* was not just a legal decision. Like *Plessy*, it was a turning point that projected a newly outspoken Blackness into the homes of white Americans.

⚜

The late fifties also saw events that would forever define both the civil rights protests and the state-sanctioned violence that followed. In August 1955, two white men lynched fourteen-year-old Chicago-born Emmett Till, visiting family in Money, Mississippi, after accusing him of whistling at a white woman. (The men confessed but were acquitted.) In December 1955, Rosa Parks refused to give up her seat on a Montgomery, Alabama, bus. Rev. Martin Luther King Jr., then a relatively unknown preacher, was thrust into the national spotlight when he led the ensuing year-long boycott against Montgomery's segregated transportation system. Then, on September 3, 1957, nine African American students arrived at Central High School in Little Rock, Arkansas, to begin classes. They were met by the Arkansas National Guard (on orders from Gov. Orval Faubus) and a screaming white mob. 'I saw all of the anger, and the ugly faces across the street, but I ignored them, and I really did consider them ignorant people,' Carlotta Walls LaNier, one member of the Little Rock Nine, told *Smithsonian Magazine* in 2017. 'To be honest with you, that is what really got me through the whole year, that I knew this was ignorance that was making these statements and not the type of people that I would associate with.'[5]

News media reports of Montgomery and Little Rock, coupled with increasingly visible protests organized by King and other civil rights leaders, shocked white America. These Black people did not fit into the Uncle Tom and mammy moulds many whites had grown accustomed to. Nor did Black blues and rock 'n' roll musicians like Bo Diddley, Fats Domino, Chuck Berry, and Little Richard, all of whom were achieving mainstream success on radio stations across the country. Their popularity catapulted Black male faces into homes across America, frightening many whites in both the North and South who saw rock 'n' roll as the devil's music.

When white artists like Elvis Presley, Pat Boone, and Bill Haley covered the songs of these artists, they began erasing their Black presence from the radio, but also, and most importantly, from the imaginations of young white women who were still seen by some as the target of Black men's uncontrollable sexual appetites. The emergence of white rock 'n' roll also served to recast the new genre of music away from Black origins. In 1959, when Berry Gordy launched Motown Records in Detroit, he set out to bring Black music into the mainstream of white America, initially by minimizing the Blackness of his artists.

Beyond the new-found visibility of Black artists, non-violent civil rights protesters like Parks and King became part of the media landscape. But they and their followers were often framed as victims. Newspapers and magazines were filled with photographs of confrontations over voting rights and school or lunch-counter integration. White readers encountered images of Parks being fingerprinted and King being roughed up during a 1958 arrest. There were more news photos showing scores of limp protesters being dragged from streets and courthouse steps, attacked by police dogs or pummelled with firehoses. These shots constructed a narrative of Black victimhood and passivity that was broadcast to white audiences across America.[6]

Of course, Parks and the women who participated in the Montgomery boycott were real-life African Americans who not only supported their families with the income they earned by running white households but bore little resemblance to the Mammies in film and on consumer packaging.[7] They did not see themselves as victims but rather protesters fighting an unjust and inhumane system. At the time, 63 per cent of the Black women in Montgomery worked in domestic service. The fact that these women could sustain a boycott of the bus system for 381 days, until they succeeded in winning desegregation, shows how determined they were to challenge Jim Crow.[8]

The juxtaposition of African American performers on radio and TV in the North and African American protesters defying Jim Crow in the South created a public image of two Black Americas. The notion of 'freedom' in the North and segregation in the South perpetuated racial stereotypes in Hollywood and on television. But while the entertainment industry was determined to preserve the popular stereotypes about Black America, the events of the day were creating a generation of Black martyrs who were very different from the original Uncle Tom.

Thurgood Marshall, who served as the NAACP's chief counsel in *Brown*, helped to move the legal needle, but it was the Civil Rights Act of 1957 that ultimately broke down the wall. This law was the first legislative act aimed at protecting the rights of African Americans since the Reconstruction period. It established a Civil Rights section of the Justice Department and set up a federal apparatus whereby prosecutors would be able to gain court injunctions against businesses and institutions that interfered with African Americans' voting rights. The act also established the Federal Civil Rights Commission.

These political victories did not eliminate the extreme contradictions in relations between white and Black America. Despite Supreme Court rulings, school integration, and the popularity of Black rock 'n' rollers, some acclaimed African American figures were nevertheless accused of un-American conduct and in some cases forced to leave the country for good.

Paul Robeson, June 1942, Washington, D.C.
Photographer: Gordon Parks.

In 1949, actor-turned-activist Paul Robeson spoke candidly about the lives of Black people in America at a Soviet Union–sponsored Paris Peace Conference. The event, which took place at the start of the Cold War, spurred the House Un-American Activities Committee to label Robeson a communist. The HUAC summoned Jackie Robinson to testify about Robeson. Two years prior, Robinson had made history as the first African American to integrate major league baseball. As such, he was the most logical person to testify against Robeson to reassure the U.S. government that 'not all Black people' felt the way he did.

The son of a former slave, Robeson had an intellect and authentic ability that enabled him to reach for all the best that white America had to offer. Born in Princeton, New Jersey, in 1898, he won a scholarship to Rutgers University at a time when such awards were virtually unheard of for Black students. He established himself as a screen presence during the Depression in films like *Sanders of the River* (1935), and in *Show Boat* (1936) his rendition of 'Ol' Man River' became the most well-known. As film historian Donald Bogle notes, 'Robeson's greatest contribution to Black film history – and the aspect of his work that most disturbed American white moviegoers – was his proud, defiant portrait of the Black man.' Because he was one of the few Black actors to triumph in an independently produced Black film, Bogle continues, 'Robeson now serves as a lead-in for the next great phase of Blacks in films – the period of the Black moviemakers, when independent directors and producers made movies to tell the world what being Black was really about.'[9]

Robeson had said African Americans would be sympathetic to communism because it was incongruent with racism. For Robeson, capitalism had been built on a racist foundation. In 1956, when Robeson himself appeared before the HUAC, he pleaded constitutional immunity when queried about alleged communist affiliations. He denounced America and the committee, accusing the latter of being unpatriotic and un-American.[10] Robeson eventually left the United States to live in Europe, though after falling ill while there, he returned to the U.S. years later. His career trajectory, which was severely limited by his outspokenness, reflects an obvious intention to not be pigeonholed as an Uncle Tom.

❧

By the early 1960s, King's philosophy of non-violence had frustrated some younger Black men who felt a more aggressive public presence was needed to achieve liberation. From college students being beaten and verbally assaulted after launching non-violent protests to 'Freedom Riders' embarking for the South to protest segregated bus terminals, the strides of the 1950s seemed to be doing little to change Black America's reality. The March on Washington in 1963 and King's famous 'I Have a Dream' speech became the battle cry for the movement at the start of a new decade, leading to the signing of the Civil Rights Act of 1964, which ended segregation in public places and banned employment discrimination on the basis of race, colour, religion, sex, or national origin. The Voting Rights Act of 1965 and the Fair Housing

Act of 1968 were also great legal triumphs. And yet a pervasive racism lingered in the streets, on TV, and in Hollywood.

The new era in civil rights also witnessed the violent deaths of key figures in the movement. Activist Medgar Evers was killed in 1963. R&B singer Sam Cooke was murdered in 1964. And Malcolm X was assassinated in 1965. By the mid-1960s, a new generation of African Americans believed that something had to change; non-violent protest was not going to be enough to help Black life in America. This milieu gave birth to the Black Panther Party, founded by Huey Newton and Bobby Seale in 1966.

Against the backdrop of violent backlash and the assassinations of central figures in the civil rights movement, militant activists like Stokely Carmichael began to position the Black Power movement as a more radical alternative to King's pacifist campaign. Carmichael also felt that King was an Uncle Tom for his unwillingness to advocate retaliatory violence against white people.[11] The Black Panthers were unapologetically Black, and proudly displayed the aesthetics and vernacular of this new identity: Afros, Black clothing, and fists raised in defiance.

Jim Crow historian David Pilgrim asserts that by the end of the 1960s, civil rights leaders 'were called Uncle Toms by more militant blacks.'[12] Whitney Young, for example, executive director of the Urban League from 1961 to 1971 and an ardent integrationist, faced charges that he was an Uncle Tom because of 'his willingness to work with whites.' The movement's slogans – 'Black Power' and 'Black Is Beautiful' – created a symbolic and literal distinction between Black men who were pro-Black and Black men deemed to be 'sellouts.' In this socio-political context, solidarity mattered to Black militants. Uncle Tom became an accusation that carried both personal and political implications. As Brando Simeo Starkey writes, 'The black community, therefore, heavily monitored behavior affecting segregation. Any black person deemed guilty of violating racial loyalty norms in the context of racial apartheid was harshly disciplined, frequently with an embarrassing *Uncle Tom* denunciation.'[13] Anyone deemed to be an Uncle Tom in this period was seen as acquiescing to segregation. Black men who even appeared to conduct themselves in deference to white authority risked facing this accusation. And those who hurled the Uncle Tom aspersion were policing the boundaries of racial loyalty.

This risk of being labelled an Uncle Tom became something Black men had to ponder deeply before they made personal or professional choices. As the pejorative was thrown around with increasing frequency, it became the most feared in-group slur.[14] Black celebrities such as Nat King Cole, Sidney Poitier, and Harry Belafonte, as well as sports icons like Jesse Owens, Jackie Robinson, Floyd Patterson, and Muhammad Ali, all 'represented' the Black community in popular culture. At various times, these figures all faced the accusation of Uncle Tomism, and, in the case of Ali, also condemned other Black men of the same crime. It was as if, at the height of the civil rights era, Uncle Tom had become an embodied figure with the potential to harm the cause of Black progress through his diffidence.

Civil rights dominated the cultural politics of the 1960s. At the same time, a new Uncle Tom was born out of in-group/out-group policing. On TV and in Hollywood films, Uncle Tom was reinvented. These Toms were presented in popular culture as enemies of Black progress. While the entertainment industry had made some strides in its depictions of Black life as it entered the decade, Hollywood mainly ignored Black protests and the inner-city riots sparked by King's assassination. The times were a-changing, and Uncle Tom was right there, changing with them.

HARRY BELAFONTE AND SIDNEY POITIER

As Americans' TVs and news magazines filled with images of a new generation of Black leaders – some preaching a message of reconciliation and others promoting a more militant form of racial politics – their movie theatres increasingly featured a new generation of Black actors and characters who were not stranded in cinematic slavery.

Ossie Davis, Harry Belafonte, and Sidney Poitier had emerged in the 1950s as America's most successful Black actors. They also became active in the broader culture. Davis and his wife, actress Ruby Dee, openly supported Paul Robeson during his HUAC hearings. Belafonte, in turn, introduced Americans to the music of the Caribbean and financially supported civil rights movements. Poitier's triumphs were primarily on the big screen. His career path mirrored that of Belafonte, but his public persona, and perceptions of his relationship to white America, followed a very different trajectory.

Belafonte and Poitier were both born in mid-1920s America (Harlem and Miami, respectively), but spent significant parts of their lives in the Caribbean. Belafonte lived in Saint Ann, Jamaica, for most of his childhood. Poitier grew up in the Bahamas.

In 1954, Belafonte starred with Dorothy Dandridge in *Carmen Jones*, a film described by film scholar Donald Bogle as 'the 1950s' most lavish, most publicized, and most successful all-black spectacle.'[1] Three years later, Belafonte's most controversial film, *Island in the Sun*, was released. During and after filming, and shortly before its release, some white theatre owners threatened to boycott *Island* for the interracial love plots involving Belafonte and Joan Fontaine, and John Justin and Dorothy Dandridge. In April 1957, when Hollywood producer Darrell Zanuck began publicizing *Island in the Sun*, Southern politicians were outraged, observes Bettye Collier-Thomas and V. P. Franklin in *My Soul Is a Witness: The Chronicle of the Civil Rights Era, 1954–1964*.[2] In Columbia, South Carolina, the following month, legislators began debating a bill that imposed a $5,000 fine for any movie theatre in the state that showed the film. While the Southern protests failed to affect *Island*'s success at the box office, picket lines appeared in some Southern cities around theatres where it was being screened.

'If you liked [me],' Belafonte recalled in an interview on his ninetieth birthday, 'you were making a political statement, and that felt good, the way it felt good to listen to Paul Robeson, and listen to what he had to say. If you were a white Belafonte fan, you felt even

Sidney Poitier, Harry Belafonte, and Charlton Heston at the March on Washington, Washington, D.C. August 28, 1963. Photographer: Rowland Scherman.

better. You were connecting with your better angels, reaching across the racial divide.'[3] During the civil rights movement – at the peak of his acting career – Belafonte became an adviser and confidante to Dr. Martin Luther King Jr. and also provided financial assistance to fund voter-registration drives and freedom rides. With Poitier, he helped organize the 1963 March on Washington.

Belafonte had nothing but praise and respect for Poitier. 'I don't think anyone [else] in the world could have been anointed with the responsibility of creating a whole new image of black people, and especially black men,'[4] he said. Despite such endorsements, Poitier's film choices troubled some Black people, who felt his roles did not speak to the Black experience.

Poitier accomplished what no Black actor had ever done: he was the first Black male actor to be nominated for an Academy Award (*The Defiant Ones*, 1958), and the first to win one for Best Actor (*Lilies of the Field*, 1963). Yet, while he and Belafonte remapped the image of Black masculinity in the 1950s and 1960s, Poitier's roles also helped usher in a new Black stereotype: the well-dressed, desexualized Black character. A string of critically acclaimed films, such as *The Blackboard Jungle* (1955), *Raisin in the Sun* (1961), *To Sir with Love, In the Heat of the Night*, and *Guess Who's Coming to Dinner* (the latter three all released in 1967) depict an impeccably virtuous Black man. In *Guess Who's Coming to Dinner*, a film about an interracial relationship, Poitier's character is so deracialized that one angry Black writer called him a 'warmed-over white shirt.'[5]

By the 1960s, Black culture was changing, especially for young Black men and women who were increasingly adopting what was known as a 'soul aesthetic.' To be a 'soul man' was to combine African cultural elements into a personal style. Clothing, like the dashiki, along with the Afro, formed part of the soul aesthetic of the Black Is Beautiful movement, which encouraged Black people to love and cherish their natural hair, features, and culture. Soul style was an in-group cultural and aesthetic movement that used clothing design, hairstyles, and even body language (stance, gait, method of greeting) to authenticate a new Black identity.[6] As Black America reclaimed its culture and redefined what being Black and proud meant, a new appreciation for African American culture also emerged.

Soul food, for instance, traces back to chattel slavery, when plantation owners fed the enslaved as cheaply as possible, often giving them leftover foods they themselves did not wish to eat. The resulting cuisine emerged as an important part of African American culture. Before the 1960s, however, soul food was largely stigmatized because of its association with the slave diet. But during the civil rights movement, it took on political and socio-cultural significance as it came to exemplify the cultural pride of a new Black middle class and its ability to assert a racial authenticity.[7] Although collard greens, black-eyed peas, hush puppies, fried chicken, and chitlins had appeared on both Black and white tables in the antebellum South, the soul aesthetic of civil rights solidified these foods as integral to the African American experience.

In the late 1960s, when Mahalia Jackson, the nation's greatest gospel singer, launched a national fried-chicken chain, the marketing strategy was directly aligned with the racial tenor of the time. It combined Black Power, entrepreneurism, religion, and soul food and envisioned restaurants that were Black-owned, Black-marketed, Black-managed, and Black-staffed.[8] While Jackson's chain only survived a few years, it reflected a general sense among Black celebrities that their politics had to align with their images within the Black community. And if they did not, these prominent figures ran the risk of being labelled a sellout or, worse, an Uncle Tom.

❧

Unlike Belafonte, Poitier's roles seemed to appease white Americans' desire for a Black leading man who met their middle-class standards. While his roles varied sharply from film to film, his sympathetically portrayed characters were often squeaky clean and notably non-sexual.

On one level, Poitier's roles were symbolic leaps forward for Black cinematic characters in terms of how he dressed and spoke. But on another level, he failed to radically dismantle the lingering memory of cinematic Uncles such as Uncle Remus or menials like Stepin Fetchit. Poitier never played a slave character, nor was he a buffoon. Instead, his characters expressed real concerns that resonated with some Black audiences. But they also suggested a survival strategy that seemed retrograde and uncomfortably reminiscent of the loyal Uncle Remus. If there was a white character in the film, Poitier was there to support, assist, and help out – just like ol' Uncle Remus helped out little Johnny on the plantation. In the way that Stepin Fetchit shielded white America from having to confront anti-Black racism, Poitier's clean-cut and well-spoken presentation, and ease among whites – even gruff and entitled older white men, like Spencer Tracy in *Guess* – served to prevent white America from seeing Black poverty, disenfranchisement, and the lasting effects of Jim Crow.

When he first came on the scene in the late 1950s, Poitier was achieving things no Black actor had ever done before. But a decade later, he had become an Uncle Tom. What changed? If the pre-1960s version of Uncle Tom was the deferential old Black man or the excessively docile railway porter, how did he morph – through Poitier's movie roles – into a new Uncle Tom that had far more sinister connotations?

❧

The 1960s Black counterculture movement, ushered in by the Black Panthers and social unrest in America's inner cities, positioned Poitier's cinematic presence as Uncle Tom–like. Reflecting on his image during the decade, Poitier later observed, 'According to a certain taste that was coming into ascendancy at the time, I was an "Uncle Tom," even a "house Negro," for playing roles that were non-threatening to white audiences, for playing the "noble Negro" who fulfills white liberal fantasies.'[9] Jim Crow historian David Pilgrim asserts that Poitier's Toms are best described as 'enlightened.' In many of Poitier's films, he writes, 'He is the smartest, most articulate character – and, more importantly, the one who delves into the philosophical issues: egalitarianism, humanitarianism, and altruism … He is a paragon of saintly virtue, sacrificing for others, who, not coincidentally, are often white.'[10]

Importantly, Black people were not accusing Poitier of being an Uncle Tom in his *real life* – he was, after all, just as involved in the civil rights movement as Belafonte and others. His Uncle Tomism arose from his film roles. According to a 1967 *New York Times* editorial entitled 'Why Does White America Love Sidney Poitier So?' the problem was that '[he's a] good guy in a totally white world, with no wife, no sweetheart, no woman to love or kiss, helping the white man solve the white man's problem.'[11]

In *The Defiant Ones*, Poitier stars alongside Tony Curtis (1925–2010) in a buddy film where they play escaped inmates who are chained together and, as a result, are forced to look past their differences and learn to respect each other. A Black man and white man in 1950s America fleeing across the country and, in so doing, becoming friends was not only far from reality but, in the eyes of some, dangerous.

In one scene, Poitier and Curtis are chasing a moving train, trying to jump on. Poitier successfully leaps on board, but Curtis cannot manage it. Poitier tries to keep his balance while grabbing for Curtis's outstretched hands to pull him on board. For a brief moment, a close-up captures their clenched hands, but Curtis eventually loses his grip. Poitier leaps from the train, and both roll down a hill. Curtis is stunned as Poitier tries to soothe and comfort him. 'When Sidney jumps off the train, the white liberal people downtown were much relieved and joyful,' James Baldwin lamented in an essay about the public's perception of the film. 'But when black people saw him jump off a train, they yelled, "Get back on the train, you fool!" The black man jumps off the train in order to reassure people, to make them know they are not hated. Though they have made human errors, they have done nothing for which to be hated.'[12]

In *Lilies in the Field*, Poitier plays handyman Homer Smith, who, while travelling in Arizona, stops by a rural farm where he is welcomed by a group of Roman Catholic nuns who have emigrated from Germany. Realizing the farm needs a lot of work, Homer launches into several repair projects for the women, who, impressed by his kindness and strong work ethic, start to believe that he has been sent by God to help build them a chapel. This narrative recalls Stowe's God-fearing Uncle Tom, who resonated with white readers because he was not a violent runaway from the plantation. As a figuratively castrated character, Poitier symbolized for white audiences in the wake of the civil rights movement a denial of the potential threat of Black masculinity.

In *In the Heat of the Night* (1967), Poitier plays a Black by-the-book Philadelphia detective who becomes embroiled in a racially charged Mississippi murder investigation. Released three years after a trio of civil rights activists were killed in Mississippi, the Oscar-winning film reached audiences just months before the spring 1968 assassinations of Martin Luther King Jr. and Robert F. Kennedy, which triggered widespread rioting. By then, Black rage had annihilated the myth that the American Dream was accessible to all Americans. Their deaths also shone a light on the inner city that white suburbanites had fled in the 1950s. In Chicago, the Democratic National Convention was the site of more Black protest. In California, Huey Newton's Black Panther Party marched across cities like Oakland wearing large Afros and leather jackets, some carrying guns. As these images of Black revolt flashed across the TV screens, Poitier's law-abiding, desexed roles provided a safe alternative depiction of Black masculinity that spoke to simpler times. His screen presence helped subdue white fears of Black Panthers making their way to the suburbs. Poitier's enlightened Uncle Tom roles became the antidote white Americans needed to remind them that, indeed, everything was going to be all right. There were still 'Good Negroes' who obeyed laws, spoke in an English whites could understand, and, like the smiling railway porters, enjoyed their company.

Poitier's enlightened Toms also imposed a price on the Black community. Hollywood seemed content with neutral Black characters who were Black on the outside but white on the inside, characters with no cultural politics and an absolute aversion to soul aesthetics. Just as white flight had created two Americas, the Black community was split by competing images of Black masculinity on the big screen and Black activism on the streets.

As the integrationist civil rights campaign yielded during the decade to a nationalist Black Power movement, racial authenticity increasingly meant policing the boundaries of not only representational Blackness in film, but also political Blackness for those in the public eye. More than celebrities like Poitier, African American sports heroes, such as Muhammad Ali, who were neither polite nor deferential, became the new arbiters of racial loyalty. Indeed, Ali, and a younger generation of outspoken Black athletes, would become the embodiment of the *new* Black male that emerged in the late 1960s as counterpoints to the likes of Poitier. These figures became anti-Toms who were mad as hell and were not going to take it anymore.

16

THE ANTI-TOM

Actor Ossie Davis (1917–2005) spent his long career in film and TV avoiding the Stepin Fetchit and passive railway porter stereotypes. Not surprisingly, he became embroiled in the civil rights movement, and its leaders – Malcolm X, Dr. Martin Luther King Jr., and many others – were his friends. As he wrote in a revised edition of Alex Haley's *The Autobiography of Malcolm X*:

> Malcolm knew that every white man in America profits directly or indirectly from his position vis-à-vis Negroes, profits from racism even though he does not practice it or believe in it. He also knew that every Negro who did not challenge on the spot every instance of racism, overt or covert, committed against him and his people, who chose instead to swallow his spit and go on smiling, was an Uncle Tom and a traitor, without balls or guts, or any other commonly accepted aspects of manhood![1]

Haley's book was based on a series of in-depth interviews he conducted with Malcolm X between 1963 and his assassination in 1965, when the book was first published. The importance of Davis to the Uncle Tom trope is that he purposefully spent his entire sixty-five-year career resisting this stereotypical portrayal of Black men in Hollywood films.

The centuries-long experience of seeing oneself constructed through the dominant culture's eyes as either a menial labourer or buffoon meant that Black men had had to develop a doubled sense of

Ossie Davis at the 1963 Civil Rights March on Washington, D.C. Photographer: Rowland Scherman.

who they were. In the 1960s, Poitier's enlightened Toms did not help. They presented one image of Blackness to white America. But on the streets, Black life was going through a political and social collective transformation that had little in common with Poitier's persona. The decades-long effects of Jim Crow were hardest felt in inner-city communities, where white flight to the suburbs had led to an increasingly isolated Black inner-city population. By the late 1960s, moreover, white academics had begun to study inner-city Black communities, further stigmatizing and pathologizing residents in these neighbourhoods.

Daniel Moynihan's 1965 government study on the 'Negro Family' directly linked the contemporary social and economic problems of the Black community to a putatively matriarchal family structure. According to the report's thesis, the source of oppression ran deeper than the racial discrimination that had produced unemployment, poor housing, inadequate education, and substandard medical care. Instead, Moynihan described oppression as a pathological issue created by the absence of male authority among Black people.[2] In one infamous chapter, 'The Tangle of Pathology,' he wrote, '[T]he Negro community has been forced into a matriarchal structure which, because it is so out of line with the rest of American society, seriously retards the progress of the group as a whole, and imposes a crushing burden on the Negro male and, in consequence, on a great many Negro women as well.'[3]

Moynihan's report was followed by others, such as economist John Kain's 1968 study, which concluded that African Americans in the inner city faced greater challenges than those who lived elsewhere. Citing 'spatial mismatch,' Kain came to a stark conclusion about the fact that Black neighbourhoods tended to be located far from job opportunities: 'Since Negroes typically have less skill and less education than whites [and] if the average skill level requirement of jobs increased with distance from the ghetto,' he claimed, 'it seems possible that the extensive growth of metropolitan areas and the rapid postwar dispersal of employment, accompanied by no reduction and perhaps even an increase in housing market segregation, may have placed the Negro job seeker in an even more precarious position.'[4]

While these studies drew strong connections between being Black, living in the inner city, and being poor, they did not address the structural factors that created ghettos in the first place and that contributed to poverty and Black families' inability to live elsewhere.

Faced with denigration masquerading as scholarship, young Black men living in inner cities became increasingly determined to change the very structure of American society. It is within this context that the Black community began to police the boundaries of racial loyalty. 'Uncle Tom' became the label used to describe those Black men deemed to be 'sellouts' to the race. The insult means these men are only interested in serving whites, the government, corporations, or 'the system' generally. The connotation is that Uncle Toms will ensure that white needs come before the needs of both the Black community and themselves. While Poitier's enlightened Toms were, of course, fictional characters on the big screen, the 'sellout' Uncle Toms of the 1960s were real people.

Importantly, the story of Uncle Tom as a kind of Judas is complicated. The integrationist civil rights leaders of the 1950s were seen as out of touch by a new generation of Black militants who had little interest in desegregation, believing instead that a complete dismantling of the state itself was the only way for Blacks to be fully emancipated. In this way, Uncle Tom divided the Black community.

⁂

Militant Black activists, who believed their cause could be advanced only through violent retaliation against white racism, began to accuse more mainstream Black civil rights leaders of Uncle Tomism. They judged men like Dr. Martin Luther King Jr. to be too passive, too religious, and too eager to integrate – in short, too much like Uncle Tom.

Black Power co-founder Stokely Carmichael, who had been a leader of the Student Nonviolent Coordinating Committee (SNCC), which led sit-ins at segregated lunch counters in the South, was most outspoken about the direction he felt the civil rights movement needed to take. In a November 1966 feature in *Ebony* entitled 'Crisis in Civil Rights Leadership,' Carmichael laments, 'The power structure doesn't want black people to have power. I'm not talking about [Alabama governor] George Wallace. I'm talking about Bobby Kennedy.'[5]

These comments were significant for a few reasons. When *Ebony* first appeared in November 1945, it carried no advertisements. But after 1946, publisher John H. Johnson persuaded white advertisers to give *Ebony* the same consideration as *Look* and *Life* in terms of ad buys. By the 1960s, the magazine was the unofficial voice of the Black middle class, providing prosperous African Americans a venue to showcase their successes as inspirational blueprints.[6]

In the 1960s, in fact, a Black middle class was emerging. Between 1960 and 1970, median family income for Black families increased from $3,161 to $6,067.[7] African Americans began to move into a wider range of professions and higher income brackets. At the same time, Black poverty continued to grow. While some professional barriers fell, unskilled and undereducated African Americans were left behind.[8] Against this backdrop, Carmichael's comments were specifically meant to strike a chord with Black middle-class readers who believed their personal advancements were evidence of collective Black progress, when, in reality, lower-income Blacks remained disenfranchised.

In September 1962, Robert Kennedy, as attorney general in the administration of his brother John F. Kennedy, was thrust into the national spotlight when he was forced to intervene in a violation of the U.S. Supreme Court's ruling on school desegregation. University of Mississippi governor Ross Barnett had denied entry to James Meredith, a Black student, when he arrived to register for classes. After a white mob erupted outside the school, Kennedy scrambled to keep the peace, sending five hundred U.S. marshals to the campus, followed by military police, the Mississippi National Guard, and U.S. Border Patrol officials. It was the Kennedy administration's first major confrontation with Southern racism. When Meredith finally became the first Black student enrolled at Ole' Miss, the Kennedys were seen as allies of the Black community.

Robert Kennedy believed that he was so 'in' with the Black community that, in the spring of 1963, he requested that eleven African American activists, including novelist James Baldwin, come to the Kennedys' family home to talk about the volcano of rage building in Northern Black communities. But he also wanted advice on what the Kennedy administration should do, from African Americans who knew what was happening. Significantly, Kennedy excluded King and the top officials from the NAACP and the Urban League. As Larry Tye, author of *Bobby Kennedy: The Making of a Liberal Icon*, observed, 'Bobby Kennedy wanted a no-holds-barred critique of their leadership.'[9]

The meeting ended terribly, as Kennedy was unprepared for the disdain expressed by the activists in attendance. They not only condemned the racism in America, but also the Kennedy administration's policies on Vietnam. Some of those who attended, like activist Jerome Smith, vented their anger: 'Mr. Kennedy,' the twenty-four-year-old said, 'I want you to understand I don't care anything about you and your brother. I don't know what I'm doing here, listening to all this cocktail party patter.' Young Black men, Smith continued, would fight to protect their rights at home, but they would refuse to fight for America in Cuba, Vietnam, or any of the other places the Kennedys saw as geopolitical threats. 'What Smith and the others said should not have come as a surprise,' Tye observed. 'Their remarks mirrored what Baldwin had written six months earlier in an acclaimed *New Yorker* article that Bobby had read.'[10]

In a November 1962 essay in the *New Yorker*, Baldwin had explained why Blacks distrusted whites in America. 'Negroes know far more about white Americans,' he wrote. 'Ask any Negro what he knows about the white people with whom he works. And then ask the white people with whom he works what they know about him.'[11] Baldwin's comments spoke to the Black rage behind the smiling grin of railway porters that many white passengers had probably not even noticed. Where integrationists like King believed that conscientious whites

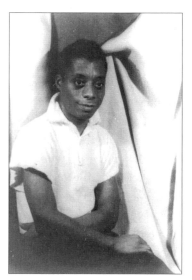

James Baldwin, September 13, 1955.
Photographer: Carl Van Vechten.

could be allies in the struggle, militants like Smith felt this was utterly impossible because white America simply did not *see* Black America for what it truly was.

When Carmichael took aim at Kennedy in *Ebony*, he was speaking to the Black middle-class integrationists who, he felt, had been taken in by the liberal politics of the Kennedys. Civil rights leader Rev. Frederick D. Kirkpatrick had even gone so far as to call Bobby a 'blue-eyed soul brother.'[12]

The *Ebony* feature ultimately shone a light on the split in the civil rights movement between militants and integrationists. In an article about a meeting of the Congress of Racial Equality, *Ebony* reported exactly how young militants felt about 'Uncle King, Uncle Whitney and Uncle Wilkins.' That's how Roy Innis, chairman of CORE's Harlem chapter, described 'an archaic structure' run by Dr. Martin Luther King Jr., National Urban League leader Whitney Moore Young Jr., and NAACP head Roy Wilkins. 'Other conference speakers,' the magazine noted, 'assailed the Negro middle class, the Negro "Ph.Ds.," the "black preachers," "the Toms" and the establishment.'[13]

Just as militants disparaged older civil rights leaders and integrationists as Uncle Toms, some Black male sports figures who publicly expressed conservative political views or denounced Malcolm X and the Nation of Islam were considered 'sellout' Uncle Toms by a new generation of outspoken and politically conscious athletes.

For example, in 1960, former baseball star Jackie Robinson, endorsed Republican Richard Nixon for president. During the campaign, Kennedy, in a much-heralded call to Coretta Scott King, agreed to help secure the release of her husband, Dr. King, who had been jailed in Georgia on a trumped-up charge.[14] Kennedy's move won widespread support among Black Americans, but Robinson remained loyal to Nixon. As a result, Robinson's legacy – as a ballplayer who had endured death threats in 1947 – was tarnished with accusations that he had become a 'sellout Uncle Tom.' In the turbulent sociopolitical climate of the 1960s, it no longer mattered that Robinson had advanced the cause of Black freedom. The question he faced from militant African American activists was 'What have you done for Black America lately?'

⁊≻

While Uncle Tomism remained standard fare in Hollywood, in the world of sports some Black athletes emerged during the social upheavals of the 1960s as anti-Toms, and none more so than Muhammad Ali, a Black athlete unlike any the world had ever seen. Outspoken, funny, and unabashedly political, Ali converted to Islam and changed his name from Cassius Clay at the height of his fame. Ali also delighted in calling his Black opponents Uncle Toms.

In 1965, he fought Floyd Patterson, a devout Christian and staunch integrationist. Patterson had criticized Ali for becoming a Black Muslim. 'Cassius Clay is disgracing himself and the Negro race,' Patterson said. 'No decent person can look up to a champion whose credo is "hate whites."'[15] Patterson was out of touch with the times; many young Black men were increasingly vocal about white racism, or the racist system from which white Americans benefited. Many in the Black community denounced Patterson as a sellout Uncle Tom.

In February 1967, Ali fought Ernie Terrell. At the pre-fight press conferences, Terrell repeatedly called Ali by his given name, refusing to acknowledge his Black Muslim name, Muhammad. After the fight, *Sports Illustrated* described it as 'a wonderful demonstration of boxing skill and a barbarous display of cruelty,' as Ali jabbed and punched around the ring, all the while shouting, 'What's my name, "Uncle Tom"? What's my name?'[16] Four years later, when Ali fought Joe Frazier in what was hyped as the 'Fight of the Century,' he similarly dismissed Frazier as a tool of the white establishment, calling him 'dumb,' 'ugly,' and an Uncle Tom.[17]

Away from the boxing ring, heightened racial consciousness was prompting some Blacks to enforce a code of loyalty and solidarity by wielding the Uncle Tom insult to disparage figures like Robinson and Patterson, who seemed overly eager to join white society.[18] By the late 1960s, Black loyalty and solidarity versus real or perceived disloyalty and deference to white authority were clearly delineated social polarities. The 1968 Olympics became a watershed moment in racial politics when Black runners John Carlos and Tommie Smith staged a symbolic protest at the medal ceremony in Mexico City.

After placing first and third, respectively, in the men's two-hundred-metre race, Smith and Carlos mounted the podium with Olympic Project for Human Rights buttons pinned to their track jackets. They each wore black socks without shoes, rolled-up pant legs, and a single black glove. When they received their medals, both men pivoted toward the rising flags. While 'The Star-Spangled Banner' played, each raised a black-gloved fist in the air and lowered their heads – a moment famously captured by photographer John Dominis. (Their symbolic act anticipates former NFL quarterback Colin Kaepernick's 2016 decision to 'take a knee' during pre-game national anthems to protest racial injustice.)

In the ensuing controversy, some observers defended the protest. In one story, *Life* magazine declared, 'They're not separatists. They do not believe in violence. They are dedicated to ending what they see as exploitation of black athletes and, in the process, gaining dignity and equality for all black people.'[19] Nevertheless, Dominis's photograph ignited furious debate in white America 'about the propriety of the athletes' actions rather than the issues they sought to address,' observes historian Martin A. Berger.[20] The debate rages to this day.

Coming just six months after King's assassination and on the heels of a summer of rioting in America's Black inner cities, the Olympic protest, coupled with calls for racial justice, meant that such gestures were viewed by African Americans as acts of Black loyalty. But to white America, their actions seemed like attacks on everything they had held dear. 'The degree of distress Smith and Carlos's peaceful and lawful protest stirred up in whites suggests the challenges blacks faced in crafting demonstrations to make visible long-ignored problems and prompt sympathy in whites,' argues Berger. 'Blacks who hoped to reach whites through protest had to navigate a narrow range of "acceptable" actions.'[21]

Those Blacks who were critical of Black protest ran the risk of being labelled Uncle Toms. Most notably, Jesse Owens, the famed sprinter who won four gold medals at the 1936 Olympics in Berlin, ardently opposed Black athletes using their platform to further the cause of Black activism. Smith and Carlos belonged to another generation, however. Grand Valley State University historian Louis Moore explains that already in November 1967, Smith and Carlos had made it known they were prepared to boycott the 1968 Olympics if the 'society and sports world' did not meet their demands. These included reinstating Ali as world boxing champion; firing International Olympic Committee chair Avery Brundage, a Nazi sympathizer; and halting the participation of South Africa and Rhodesia (present-day Zimbabwe) if those countries insisted on bringing all-white Olympic teams.[22]

Upon hearing about the planned protest by Carlos and Smith, Owens did not mince words. 'There is no place in the athletic world for politics,' he told a reporter, adding, 'I deplore the use of the Olympic Games by certain people for political aggrandizement.'[23] Throughout 1968, in fact, Owens continued this line of attack in print media and on television after the duo's protest. Critics routinely denounced Owens as an Uncle Tom. Four years later, he wrote a memoir in which he conceded that Black athletes had to be activists. But, to his critics, Owens's change of heart came too late because his words had stood in the way of Black progress.

In the realm of sports, the threat of Uncle Tom always loomed once a Black male athlete reached the highest echelons and became embedded in mainstream popular culture, a hero for *everyone*, not just the Black community. In fact, Uncle Tom and the spectacle of modern professional sports are so intertwined that, in the present day, Black

Uncles still emerge, although they often bear little resemblance to the Uncles of the past.

Consider the sports comedy film *Uncle Drew*, directed by Charles Stone III and written by Jay Longino. After it hit theatres across North America in 2018, *Uncle Drew* can be read as a piece of pop culture that had found a way to bind contemporary consumer product advertising, Black sports heroes, and the remarkably enduring influence of Uncle Tom.

Uncle Drew features NBA star Kyrie Irving, an Australian-born American point guard, in the title role, along with former NBA icons Shaquille O'Neal, Chris Webber, Reggie Miller, and Nate Robinson, as well as former WNBA MVP and Olympian Lisa Leslie. 'What struck us was [Irving's] charm, his charisma and his ability to have a little fun and not take himself too seriously,' Lou Arbetter, general manager of Pepsi Productions, told CNN.[24] Pepsico had created the Uncle Drew character in 2012 to sell Pepsi Max, and then, in a first, commissioned the film.[25]

Uncle Drew is an elderly Black man who walks with a limp. He reminisces about players from basketball's past and complains about the youth being too flashy, too loud, and not doing the things that folks in his day did – like practising the fundamentals of the game. In an extended ad for Pepsi Max, Uncle Drew takes to the court during a pickup game. At first, he moves slowly and misses his shots and passes. His nephew, Kevin, calls him an 'old man.' Eventually, Uncle Drew gets his game back and begins to take over the court, including an alley-oop off the backboard to himself for a dunk. Viewers then see a flashback to young Irving in a makeup studio, where he is being transformed into Uncle Drew. At the end, Irving declares, 'Transformation is complete.'

Everything about this feature-length exercise in product placement echoes Uncle Tom's transformation from literary character to commodity spokesperson to advertising and film star. *Uncle Drew* demonstrates how, in the twenty-first century, we can still locate the legacy of Uncle Tom tucked inside works that are ostensibly stories that have nothing to do with the original.

The morphing of Uncle Tom from 'sellout' insult to Uncle Drew, an unrecognizable trope of Black masculinity, really begins in the 1970s. The decade introduced new Black film characters who bear little resemblance to the Tom stereotypes of the 1960s and before.

Black masculinity is given new life with Melvin Van Peebles's *Sweet Sweetback's Baadasssss Song* (1971), the first-ever Black action film, and a precursor to Richard Roundtree as John Shaft, a tough, renegade Black detective who lives in a stylish book-lined New York apartment and has the confidence to take down anyone who crosses his path. Shaft is so sophisticated and charismatic that he can sleep with either white or Black women – a taboo-breaking plot detail that actors like Belafonte could only hint at in his onscreen love scenes a generation before.

With his long black trench coat, short Afro, and tightly fitted turtlenecks, John Shaft was no Uncle Tom; like Van Peebles's Sweetback, Shaft was a true anti-Tom. Such characters had never appeared on the silver screen before and spoke to a desire to put Tom to rest once and for all. In a 1971 concert recording, Curtis Mayfield echoed this sentiment in 'We're a Winner': when there is no more Uncle Tom, Black people will finally have moved on up. This anti-Tom lyric offered further evidence of the deep contempt that many Black men felt for a fictional character that had continued to define them in a white world.

These films were lumped into a genre that came to be called 'blaxploitation,' as the later movies of this form degenerated into a series of studio-supported action films usually set in the Black 'ghetto.' Critics condemned both the movies, for promulgating negative Black imagery, and the Hollywood exploitation machinery that created them.[26] The merchandising industry, in turn, capitalized on the genre with a flood of commodity spinoffs. Despite these attacks, the blaxploitation genre's sexy leading men – Mario Van Peebles (*Sweetback*), Richard Roundtree (*Shaft*), and Ron O'Neal (*Super Fly*) – were considered heroes in Black communities, even though Hollywood's celebrity machine mostly ignored them. In any case, these films ultimately primed audiences for the desperately needed change that was to come on the small screen in the 1970s.

GOOD TIMES' COONFOOLERY

Television was the first medium to promote the two-parent African American family. These depictions grew out of the sitcoms created by the acclaimed writer and producer Norman Lear. The first was *All in the Family* (1971–79), a groundbreaking series about a working-class white family living in Queens, New York. It starred Carroll O'Connor as Archie Bunker, an outspoken racist married to the overly deferential Edith (Jean Stapleton). The comic foil is Archie's hippie son-in-law, Michael 'Meathead' Stivic (Rob Reiner). After a few cameo appearances as Edith's cousin, Bea Arthur was given her own spinoff, *Maude* (1972–78). As the feminist response to Bunker, Maude was also outspoken and middle-aged, but politically liberal, feminist, and more accepting of racial difference than Bunker.

Maude reflected America's changing gender roles, but it reproduced one of the country's oldest tropes about race: the Black woman working as a maid for a white family. Portrayed by Esther Rolle, Florida Evans became such a popular character on *Maude* that, in 1974, she was chosen to star in her own spinoff, *Good Times*. The show followed the exploits of a happily married African American couple and their children. They were not trying to make it in a suburban white community, but instead lived in a low-income inner-city neighbourhood, with its 'ordinary layoffs' and good times.

Good Times and others that followed functioned like beacons of hope in the representation game. Another Lear production, *Sanford & Son* (1972–77), starred comedian Red Foxx as Fred G. Sanford, a widower, and his son, Lamont Sanford (Demond Wilson), who together ran a junk dealership in the Watts neighbourhood of Los Angeles. It brought white viewers into African American neighbourhoods that, only a decade prior, had been synonymous with civil-rights unrest, police violence, and riots. Both shows appeared to offer an authentic glimpse into these Black worlds, but as television scholar Herman Gray has observed, these snapshots of poor urban communities populated by African Americans, who were often unemployed or underemployed, were created by white liberal producers who thought they were delivering 'authentic' accounts of life in the Black urban ghetto.[1]

What's more, the fact that Americans watched these shows in the privacy of their homes, rather than in theatres, meant the situations seemed more 'real' and personal, even though the values of these characters were white-identified, and not wholly reflective of Black community mores.

Good Times, which premiered on CBS on February 8, 1974, was co-created by Lear, Eric Monte, and actor Mike Evans (who played Lionel on *The Jeffersons*, another *All in the Family* spinoff). Set in a Chicago inner-city housing project, *Good Times* initially centred on Florida, a tough but loving mother to three children, and her husband, James (John Amos Jr.), a hardworking blue-collar worker who was often between jobs. While Rolle and Amos (who would go on to star as the adult Kunta Kinte in the 1977 ABC miniseries *Roots*) began the series as its stars, their children soon became the show's focus. The couple's daughter, Thelma (Bern Nadette Stanis), was a good and studious child. Initially, the producers thought the youngest son, Michael (Ralph Carter), would be the show's 'breakout' character, because he was cute and had appeared in the Broadway musical *Raisin*, based on the Lorraine Hansberry drama *A Raisin in the Sun*.[2]

Good Times, however, became the career-defining role for Jimmie Walker, who played the show's eldest son, James Junior, a.k.a. J.J. Evans. The character ended up overshadowing Rolle and Amos in terms of popularity, which eventually drove both to quit the show in protest; plots that showcased Michael's or Thelma's commitment to education or Florida and James's efforts to provide for their kids were consistently hijacked by what some critics have called J.J.'s 'coonfool-ery.' Walker's character was a virtual reproduction of what *Ceramic Uncles & Celluloid Mammies* author Patricia Turner describes as 'a classic minstrel dandy ... depicted with garish clothes, an unswerving commitment to the pleasure principle, and a propensity to misuse the English language.'[3]

As the *Good Times* seasons went on, J.J.'s 'dy-no-mite!' line came up so frequently that it gradually took over the entire show. When audiences were engaging in plot lines of importance to Thelma or Michael, J.J. would literally jump into camera range – like a live-action Black pixie – and utter the famous phrase. It was an attention-seeking stunt that upstaged Thelma and Michael, and Florida and James. The expression's popularity echoed that of the phrase 'Holy mackerel!' which had been a signature line in *Amos 'n' Andy*.

With J.J.'s character deteriorating into a caricature akin to Stepin Fetchit, Rolle and Amos felt compelled to speak out about the show's direction. '[T]he differences I had with the producers of the show was that I felt too much emphasis was being put on J.J. and his chicken hat and saying "dy-no-mite" every third page,' Amos said in an inter-view with the American Archive of Television in 2015.[4] He also admitted that Lear had grown tired of his complaining. One day, Amos received a call during season three's hiatus and learned that he was no longer needed on the set of *Good Times*.

In the first episode of season four, Florida receives a telegram informing her that James has been killed in a car accident while travel-ling down South to find work. Just like that, the two-parent African American household became a stereotype: a single Black mother trying to make it while living in the projects without a man.

Soon after Amos's departure, Rolle became vocal about her discon-tent with the direction of the show. '[J.J.'s] 18 and he doesn't work,' she told *Ebony* in September 1975. 'He can't read and write. He doesn't think. The show didn't start out to be that.'[5]

The *Ebony* feature, entitled 'Bad Times on the "Good Times" Set,' did not just broadcast Rolle's frustrations with the show; it also raised tough questions about J.J.'s coonfoolery. 'The crux of it all seems to be a continuing battle among the cast members to keep the comedic flavor of the program from becoming so outlandish as to be embarrassing to blacks,' the *Ebony* editorial asserted, observing how the show initially dealt with themes such as juvenile alcoholism, gang violence, bussing, menopause, and high blood pressure among African Americans. Over time, however, it had veered toward plots and characters that seemed more like 'old-time black minstrelsy' than anything else. *Ebony* went to on offer an important commentary on representation and where the responsibility lay: 'What is being revealed is a healthy awareness on the part of black performers, that they are responsible for cleansing the strained image of blacks so long perpetrated on stage and screen.'[6]

Ester Rolle told the magazine that it was not just J.J.'s buffoonery that bothered her. She balked at the show's increasingly disparaging depiction of Blackness. 'Negative images have been quietly slipped in on us through the character of the oldest child,' said Rolle. 'I resent the imagery that says to black kids that you can make it by standing on the corner saying, "Dy-no-mite!"'[7] The issue was not just J.J.'s jokes; rather, it was that the gags had completely overtaken *Good Times* at the expense of it being the story of a Black family to whom so many viewers could relate. While there may have been 'real' J.J.s, out there, there were far more Floridas, Jameses, Michaels, and Thelmas. But the show minimized their stories and went for cheap laughs.

By the middle of season four, Rolle was fed up. She told the producers about her frustrations and demanded a raise and better scripts, including a plot line that would give Florida a new love interest (Moses Gunn as shop owner Carl Dixon).[8] Those changes were not enough. By the end of season four, Rolle quit.

After six seasons, *Good Times* was cancelled. By its end, the show was no longer about the Black family that had made it so popular. While Rolle returned briefly in the last season, she could not save the show. The good times had come to an end.

Aside from the coonfoolery of Jimmie Walker, television in the 1970s appeared to have left Uncle Tom behind. These were 'new Blacks,' who embraced living in poverty and who 'kept it real' with their families and their friends. They relished letting *whitey* know exactly what they thought of him in exchanges that produced great laughs among audiences and critics alike. However, the same tropes that confined Black masculinity – promiscuity, laziness, and a propensity for blue-collar work – persisted in Black-centred sitcoms. These images had been part of the domestic landscape in packaging, cartoons, and film for decades, but television just made them so much more immediate and believable.

The Black caricatures on TV in the 1970s served as stand-ins for how young Black men were perceived; they were never just characters in a sitcom. For some young Black men who consciously adopted J.J.'s 'dy-no-mite' as an empowering catchphrase – arguably as a replacement for the 'yessah' of a previous era – it may have seemed as if life had changed for the better. But its pop culture appeal was merely a case of history repeating itself.

By the end of the decade, television sitcoms like *The Jeffersons*, *Benson* (1979–86), *Webster* (1983–89), *Diff'rent Strokes* (1978–86), and *Gimme a Break* (1981–87) were focusing on Black upward social mobility and middle-class affluence. They supplanted Black urban poverty as both setting and theme in an earlier generation of shows. J.J. embodied Black masculinity on the small screen in the 1970s, but in the 1980s and the era of Ronald Reagan, television opened a space for yet another Uncle Tom to emerge. This new Tom turned out to be a capitalist.

⁂

The story behind television's ambiguous embrace of Black life may have surfaced new questions about representation, but it actually traced back to a much earlier period in the history of American pop culture: the radio shows of the 1920s, and *Amos 'n' Andy* in particular. By 1951, *Amos 'n' Andy* had jumped from radio to the new medium of television. Other popular radio shows like *Beulah* and *The Jack Benny Program* were similarly turned into television shows. All three shows played a crucial role in the construction and recasting of racial stereotypes of Black Americans.

In *Beulah* (1950–53), the title role played by Hattie McDaniel, Louise

Beavers, and Ethel Waters over the course of the show's four seasons, a Black woman is a dedicated, loving housekeeper and it is her job to nurture a white middle-class family. Following the pattern established by her film and fictional predecessors, she cheerfully dispenses home-spun wisdom and nutritious meals to the white children and their parents.[9] Just as *Amos 'n' Andy* reproduced earlier stereotypes of Black masculinity, the Black women characters in *Amos 'n' Andy* and *Beulah* were pigeonholed as Mammies. Although these were negative depictions, characters like Beulah resonated deeply with how many Black women felt in the 1950s.

There was also Ernestine Wade, a Mississippi-born singer and actress, who played the role of Sapphire, the demanding wife of George 'Kingfish' Stevens, one of the lead comic figures in *Amos 'n' Andy*. 'Grown black women had a different response to Sapphire;' observed critical race scholar bell hooks. '[T]hey identified with her frustrations and her woes. They resented the way she was mocked. They resented the way these screen images could assault black womanhood, could name us bitches, nags. And in opposition they claimed Sapphire as their own, as the symbol of that angry part of themselves white folks and Black men could not even begin to understand.'[10]

It is important to point out that when Gosden and Correll sold the rights to *Amos 'n' Andy* to CBS, they also gave up playing the title characters. Instead, *Amos 'n' Andy* became television's first all-Black show. But while the television version used Black actors in the main roles – Alvin Childress as 'Amos,' Spencer Williams as 'Andy,' Tim Moore as 'Kingfish,' and Wade as 'Sapphire' – they reproduced the same voices and speech patterns established by Gosden and Correll. These were the caricatured minstrel show renditions of Black actors performing blackface routines originally created by white actors in blackface.

The television version drew immediate criticism. The NAACP mounted a nationwide protest shortly after it debuted, describing the show as 'a gross libel of the Negro and distortion of the truth.'[11] These protests were unrelenting and undoubtedly contributed to the show's cancellation in 1953. However, reruns continued in syndication until CBS finally withdrew them in the mid-1960s in the face of further NAACP protests.[12]

Like *Uncle Tom's Cabin*, *Amos 'n' Andy* has never really left popular memory, despite its short run. In 2000, for example, the *Los Angeles Times* reported that civil rights activists protested outside a Los Angeles radio station that was considering broadcasting the original radio program. While KNX, which ran the radio station's nostalgic offerings, said at the time that it had no plans to schedule a run of original *Amos 'n' Andy* episodes, a website poll of its listeners revealed the show finished second (behind *The Jack Benny Program*) in a canvass about popular vintage programs. Just as film audiences in the early twentieth century longed to see a film adaptation of *Uncle Tom's Cabin*, a novel written in the 1850s, the original *Amos 'n' Andy* continued to exert its cultural influence seventy years after it initially aired on radio. This story points to how nostalgia for antiquated depictions of the past can linger for generations.

In 2016, the African American writer Trey Ellis, best known for his influential 1989 essay entitled 'The New Black Aesthetic,' wrote a screenplay called *Holy Mackerel!* It was performed live at a reading in Los Angeles, featuring *Grey's Anatomy's* Jesse Williams as Amos, *Forrest Gump's* Mykelti Williamson as Andy, and comedian and actor David Alan Grier as Kingfish. The play explored the rise and swift downfall of the *Amos 'n' Andy* television show and its Black cast. In an interview with Aisha Harris, Ellis recalls that when Harvard professor Henry Louis Gates Jr., and *New York Times* reporter Henry Finder approached him with the idea of doing a fictional film about *Amos 'n' Andy*, he recoiled. 'That seems like Stepin Fetchit, Uncle Tom … I don't want to open that door.'[13] Yet, as he read more about the television show, the Black actors, and how beloved it was by working-class Black people – even though upper-class Blacks publicly reviled it – Ellis realized he needed to explore it in more depth. When asked if *Amos 'n' Andy* can be credited with helping Black actors on television get to where they are now Ellis responded, 'In 1950 there were 500 African American members of the Screen Actors Guild … By 1960 there were 25. So black acting was absolutely decimated. Because it wasn't totally "positive," the NAACP shut it down, and Hollywood's response has been for a long time – it's either really segregated shows like *Good Times* or

Sanford and Son featuring an all-black cast, once in a while."[14]

The point is that integration, civil rights activism, and NAACP protests in the 1950s and 1960s did change America socially and culturally, but these forces had minimal impact on television.

There were few representations of Black America on television in the 1950s and 1960s that did not feature an apolitical, asexual, and/or integrationist character. Shows like *The Nat King Cole Show* (1956–57), *I Spy*, starring Bill Cosby (1965–68), and *Julia*, starring Diahann Carroll (1968–71), all projected onto the small screen some of the first representations of Black people that were not stereotypes of Stepin Fetchit or *Amos 'n' Andy*.

Nevertheless, these early characters still fit neatly within the category of Uncle Tomism in that they avoided aggression (except when in aid of whites) and depictions of poverty. While Carroll's character in *Julia* is a single mother, she works as a nurse in a doctor's office, speaks impeccable English, dresses conservatively, and lives in a clean and well-tended apartment. Even her romantic partners – played by Paul Winfield, who was best known for his role in *Sounder* (1972), and football-player-turned-actor Fred Williamson – are similarly well turned out.

However, the sanitized representations of Black television characters gave way to a new approach in the 1970s, one that echoed the shifts brought about by Black action films. Shows like *Good Times*, *Sanford and Son*, and *What's Happening!!* (1976–79) all took viewers into the everyday experiences of Blacks 'in the ghetto,' with narratives focused largely on the seemingly authentic experiences of working-class African Americans. ABC's Black policewoman drama *Get Christy Love!*, which ran for one season (1974–75) and starred Teresa Graves in the title role, followed a crime-fighting Black action heroine. Christy attempted to bring to television the appeal of Black action heroine films like *Cleopatra Jones* (1973), starring Tamara Dobson, and *Foxy Brown*, starring Pam Grier (1974). Graves's Christy, however, stands as the one exception to the representation of Black women on television during the decade. Still, *Cleopatra Jones*, *Foxy Brown*, and *Get Christy Love!* together marked a key moment in Black women's imagery within the popular culture of the Watergate era.

UNCLE TOM AND BLACK CAPITALISM

The late 1970s and 1980s represented a crucial moment in the history of Black America. In this post–civil rights, desegregated time, the rise of Black conservatism was not just about political affiliation. It also displayed a unique form of amnesia about the fight for equality and the eradication of institutional and systemic racism that had been the generations-long impetus for the civil rights movement. Rather, the meteoric rise of individual African American men during these years was interpreted as a kind of collective triumph, a signal that the entire race had 'overcome' the struggle. The reality, however, was that these triumphs did not trickle down to the community, which remained just as impoverished and disenfranchised at the end of the 1980s as it had been when Ronald Reagan declared, in 1984, that 'morning in America' had begun.

The ascendancy of Black conservatism in the 1980s is bracketed by the emergence of soul singer James Brown as an unexpected booster of Richard Nixon and the 1991 nomination of Clarence Thomas to the U.S. Supreme Court. Thomas rapidly became a poster child for a certain type of Uncle Tomism, but he did not emerge from a vacuum. His public persona and ideas reflected the decades-long shift that some African Americans had made to the right and, simultaneously, the growing sentiment among this group that they had achieved their success on their own merits. Their rhetoric of self-sufficiency, first championed by Black activists, had been reconfigured into a Republican talking point that extolled Black capitalism. Policies that could have really moved African Americans forward as a collective ultimately got lost in the shuffle as the neo-liberal ideology of the moment took centre stage.

❧

On April 5, 1968, James Brown was set to perform at Boston Garden. It was the night after Dr. Martin Luther King Jr.'s assassination in Memphis. The self-described 'godfather of soul,' at the height of his career, was poised to take the stage in a city where racial tensions were running high. A year prior, the Commonwealth of Massachusetts had ordered the city to desegregate its public schools through forced school-bussing. Now, municipal officials worried that if thousands of young African Americans converged downtown, violence would surely ensue.[1]

By that morning, just hours after King's death, the concert was already being promoted as a tribute, to be broadcast live on radio and television. Suddenly, it had become more than just a musical event. When he took the stage, Brown was either going to ignite an explosive powder keg of violence or he was going to become a catalyst for much-needed collective healing, reminding fans of all that King had stood for.

As Brown began the last song of his set, 'I Can't Stand Myself (When You Touch Me),' a man jumped on the stage, only to be violently pushed off by a white police officer.[2] But a group of teenage boys followed his lead. Suddenly, audience members surrounded Brown, and, for a moment, the police waited in anticipation of pandemonium. Brown, however, was fully in control of the crowd.

He stopped the band and called for the house lights to go on. While he asked the boys to leave the stage so he could finish the show, Brown also spoke directly to his people: 'We are black! Don't make us all look bad! Let me finish the show.' He continued: 'You're not being fair to yourself or me or your race. Now, I asked the police to step back because I figure I could get some respect from my own people. It don't make sense. Are we together or are we ain't?'

With those words, the boys climbed down, and the show went on. But the concert would go down as the night James Brown became a key figure in the civil rights movement at precisely the moment when its most visible leader had been killed.

A few months later, in August 1968, Brown released 'Say It Loud, I'm Black and I'm Proud.' The single became a battle cry for the Black Power/Black Pride movement. In the song's call-and-response chorus, Brown demands, 'Say it loud,' and a group of young Black children respond, 'I'm Black and I'm proud.' The song was recorded in the Watts and Compton areas of Los Angeles. Neighbourhoods appearing on the evening news in the homes of white Americans were now situated as sites of Black pride.

Also, in August, at the Democratic National Convention in Chicago, Brown campaigned for presidential candidate Hubert Humphrey, who, as a senator, had been integral to the passage of the Civil Rights Act of 1964. Humphrey was hardly a radical about racial justice, and he had alienated many radicals and liberals alike who felt the party no longer aimed to make institutional change the foundation of Democratic policies.[3]

By the early 1970s, in fact, Brown had drifted further right. His 'self-made' narrative, which had defined his success, made him increasingly sympathetic to the Republican Party. In 1972, Brown became a loud supporter of President Richard Nixon, and endorsed his re-election campaign. He was not alone.

Nixon counted other prominent Black figures among his supporters, including actor and singer Sammy Davis Jr. former civil rights activist Floyd McKissick (a one-time director of the Congress of Racial Equality), and Rev. Albert Sampson, once an aide to the Rev. Dr. Ralph David Abernathy, president of the Southern Christian Leadership Conference, King's advocacy group.

In an October 1972 editorial entitled 'Black Supporters of President Under Fire,' the *New York Times* noted that WHUR, the radio station at Howard University, a historically Black college, had broadcast a scathing attack on Brown. Protesters pledged to picket an appearance in Baltimore.[4] The same fate befell other Black supporters of Nixon, including former football star turned actor Jim Brown. The *Times* also ran an incendiary image of Sammy Davis Jr., a member of Frank Sinatra's 'Rat Pack,' embracing Nixon from behind as he addressed supporters at a youth rally in Miami during a campaign stop in August 1972.

These Black Nixon supporters were all labelled 'Uncle Toms,' 'sell-outs,' or 'political prostitutes.'[5] The question is, why, in the late 1960s, did a Black man's Republican political affiliation turn him into a sellout Uncle Tom? Prominent African Americans had supported the Republican Party earlier in the twentieth century without inciting controversy, among them Claude Albert Barnett, founder of the Associated Negro Press. The ANP had played a vital role in the expansion of Negro newspapers by providing an editorial critique of Jim Crow.

Barnett, a Republican for most of his life, once said that in the early twentieth century, '[the Republican Party] was the only one offering anything to Negroes in the form of jobs, public offices, and legislation.'[6] By the 1930s, however, most African Americans would leave the GOP. In *Farewell to the Party of Lincoln: Black Politics in the Age of FDR*, historian Nancy J. Weiss asserts that working-class African Americans became increasingly receptive to President Roosevelt's proposed 'New Deal' (aimed specifically at helping working-class Americans of all races). Despite Roosevelt's personal racism, the Democratic Party's roots in the South, and the discriminatory distribution of New Deal relief, masses of African Americans left the GOP for the Democrats at this time.[7] The vast majority did not return.

Sen. Barry M. Goldwater's run for president (against Lyndon B. Johnson) in 1964, and his strategy to appeal to segregationists in the South, further hampered attempts to lure African Americans back to the GOP. King himself denounced Goldwater for a 'philosophy which gives aid and comfort to the racists.'[8]

One of the reasons Nixon was able to lure some Blacks back to the party is because of his 'Black capitalism' program. In her examination of Black capitalism, University of California Irvine law professor Mehrsa Baradaran explains that Nixon sold the program as the 'natural' cure for the problem of Black poverty. Both Nixon and his Black supporters believed the bootstrap policy would 'help Negroes help themselves.'[9] As Baradaran explains, demands for federal aid and governmental assistance for the ills of the Black ghetto were framed as anti-capitalist and anti-American.

'Instead of government jobs and government housing and government welfare,' said Nixon in his 1968 acceptance speech at the Republican nominating convention, government should use its tax and credit power to drive 'the greatest engine of progress ever developed in the history of man – American private enterprise.'[10]

Nixon also advocated for 'black ownership ... black pride, black jobs,

Sammy Davis Jr. meeting with Richard Nixon, 1973. Photographer: Robert L Knudsen.

black opportunity, and yes, black power in the best, the constructive sense of that often misapplied term.'[11] He sought to co-opt the oppositional elements of Black Power – self-sufficiency and economic independence from the state – and recast them as mainstream proposals for Black capitalism.[12] As part of the program, Nixon, less than two months into his first term, established the Office of Minority Business Enterprise (OMBE). It aimed to establish a national network of business development organizations and provide seed funding to minority businesses.

Nixon's Black capitalism agenda has been described as a 'push for a segregated black economy, thereby justifying his neglect of other proposals for meaningful reform. Capitalism, and specifically "black capitalism," became yet another rhetorical weapon used to rationalize economic inequality.'[13] For example, his strategy included opposing all forms of legal race discrimination while rejecting any government efforts at integration. For most of the 1970s, OMBE did nothing to help other disadvantaged groups, such as women, and minority business leaders also found the agency unresponsive and fragmented.[14]

🙂

One of the long-lasting impacts of Nixon's presidency was his tough-on-crime strategy and 'law and order' rhetoric. He claimed that he wanted to restore peace to an America that was unravelling due to civil unrest and protest. Yet instead of engaging with Black activists, women's liberationists, and gay rights advocates – all groups that had, prior to the late 1960s, lacked any kind of public visibility – Nixon's now-familiar approach was to send signals to the so-called 'silent majority' that protesters were trying to destroy their values.

In his 1968 campaign, for example, one ad featured a series of photos of angry and bloodied protesters, police with guns, and burning buildings. The soundtrack was a snare drum and dissonant piano chords underneath Nixon's stern voice-over:

> It is time for an honest look at the problem of order in the United States. Dissent is a necessary ingredient of change but in a system of government that provides for peaceful change there is no cause that justifies resorts to violence. Let us recognize that the first civil right of every American is to be free from domestic violence. So, I pledge to you, we shall have order in the United States.[15]

Throughout his first term, Nixon also championed a 'war on drugs.' In a January 1972 speech on the establishment of the Office for Drug Abuse Law Enforcement, he said, 'Today our balanced, comprehensive attack on drug abuse moves forward in yet another critical area as we institute a major new program to drive drug traffickers and drug pushers off the streets of America.'[16] Seven months prior, he had called drugs America's 'public enemy number one' and as such, the goal of this new office, with the aid of government resources and expanded authority to the Department of Justice, was to orchestrate – in his words, 'a concentrated assault on the street level heroin pusher.'

This policy led to increased surveillance and police presence in Black communities, but also an overregulation of the informal Black economy (e.g., off-track betting), which resulted in excessive sentences for non-violent crimes – all of which hit poor Black people the hardest.[17] According to a *Time* magazine feature on rising prison populations, from 1960 to 1980, violent crime soared 270 per cent, peaking at 758 violent offences per 100,000 people in 1991.[18] However, African American and Latino communities bore the brunt of this crime wave, and also paid the price. Black and brown people were charged with crimes at a rate 24 per cent higher than white Americans.

The Nixon Administration emphasized individual responsibility, self-determination, and the pursuit of wealth accumulation without social policy reform or state intervention. The implication was that the poor were poor by choice.

As upwardly mobile African Americans tried to exit the inner cities, many still faced discrimination. Real estate agencies and banks continued to engage in discriminatory practices that rendered certain neighbourhoods off limits to Black people, whether or not they could afford the property – practices that severely limited the ability of African American families to accumulate home equity in the way that working-class whites could.[19] Only in 1974 did the passage of the Equal Credit Opportunity Act finally outlaw racial discrimination in mortgage lending; the 1977 Community Reinvestment Act banned redlining.[20]

With the economic stagnation of the 1970s, Black men in the inner ghettos were hardest hit by un- or underemployment, Black women were increasingly raising children in single-parent, low-income households, and schools became rundown, underfunded breeding grounds for gangs and drugs.

❧

This social context became the backdrop for the most important Black-centred cinema in the decade. *Cooley High* (1975) was a coming-of-age film about the hijinks of Black male teenagers in 1960s Chicago. It followed Leroy 'Preach' Jackson (Glynn Turman) and Richard 'Cochise' Morris (Lawrence Hilton-Jacobs) as they consumed alcohol, flirted with women, and got into entanglements with police officers.

Sparkle (1976), a rags-to-riches film set in Harlem in 1958, was about three sisters (Irene Cara as Sparkle Williams, Lonette McKee as Sister Williams, and Dwan Smith as Delores Williams) and the struggles that came with a life in the limelight. Though the film is centred on Sparkle, the story also shows how Sister comes to be entangled in a messy, sadomasochistic relationship with a smooth-talking gangster, Satin Struthers (Tony King). She eventually dies from a drug overdose. *Sparkle* then becomes more of a dim tragedy than a celebration of Harlem's music scene in the 1950s.

Both films, especially *Cooley High*, are considered classics for the ways in which they captured an everyday Black sensibility in urban America. But what they also did was locate poverty, drug use, and police surveillance in Black communities as things of the past. Even though the themes in each film were unfolding in the lives of young Black men and women in the 1970s, on the big screen they were scripted as another time and another place in America.

Claudine (1974), however, was the exception. The film starred Diahann Carroll as Claudine Price, a single Black mother living on welfare in Harlem while raising six children (her oldest son Charles is played by Lawrence Hilton-Jacobs, who became famous in the role of Freddie 'Boom Boom' Washington on the ABC comedy series *Welcome Back, Kotter* [1975–79]). Claudine is forced to lie to the welfare agent who makes frequent, unannounced visits to check in on her housekeeper job and her relationship with garbage collector Rupert 'Roop' Marshall (James Earl Jones) so she can receive social assistance, which is not even enough to live on.

Produced by Third World Cinema, Ossie Davis's short-lived production company, *Claudine* still feels authentic to its time. It is a love story that spoke directly to the financial challenges many Black families faced during the decade. Themes of Black love and family, as well as the financial worries of living in poverty, are told from the point of view of a Black woman. The film grossed $6 million at the box office. *New York Times* film critic Vincent Canby described it as 'the first major film about contemporary black life to consider the hopes, struggles, defeats and frustrations of blacks who aren't either supercops, supermusicians, superstuds, superpimps or super-pushers.'[21] These sympathetic but realistic narratives would soon be eclipsed by the more dominant voices of Black conservatives.

In 1977, African American author George Samuel Schuyler died. Charles Pete Banner-Haley, author of *From du Bois to Obama: African American Intellectuals in Public Forum*, describes Schuyler as the 'Godfather' of Black conservatism. Of his Depression-era novel, *Black No More*, Banner-Haley writes, 'Schuyler actually believed that black people would be better off just going about their business of being good, God-fearing, hard-working individuals who used their talents to survive and prosper. Race should just be ignored.'[22]

In his introduction to the 2018 reissue of the book, novelist Danzy Senna observed that Schuyler's Black conservatism changed in the decades following *Black No More*'s release in 1931. '[His] healthy skepticism toward authority and his absurdist, freewheeling humor gave way to rigidity and humorless far-right extremism,' writes Senna.[23] By the 1960s, he was railing against Black leaders from Dr. Martin Luther King Jr., to Malcolm X. Schuyler remained firm in his belief that 'after all, the welfare of Negroes is primarily the responsibility of Negroes.'[24]

Besides Schuyler, there were few other prominent Black conservatives between the 1930s and the 1970s. But the Stanford University economist Thomas Sowell, a North Carolina–born and Harlem-raised exponent of free-market thinking, changed all that.

'In scores of books and articles throughout the 1980s,' writes history professor Michael L. Ondaatje in *Black Conservative Intellectuals in Modern America*, 'Sowell argued that, in breaking with the principle of color blindness, color-conscious policies had created new victims of racial discrimination: white victims.'[25] Now remembered as the unofficial godfather of the 'Black right,' Sowell in 1980 said, 'Being a black conservative is perhaps not considered as bizarre as being a transvestite, but it is certainly considered more strange than being a vegetarian or a bird watcher.'[26] These comments, quite clearly offensive today, point to how divisive some Black conservative language can be.

Educated at Harvard and the University of Chicago, Sowell studied the economic theories of Karl Marx and for a time considered himself a leftist. But during the civil rights movement, he, like Schuyler, had an ideological change of heart. Sowell failed to see the benefits that could be gained from government intervention in systemic racism. In a 1999 interview, for example, Sowell explained why he had opposed the Civil Rights Act of 1964: 'What happens is that there's a sweeping under the rug of black success that does not fit the ideological vision,' he stated. 'Of course there were things that needed to be gotten rid of – the Jim Crow system in the South. My point is that people expected social and economic results which were not to be expected from that source.'[27] Banner-Haley opines that for Sowell, 'the capitalist system, kept open to all, would provide the opportunities for any individual who took advantage of it to succeed.'[28]

As more and more African Americans entered colleges, a Black middle class began to emerge, giving rise to a new generation of Black conservatives. These folks were university-educated and sought to be judged by the quality of their skills, not the colour of their skin. Most of all, they wanted to achieve financial success not because of government assistance but through the merits of their hard work.

Philosopher Cornel West's 1993 book, *Race Matters*, was one of the first to engage with these ideas and to offer a reasoned assessment of the political significance of Black conservatism. A socio-cultural critic, he explained the rise of Black conservatism in the context of the structural shifts that had taken place in America between the 1960s and 1980s: the collapse of American liberalism, the structural transformation of the national economy, and the breakdown of Black communities across the country.[29]

Despite the fact that many middle-class Blacks had achieved their positions by means of affirmative action programs in the 1970s and 1980s, 'the new black conservatives voiced … feelings [for race-free hiring criteria, and a dismantling of equity mechanisms] in forms of attacks on affirmative action programs,' West explained.[30] Black conservatives, he argued, seemed to justify actual practices of discrimination by overlooking one fundamental fact: affirmative action policies were political responses to the refusal of most white Americans to judge Black Americans on the basis of merit, not on race.

The concept of affirmative action traced back to President Kennedy, who first used the term in a 1961 executive order urging federal contractors to eliminate discrimination in their recruitment, hiring, and promotional practices.[31] As official policy, affirmative action later aimed to level the playing field by giving preferences for jobs, university admissions, or government contracts to members of historically oppressed racial (and gender) groups.

In the 1980s, Reagan's agenda, which aligned with governments across the Western world, stressed deregulation, privatization, and globalization, as well as making a rhetorical shift toward individual responsibility as key to the expansion of a free-market enterprise system. Accordingly, governments no longer sought to regulate society. Instead, individual citizens were encouraged to self-actualize and seek fulfillment through the market system.

Despite the rhetoric, suburbanization and declining manufacturing fuelled skyrocketing inner-city crime and high rates of unemployment. And for the growing numbers of middle-class and upwardly mobile African Americans who had never lived in the ghetto, the conversation about racial identity and politics was changing.

꒜

This new ideology would seep into film, but the results bore little resemblance to the realism of the work of Ossie Davis. Hollywood offered up a very different vision of what it meant to be Black in the 1980s, and one that drew again on the tropes of earlier eras.

Trading Places (1983), a comedy directed by John Landis, starred comedian Eddie Murphy, who had catapulted to fame on *Saturday Night Live*. It was one of the first films in the 1980s to depict the 'rags-to-riches' potential that African Americans now supposedly enjoyed in Reagan's America. In the film, Murphy plays Billy Ray Valentine, a con man who makes his first appearance pretending to be a blind, legless veteran. His white co-star, Dan Aykroyd (Louis Winthorpe III), plays a stuck-up commodities broker. The film's premise is simple: two rich white men, Randolph and Don Duke (Ralph Bellamy and

Don Ameche), make a bet to see what the results would be if they switch the lives of two people on opposites sides of the tracks – a white rich guy (Winthrope) and a Black man in poverty (Valentine).

In their experiment, the Dukes frame Winthrope as a criminal, while Valentine is given a 'leg up' by their generosity. Eventually, he becomes well-versed in the business of commodity trading. In the end, Winthorpe and Valentine mastermind a get-rich-quick scheme that bankrupts the Dukes, as they go on to become millionaires. Aykroyd's character tellingly appears in blackface at one point during the switcheroo.

The plot of *Trading Places* was different from Murphy's other box office successes – *48 Hrs.* (1982) and *Beverly Hills Cop* (1984) – but, like Sidney Poitier's films from the 1960s, all three share a common theme: the experiences of a Black man who finds himself alone in a white world. But what distinguished Murphy in these roles was that he came across as an attractive Black man with strong sexual desires and street cred.

In *Trading Places*, writes film critic Krin Gabbard, 'Valentine has a few connections to the black community in the early scenes when he buys drinks for a group of prostitutes and tough-looking black men he met in prison. The filmmakers can only conceive of black culture in terms of freeloaders and ex-convicts.'[32] Separated from the Black community, Valentine acquires the assets and power of white capital, and then he is never again in the presence of Black people until the final moments of the film.

Similarly, in *Beverly Hills Cop*, Murphy as Axel Foley leaves Black Detroit for Los Angeles to pursue the killers of his white friend, Mikey (James Russo). All the significant people in his world are now white. In the scene where Axel checks into his hotel, he uses accusations of racism as a threat to intimidate the white staff. As film scholar Donald Bogle observes, 'At this point in American history, some white Americans were complaining that blacks found racism in places where it did not exist. This scene, better than almost any other in American films of the 1980s, supports such attitudes.'[33] Additionally, because Axel's ploy with the hotel staff succeeds (he gets a room), the scene validated the idea that race was a card that, when played, would give Black people an unfair advantage.

Other 1980s hit films – Richard Pryor's 1985 film *Brewster's Millions*, about a hack Black baseball player who inherits money from a white relative he's never met, or *Lethal Weapon* (1987), starring Mel Gibson (Martin Riggs) as a hot-tempered, reckless, alienated white detective working with even-keeled partner Danny Glover (Roger Murtaugh) – drew attention away from America's ongoing structural inequalities. Such movies primed viewers to see their own actions (and inactions) as the answer to (and reason for) for Black poverty. Systemic racism had no place in these fictional settings.

The era of Reagan, the New Right, and the Moral Majority, included Wall Street crashes, endemic homelessness, and increasing poverty. Yet it all gave rise to an evidently compelling form of political conservatism.[34] For many Black Americans, the decade therefore became a time to move fully into the system rather than to remain outside of it. Jesse Jackson's presidential run in 1988 exemplified the shift in outlook. But these changes in Black cultural politics meant that Black critics had their eyes trained keenly on Black capitalists as well as interlopers who aspired to gain entry to the world of white conservative politics.

☙

President George H. W. Bush's nomination of Clarence Thomas to the U.S. Supreme Court in 1991 represented a cataclysmic change in the role that Black conservatism would play in setting institutional and political agendas in America. His nomination also represented the continuing power of Uncle Tom as a figure who could still be called upon to help explain Black men who appeared to be out of step with the collective Black consciousness. As if to signal a changing of the political guard, Thomas's appointment, and the ensuing Senate Judiciary Committee hearings, introduced the American public to a consortium of Black supporters of the Reagan/Bush consensus in national politics. Their goal, many believed, was to tear down the liberal legal principles that Thurgood Marshall, who stepped down from the bench in 1991, had fought for decades to establish.[35]

Thomas was born in Pin Point, Georgia, in 1948. After graduating with a law degree from Yale in 1974, he became Missouri's assistant attorney general, under State Attorney General John Danforth. As the decade progressed, he became increasingly conservative. 'Perhaps it was his strong religious beliefs that pushed him to abandon separatism and accept integration,' writes Banner-Haley, or 'it may be that his impoverished childhood in Georgia coupled with the strong discipline that he received from his grandparents and subsequent schooling made him a strong believer in lifting oneself up.'[36]

Like Sowell before him, Thomas became disillusioned with the Democratic Party during the civil rights era, believing that government interventionist policies would not benefit Black people.

The Enigma of Clarence Thomas (2019), a biography by political theorist Corey Robin, charts Thomas's move to the right and his ascendency into national politics. He served in the Reagan administration as an assistant secretary of education and in 1981 chaired the Equal Employment Opportunity Commission (EEOC). Under Bush, he was appointed to the U.S. Court of Appeal for the District of Columbia and then nominated to the Supreme Court.

'Thomas is not a conservative man who happens to be black,' Robin writes. '[He] is a black man whose conservatism is overwhelmingly defined by and oriented toward the interests of black people, as he understands them.'[37] While this is an empathetic framing of Thomas, others have not been as kind.

For Brando Simeo Starkey, the case against Thomas starts with the question of why he promulgates the myth that he grew up impoverished and by sheer grit made it to the Supreme Court. After investigating his life, judicial opinions, and statements, and weighing the evidence, Starkey concludes that 'the scales are lopsided': 'Justice Thomas is an *Uncle Tom*. He is uncommitted to the black plight.'[38] Starkey challenges Thomas's rags-to-riches story, and questions why, even as he has benefited from affirmative action, the justice has continued to assail it as bad policy for other Black people.

The spectacle of his 1991 Senate confirmation hearings reignited the Uncle Tom discourse that has long hung over Black life. But questions arise: How did Uncle Tom morph under the new conservatism? And why did the all-white, all-male Senate Judiciary Committee, in questioning Anita Hill, a Black woman alleging sexual harassment against Thomas, shift conversations about race?

❧

On October 11, 1991, Hill was called to testify during Thomas's confirmation hearing.

At the time, she was a young, conservative law professor who taught at the University of Oklahoma. She had worked under Thomas first at the Department of Education and then at EEOC. According to Hill, shortly after she began working at EEOC, Thomas started harassing her with obscene jokes, asking her out repeatedly, and frequently making graphic sexual comments to her. Some thirty million Americans watched the hearings, which were televised live.[39] The session's racial undertone – white male senators questioning dozens of African American men and women about Thomas – was compounded by the optics of a Black man being accused of sexual improprieties with a Black woman in an America where both Black men and women have been sexualized and criminalized by white men. It was disturbing to watch and brought up the worst stereotypes about Black men – the oversexed brute – that many had spent decades pushing against, especially in the unforgiving context of America's 1980s conservatism.

When Sen. Joe Biden, then chairman of the Judiciary Committee, asked Thomas if he had anything to say about Hill's allegations, the nominee had an unforgettable reply:

I would like to start by saying unequivocally, uncategorically, that I deny each and every single allegation against me today … And from my standpoint as a black American, as far as I'm concerned, it is a high-tech lynching for uppity blacks who in any way deign to think for themselves, to do for themselves, to have different ideas, and it is a message that unless you kowtow to an old order, this is what will happen to you. You will be lynched, destroyed, caricatured by a committee of the U.S. ... rather than hung from a tree.[40]

Despite Hill's testimony, and that of four corroborating witnesses, the Senate voted to confirm Thomas 52–48, one of the narrowest margins in history. Following the hearings, Black liberals denounced Thomas as an Uncle Tom.

Black conservatives since Thomas have frequently been accused of aiming to please whites only to elevate themselves – socially, politically, and economically. Jim Crow historian David Pilgrim charges that 'they publicly say about race what conservative whites dare not say: crime and welfare are black phenomena, affirmative action is reverse discrimination, and white racism is not the cause of black problems. They wear the "Uncle Tom" label as a badge of pride – at least publicly.'[41]

Many high-profile Black conservatives have had to contend with these accusations. In 2004, Wisconsin radio show host John Sylvester dismissed Condoleezza Rice, George W. Bush's secretary of state, as an 'Aunt Jemima' for participating in his administration. Rice had previously served as Bush's national security adviser. But in 2004, Bush appointed her to replace Colin Powell, the first African American to serve in this position (as well as chair of the joint chiefs of staff). Sylvester, who is white, told the Associated Press at the time that he used the term 'to describe Rice and other blacks as having only a subservient role in the Bush administration.'[42]

Many listeners complained about his comments, but Sylvester defended them, noting that he had a long history of commitment to civil rights and had supported Madison's Black community. In other words, the radio host believed that his work in Black community and support of Black issues gave him the right to become an interloper, policing the boundaries of Black loyalty.

The racial loyalty of Powell, like Rice, had previously been called into question. Civil rights activist and singer Harry Belafonte likened him to a 'house Negro' and 'yassuh-boss' Uncle Tom. 'When Colin

Powell dares to suggest something other than what the master wants to hear, he will be turned back out to pasture,' Belafonte said in a 2002 radio interview.[43] Belafonte, who was at odds with the Bush administration over its position on the Iraq War and its dubious record on civil liberties, saw Powell as an Uncle Tom figure because he seemed 'scared to confront' Bush on his policies.

This exchange would not be the last time that the Bush administration was accused of reproducing relations of servitude. In 2006, during a speech on Martin Luther King Jr. Day, then Sen. Hillary Clinton told a mostly Black audience at a Harlem church that Republican leaders had run the White House 'like a plantation.'[44] Her accusation echoed comments made in 1994 by then GOP House Speaker Newt Gingrich shortly before Republicans won a majority in the House. On the eve of the Republicans' 1994 mid-term victory in the House, he said Democrats 'think it's their job to run the plantation,' and that 'it shocks them that I'm actually willing to lead the slave rebellion.'[45]

These highly publicized comments linking the White House, plantation slavery, and African Americans demonstrate the fluidity with which the past can intrude on the present. They also reflect the inherent contradictions that come with Black success in politics. After all, what are the politics of racial loyalty when public officials must serve as spokespeople for white leaders who are invariably male and wealthy. 'Are they Black enough' is not merely an opinion or criticism; in politics, it has real-life implications for the well-being of the Black community.

❧

Within weeks of Thomas's confirmation, *Emerge*, the Washington-based magazine that made waves with its aggressive and sometimes flamboyant coverage of Black culture and politics (and ceased publishing in 2000), ran a cover of the newly confirmed Justice Thomas with a handkerchief tied around his head.[46] The implication was that Thomas was unsympathetic, and even hostile, to the struggles of his own people and, what's more, committed to protecting the interests of white people.

Author June Jordan condemned Thomas as a 'virulent Oreo phenomenon,' a 'punk ass,' and an 'Uncle Tom calamity.' Black feminist Julianne Malveaux fumed, 'these people such as Thomas who claim to have pulled themselves up by the bootstraps are very likely to use the bootstraps to strangle [other Blacks].' Invoking an old slave-owner image, Spike Lee also called Thomas 'a handkerchief-head, chicken-and-biscuit eating Uncle Tom.'[47]

In November 1996, *Emerge* took its vitriol against Thomas even further when it featured him on its cover as a grinning lawn jockey from the Jim Crow era, with the headline 'Uncle Thomas: Lawn Jockey for the Far Right.' George E. Curry, *Emerge* editor-in-chief, said the following about the two covers:

> I apologize. Exactly three years ago, shortly after I took over as editor of *Emerge*, we ran a cover illustration of U.S. Supreme Court Justice Clarence Thomas, resplendent with an Aunt Jemima–like handkerchief on his head. In retrospect we were far too benevolent. Hence, this month's cover with Clarence appropriately attired as a lawn jockey. Even our last depiction is too compassionate for a person who has done so much to turn back the clock on civil rights, all the way back to the pre–Civil War lawn jockey days.[48]

These illustrations not only spoke to Justice Thomas's subservience to the Republican Party and new conservatism, they also sent a message to African Americans that he was a race traitor – the most despised version of Uncle Tom of them all.

In his defence, Thomas has said, 'I am not an Uncle Tom … I have not forgotten where I came from … I feel a special responsibility to help our people.'[49] However, his use of 'I' says a lot about his inability to see and/or acknowledge the collective 'we' that lay at the centre of liberal Black politics. As journalist Jack E. White argued in a 1995 article entitled 'Uncle Tom Justice,' Thomas became the high court's 'most aggressive advocate of rolling back the gains [Thurgood] Marshall fought so hard for … Thomas owes his seat to precisely the kind of racial preference he goes to such lengths to excoriate. And as long as he is on the court, no other black need apply: Thomas fills a quota of one.'[50]

❧

According to *Time*'s sneak peak of the documentary *Created Equal: Clarence Thomas in His Own Words* (released in 2020), Thomas addressed his experience as a prominent Black conservative. 'There's different sets of rules for different people,' he says in the film. 'If you criticize a black person who's more liberal, you're a racist. Whereas you can do whatever to me, or to now [HUD Secretary] Ben Carson, and that's fine, because you're not really black because you're not doing what we expect black people to do.'[51] As recently as 2017, Rep. Bennie Thompson, a Mississippi Democrat, stood by racially charged comments he made about Thomas's Uncle Tomism. 'For some it is [a lie],' Thompson told CNN, 'but to others it's the truth.'[52]

The most revealing part of the Uncle Tomism that clings to Thomas is how Stowe's Uncle Tom still enters the conversation. As one African American blogger wrote in 2018, '[Thomas] isn't an "Uncle Tom." Uncle Tom was a hero who sacrificed his life so some other slaves could escape the plantation. Too old to run himself, they killed him for refusing to tell where they were.'[53] *Chicago Tribune* columnist Dahleen Glanton, who is African American, also invoked Stowe's Tom as a foil to Thomas. 'I understand the deep disdain blacks feel for Thomas,' said Glanton in a 2016 article, adding that anyone who thinks of him as an Uncle Tom should take a closer look at Stowe's *Uncle Tom's Cabin*. She goes on to argue that Uncle Tom was a 'noble character' who used his perceived ignorance to promote his own anti-slavery convictions. While he was strong, courageous, and inspirational in the novel, she asserted that those original character traits have been 'misconstrued to be one of the hated, most disrespected black characters in American literature.'[54]

Thomas is not, in fact, Stowe's Uncle Tom. Because through his actions and, most importantly, his institutional power, he has hindered, not aided, the Black community, he represents a new chapter in the continuing metamorphosis of Tom: a conservative Uncle. And while conservative Uncles are not new, they wield a new kind of power acquired during and since the Reagan era and therefore, according to some critics, require constant monitoring by the Black community.

Crucially, television in the 1980s played a pivotal role in crafting a new, more pernicious Tom. The construction of Blackness on television was fundamentally defined by one sitcom that premiered during the Reagan era: *The Cosby Show*. Indeed, while Thomas focused on dismantling protections for Black civil rights on the Supreme Court in Washington, Bill Cosby presented a conservative fantasy of the Black American dream on TV.

THE 1980S, BILL COSBY, AND SMOKESCREEN TOMS

On November 6, 1984, President Ronald Reagan was re-elected in a landslide victory. The Reagan administration, which had become a model for conservative governments in Britain, Canada, and elsewhere, believed in limited government, rolling back many of the social policies that had been put in place during the Democratic administrations of the 1960s. In the 1980s, governments prioritized corporate interests over civil rights, implementing a set of policy choices that had its greatest impact on poor, inner-city Black communities.

Between 1965 and 1981, the U.S. federal budget grew from 18 per cent of GNP to 23 per cent, doubling in real terms from $330 billion to $660 billion (1981 dollars).[1] Previous governments had allocated substantial amounts to social security, unemployment insurance, child benefits, Medicare and Medicaid, education, training, and other social services, but in 1982, the Reagan budget proposed $44 billion in cuts to all those programs.

Prior to the 1960s, many immigrants to America had come from Europe. By the 1980s, countries like Mexico, the Philippines, Vietnam, China and Taiwan, and Korea accounted for most immigrants. Piggybacking on the country's shifting demographics, Reagan celebrated this new 'multicultural' America. 'Our nation is a nation of immigrants,' he declared in a 1981 speech. 'More than any other country, our strength comes from our own immigrant heritage and our capacity to welcome those from other lands.'[2]

In *Morning in America: How Ronald Reagan Invented the 1980s*, presidential historian Gil Troy writes, '[T]he 1980s would be Reagan's decade because Reagan skillfully rode and often took credit for one independently generated cultural wave after another.'³ The Reagan decade saw the founding of CNN, MTV, and USA *Today*, as well as the reign of prime-time soaps like *Dallas* and *Dynasty* on television. There were many other shifts and changes in America in the 1980s that had nothing to do with Reagan, such as the advent of microwave popcorn in 1983. But he often attributed these innovations to the fact that by removing regulations and reducing checks on corporate enterprise, his administration had enabled the free-market system to function at its best – hence America's success.

'The American miracle of which the world now speaks is a triumph of free people and their private institutions, not government,' Reagan proclaimed in a nationwide televised speech in 1985. 'It was individual workers, businesspeople, entrepreneurs, not government, who created virtually every one of our seven million new jobs over the past two years.'⁴ His words extolled the virtues of buying more and spending more, while attributing individual success to just that: the individual.

As America became swept up in the rhetoric of laissez-faire economics, Black conservatives also got caught in the web of free-market capitalism. With the Black conservative network growing in size and strength, empowered by the Reagan administration's staunch rejection of any suggestion that its policies were racist, many distanced themselves from the ideas, policies, and institutions that framed the issues confronting Black America in collectivist terms. The new conservatism ascribed social mobility and empowerment to the agency of the individual.⁵ As Reagan told the NAACP, 'The well-being of blacks, like the well-being of every other American, is linked directly to the health of the economy.'⁶

Before he was named to the Supreme Court, Clarence Thomas famously rejected the notion that white racism was an insurmountable obstacle to Black progress in America, attributing the success of individuals to 'better choices.' In a November 1987 interview with *Reason* magazine, Thomas, then chairman of Reagan's Equal Employment Opportunity Commission, described Malcolm X's rhetoric as 'anti-white,' while admitting he was also partial to Malcolm because of his 'self-help teaching.' He steadfastly rejected arguments, from the NAACP and others, that government programs would assist Black Americans in overcoming systemic racism. 'When Ronald Reagan is gone, why are you going to tell them that it's hopeless? Because the government isn't spending enough money? It will always be hopeless if that's the reason.' Thomas always came down on the side of self-determination. 'What you do have control over is yourself. They should be telling these kids that freedom carries not only benefits, it carries responsibilities... You've got to learn how to take care of yourself, learn how to raise your kids, how to go to school and prepare for a job and take risks like everybody else.'[7]

❦

The Reagan-era rhetoric of individualism formed the socio-political backdrop for *The Cosby Show*, a sitcom that exemplified the ideology of that moment.

When it premiered on September 20, 1984, *The Cosby Show* became the first prime-time television sitcom to feature a Black family that included two university-educated parents raising five children in a desegregated middle-class neighbourhood. The program transformed American culture while shifting the viewer's gaze away from the Reagan administration's policies, which had created two starkly different realities for Black America.

On the one hand, there was an increasingly poor, inner-city Black population living with increased police surveillance and the huge socio-economic impact of declining government transfers. On the other hand, an entire generation of African Americans – what historian Michael L. Ondaatje calls the 'new Black vanguard' – became upwardly mobile, attained wealth, and established middle-class communities. Many attributed these gains to individual choices and self-determination, not government programs or policies.

Set against this backdrop, *The Cosby Show* was bigger than TV. It depicted a vision of the new Black experience, showcasing those born and raised in middle-class environments, and who were college-educated, upwardly mobile, and, most importantly, apolitical.

The growing chasm in Black America was the focus of Spike Lee's *School Daze* (1988), a satire set at a white-financed, all-Black Southern college whose motto is 'Uplift the Race.' The student body is divided along racial and class lines. The Wannabees, light-skinned Blacks who disregard their cultural roots in favour of an idealized form of whiteness with nails, big hair, and glitter to match, are placed in opposition to the Jiggaboos, dark-skinned rebels who are outside the mainstream of school life. *School Daze* was uncompromisingly Black, and Lee made no concessions to please white audiences.

The Cosby Show, by contrast, presented only one side of the picture. When the program launched, Cosby was well-known to American audiences. Born in Philadelphia in 1937, he was the first Black performer to have a starring role in a dramatic TV series, *I Spy* (1965–68). From 1972 to 1985, his cartoon, *Fat Albert and the Cosby Kids,* was a favourite among children of all races. By the 1980s, he had become a pitchman for Jell-O, Coca-Cola, and other American products. Cosby was earning $10 million a year at the time. In 1985, he received the decade's highest Q rating, an industry measurement used to assess a celebrity's 'likeability.'[8]

The Cosby Show was culturally significant because of the space it cleared on television for the representation of a Black family implicitly aided by Reagan's free-market policies. Yet, as TV scholar Herman Gray observes, Cosby seemed unable, or unwilling, to reconcile the show's universal appeals to family, the middle class, professional mobility, and individualism with the realities of Black social, cultural, political, and economic life.[9]

Located in Brooklyn, the Cosby home was headed by Cliff Huxtable, a well-to-do obstetrician with a home-based clinic. The son of a prominent jazz trombonist, he is married to Clair (Phylicia Rashad), a high-powered New York attorney. Together, they have five children: Sondra (Sabrina Le Beauf), Denise (Lisa Bonet), Theo (Malcolm Jamal Warner), Vanessa (Tempestt Bledsoe), and Rudy (Keshia Knight Pulliam). By season six, Sondra, a Princeton graduate, is married to another Princeton alum, Elvin (Geoffrey Owens), and raising twins. Denise is married to Navy man Martin (Joseph C. Phillips), and their daughter, Olivia (Raven Symoné) has taken over Rudy's role as Cliff's 'cute' child sidekick. Vanessa, Theo, and Rudy, also educated at elite colleges, all appear with the occasional boyfriend or girlfriend.

The show focused repeatedly on the education of the Huxtable children and their significant others. These themes were so consistent that Cosby, who had earned both a master's degree and a doctorate at the University of Massachusetts–Amherst, insisted that scripts for each episode be reviewed by the acclaimed African American Harvard psychologist Alvin Poussaint in order to ensure that, as Patricia Turner says, 'no insidious negative stereotypes had slipped into the pages.'[10]

TV Guide noted that the show was 'TV's biggest hit in the 1980s, and almost single-handedly revived the sitcom genre and NBC's ratings fortunes.'[11] Cliff Huxtable was often described as the 'Greatest Television Dad' of all time.[12] But accusations of Uncle Tomism followed after the show's debut. '*Leave It to Beaver* in Blackface,' sneered a *New York Magazine* feature in October 1984. 'Cosby sells reassurance,' the magazine observed. 'He's been selling it – in commercials, in the Fat Albert cartoons, on talk shows – ever since the demise of the *I, Spy* series…. And he's selling it again, very successfully.'[13] The *Village Voice* went so far as to say that Cosby 'no longer qualifies as black enough to be an Uncle Tom.' Cosby bristled at these criticisms: 'Does it mean only white people have a lock on living together in a home where the father is a doctor and the mother a lawyer and the children are constantly being told to study by their parents?'[14]

In a November 1984 interview with the *Washington Post*, Poussaint said he was not sure what the criticism was about. 'Sometimes it seems they want the show to be "culturally" Black in the sense that they think of cultural Blackness – like the Jeffersons or *Good Times* – and sometimes it seems they would be happier to see them cussing out white people, a sort of protest sitcom,' he said. 'Some seem to feel that because the family is middle-class with no obvious racial problems, that constitutes a denial or dismissal of the black poor.

And some seem to feel somehow threatened.'[15] Significantly, as the *Post* reminded readers, perhaps they do not know there are growing numbers of Black families whose lifestyles are a lot closer to the Huxtables' than to the Jeffersons'. 'You don't have to be poverty-stricken or bitter or smart-ass to be authentic.'

As some African Americans were gaining increased access to schools, jobs, and neighbourhoods that had long been off-limits, Cosby was offering a reassuring image to whites. He was the Black buddy or the neighbour everyone wanted to know. As such, he was resurrecting the older unthreatening image of Black masculinity that catered to white America's desire to live in a nation where racism, discrimination, and division no longer existed.[16] Similarly, all the Huxtable children assimilated into the dominant culture, attending elite schools and speaking a standard English. As an instantly recognizable figure from his work as a comedian, Cosby was also highly marketable, entertaining, and eminently likeable, to both white and Black audiences. Notably, Cosby's book *Fatherhood* sold 2.4 million hardcover copies in 1986.[17]

Cliff was friendly and deferential, loyal both to the dominant societal values, such as law and order, and to the individuals who upheld them, but he was also a capitalist. It is the latter of these conservative ideals that helped to distinguish Cosby's brand of Uncle Tomism from earlier versions. He projected a non-threatening Black identity, defined neither by his sexual prowess nor by any hint of violence. But Cliff/Cosby was also deeply embedded in the free-market capitalist system. Immediately after *The Cosby Show* aired, for example, Cosby would appear in a commercial for Jell-O. He sold fatherhood and then consumerism.[18] The new rendition of Uncle Tom was as a capitalist.

Within the capitalist 1980s, in fact, Cosby's image helped to sell all sorts of products. He was not alone. In this consumerist climate, Black men like Cosby could be repackaged as 'Black buddies' and receive lucrative endorsement contracts. They made lots of money and joined the ranks of wealthy white Americans. *The Cosby Show*'s vision of multicultural Brooklyn – a far cry from Archie Bunker's working-class Queens of the 1970s – underscored Reagan's rhetoric about the new America. It was a place where, as Troy writes, 'on the same block in Flatbush or Flushing you could buy kimchi, paratha, and a potato knish from Gus the knish-man, whether you were black, brown, or white.'[19]

Cosby updated the affable and agreeable Uncle Tom trope into something that was not offensive to most people in Reagan's America. He *knew* who he was. Cliff Huxtable was not a 'sellout' to his culture or race. He had a Black wife and Black children, for crying out loud! In fact, when I watched *Cosby* as a kid, the show introduced me to African American art and jazz and Black fraternities and sororities that I otherwise would not have known about. However, when I peeled away the aesthetics of the show, I could see that at its core lay a version of Uncle Tom that aimed to accomplish one goal: diverting attention away from the collective social ills in disenfranchised Black communities that had been caused by neo-conservative policies. Cosby's Uncle Tom served as a smokescreen.

～

During the 1980s, aggressive policing and drug/three-strikes laws saw an ever-growing percentage of Black men convicted and incarcerated – a socially ruinous trend that created a disproportionate number of single-parent Black households. Disturbing images of working-class Black men flooded the media during Reagan's 'War on Drugs' and presented a stark contrast to Cosby's squeaky-clean image. Washington's drug war created that social dividing line. When crack cocaine appeared, it became the perfect target for the Reagan administration. As Black feminist scholar Patricia Hill Collins notes, crack was primarily appearing in Black inner-city neighbourhoods, and the media representations of crack addicts constructed an intensely punitive climate, with the criminal justice system incarcerating tens of thousands of Black men and women for even minor possession offences.[20]

Writing in 1989 in the *New York Times*, Harvard professor Henry Louis Gates Jr., called the 1980s the 'Cosby decade' – to the detriment of Black America. 'Today,' he observed, 'blacks are doing much better on TV than they are in real life, an irony underscored by the use of black public figures (Cosby as well as Michael Jackson, Michael Jordan, Bobby Ferrin) as spokesmen for major businesses ... As the dominant representation of blacks on TV, it suggests that blacks are solely responsible for their social conditions, with no acknowledgement of the severely constricted life opportunities that most black people face.'[21] In many ways, Cosby's success echoed the popular appeal of *Amos 'n' Andy*: in both cases, the representation itself is not what appealed most to people, it was the idea of the representation on TV at that moment. Cliff, a child of college-educated parents, was a believable figure in Reagan's 1980s, as were Amos and Andy's tales of migration, entrepreneurial outlook, and taste for hijinks in 1950s America. But the role both played in American culture, and the status they took on as being truly representative of Black life, was not.

The 1980s were marked by the fraught politics of drug enforcement. While media coverage of crack led to an increase in law-enforcement funding, author and civil rights advocate Michelle Alexander points out, in *The New Jim Crow: Mass Incarceration in the Age of Colorblindness,* that 'there is no truth to the notion that the War on Drugs was launched in response to crack cocaine.'[22] In fact, in poor Black neighbourhoods, illegal drug use was declining. Yet the media coverage greatly influenced public opinion about the link between drugs and Black communities. The resulting moral panic led to the passage of draconian penalties for drug possession. Tellingly, in 1985, polls found that only 2 to 6 per cent of Americans saw drug abuse as the nation's 'number one problem'; by 1989, the same polling question showed concern over drugs had peaked at 64 per cent.[23] Those laws rapidly boosted prison populations, with African Americans affected most conspicuously. The number of incarcerated African Americans nearly quadrupled and continued to increase steadily until 2000, at which point the number of Blacks in U.S. prisons was twenty-six times higher than in 1983.[24]

Cosby's sitcom Uncle Tom was pulling a veil over the root causes of African American disenfranchisement and did so according to 1980s neo-liberal precepts that made individuals entirely responsible for their own successes and failures. Cosby's Tom appeared to 'represent' the Black community, but in reality, the depiction only served a new conservatism that refused to acknowledge racism or structural barriers.

The War on Drugs framed working-class Blacks as a dire threat to white America, while *Cosby* positioned upper-middle-class Black men, especially affable ones, as safe and welcomed. This dichotomy explains why, even though the Huxtables lived in predominantly Black Brooklyn, the show never addressed any of the racial issues that would have affected Black men living in New York at the time. A case in point: the tragic story of the Central Park Five – a group of African American and Latino boys wrongfully accused and convicted of raping a white woman in 1989 – never appeared in the Huxtables' dinnertime conversations. The result was a stark juxtaposition between the show's soothingly bourgeois plot lines and what NYU film scholar Ed Guerrero once described as the 'real-time, genocidal slaughter of urban blacks on the nightly eleven o'clock news.'[25] In fact, even though Clair is a lawyer, she never once mentions Anita Hill's allegations against Clarence Thomas or the beating of Rodney King by the LAPD, both of which occurred in 1991.

Taking their cues from *Cosby*, leading Black male characters on the decade's other Black middle-class shows maintained the image of a 'Black buddy' who apparently could live without fear in America's *new* colour-blind society. These included Sherman Hemsley as Ernest Frye, a widowed deacon of the First Community Church in Philadelphia on *Amen* (1986–91); Hal Williams as Lester, husband, father, and owner of his own construction company on *227* (1985–90); and Reginald Vel Johnson as Carl Winslow, husband, father, and Chicago police officer on *Family Matters* (1989–98). They all served up apolitical renderings of Black middle-class family life in America.

Will Smith, who starred in *Fresh Prince of Bel Air* (1990–96), took up the Huxtable mantle, updating the Black buddy trope for the 1990s. He affirmed for television sitcom audiences that race relations in America had never been better. Shows like *A Different World* (1987–93), *Living Single* (1993–98), and *Martin* (1992–97) all made more explicit references to Blackness as a culture and African Americans as a distinct community in America with its own speech, rhythm, style of dress, and music. But once they ran their course, they disappeared quickly and were not replaced.

Fresh Prince, another rags-to-riches tale, followed Will, a street-smart teenager from West Philadelphia who is sent to live with his wealthy Los Angeles relatives: Uncle Phil (James Avery) and Aunt Vivian (Janet Hubert and Daphne Maxwell Reid) and cousins Carlton (Alfonso Ribeiro), Hilary (Karyn Parsons), and Ashley (Tatyana M. Ali). Carlton is a young conservative who speaks a standard English, wears whites and pastels, and lacks any authentic Black sensibilities that could be seen as street cred. Will, on the other hand, plays the role of the *new* young Black male who is part of the hip-hop generation (those who came of age in the 1980s and 1990s and who spoke with street slang, dressed in baggy clothing, and wore their hats to the side). Like Cosby, who had a film career prior to television, Smith took up the mantle as America's Black buddy on the big screen playing roles that were a far cry from inner-city Will.

Smith's cinematic roles are often described as the safest images of Black masculinity available to the film industry. His 1990s movie credits – *Six Degrees of Separation* (1993), *Independence Day* (1996), *Men in Black* (1997), and *Enemy of the State* (1998) – cast him in the well-established trope of the buddy duo that can be traced back to Sidney Poitier in *The Defiant Ones*, Cosby on TV's *I Spy*, and Danny Glover in the *Lethal Weapon* films alongside Mel Gibson. These characters adhered to normative Black aesthetics (i.e., hip-hop culture, street cachet, and Black women as romantic partners), but they also reflected white standards of Hollywood masculinity – physically strong rebels who protected women and children from harm.[26]

Despite Smith's highly visible role in pop culture in the 1990s, his fame and influence never exceeded Cosby's. In fact, Cosby's influence was such that the U.S. Census Bureau recruited him and other prominent Black figures, like Magic Johnson, Alfre Woodard, and Miss America Debbye Turner, to encourage increased Black participation in the 1990 census.[27]

Who would have guessed that Cliff Huxtable would end up modernizing the images of Uncle Tom and Uncle Ben in a desegregating America? For a time, that was Bill Cosby's primary legacy.

๛

In recent years, of course, the Cosby myth – and his role as a smokescreen Uncle Tom – has been irrevocably debunked and finally erased. There had long been rumours around Hollywood and in some media circles about Cosby and sexual misconduct during the show's run. In the early 2000s, sexual assault allegations against him began to surface. Most notably, in 2005, Tamara Green, a California lawyer, appeared on the *Today Show* alleging that Cosby drugged and sexually assaulted her in the 1970s. While many people chose to ignore such accusations, these stories represented the first crack in what was quite possibly the cleanest image in Hollywood. Everyone was incredulous: how could 'America's dad' be a sexual predator? Eventually, more than sixty women, Black and white, publicly accused Cosby of attempted assault, rape, drug-facilitated sexual assault, sexual battery, and/or sexual misconduct. In September 2018, a jury found Cosby guilty of three counts of aggravated indecent assault and sentenced him to three to ten years in prison.

Cosby's title as America's Greatest Dad and Black buddy (and Uncle Tom) has been revoked. His conviction, moreover, reified the worst caricature of Black men. He had become the Black brute, made infamous in D. W. Griffith's 1915 *The Birth of a Nation*, which characterized Black men as dangerously violent and sexually aggressive. As a new anti-Tom, Cosby was revealed as a deceitful predator who was there to harm, not defend or mollify, white America. Cosby's trial and the allegations against him ultimately erased his pudding-pop buddy image of the 1980s. And while it also tarnished *The Cosby Show*, its cultural legacy remains in the form of the Black buddy as a refashioned Uncle Tom.

The complex and narrow representational space that has been reserved for middle-class African American men since *Cosby* speaks to the ways in which ideas about Black buddies fit within narrow definitions of Black masculinity. In the end, Cosby is the embodiment of Uncle Tom's long journey through popular culture. Like Tom, he descended from hero to villain. Unlike Tom, though, his comeback is unlikely.

20

A POLITICALLY CORRECT UNCLE TOM
AND AN IN-YOUR-FACE TOPSY

On June 14, 1987, *Uncle Tom's Cabin*, a made-for-TV movie, premiered on Showtime. This new version of Stowe's novel has largely faded from collective memory, in contrast to the 1977 miniseries *Roots*, which was based on Alex Haley's 1976 bestseller and became a pop-cultural milestone.

If we consider the historical mutation of Stowe's novel and its main character, the 1987 film version points to the ways in which Uncle Tom was once again called upon to offer up a glimpse of an allegedly simpler time in Black life. In this 1980s version, this bygone time contrasted sharply with the six-o'clock-news headlines about crack cocaine in inner-city neighbourhoods and narratives of unbridled Black criminality.

This rendition was the first and only television adaptation of Stowe's novel. In it, Avery Brooks (best known for his role as Benjamin Sisko on *Star Trek: Deep Space Nine*) plays Uncle Tom while Phylicia Rashad (*Cosby*'s Clair Huxtable) is cast as the enslaved runaway Eliza. The then-unknown Samuel L. Jackson plays George, Eliza's husband, and Edward Woodward is cast as the cruel plantation owner Simon Legree. The film was produced by Edgar Scherick, best known as the creator of ABC's *Wide World of Sports*, and directed by Stan Lathan, a pioneering African American director who entered network television in 1973. He directed several episodes of *Sanford and Son* and the 1984 feature *Beat Street*, one of the earliest films about hip-hop culture.

The project revived a work of fiction that had largely faded from view. *Uncle Tom's Cabin*, the novel, was not part of the popular imagination in the 1980s. In 1987, the *New York Times* reported that at Jackson State University, in Mississippi, the only copy of the novel in the college library had not been checked out in twenty years – an illustration of the lack of interest in Stowe's original text. The question is, why revive *Uncle Tom* almost 140 years after its original publication, when the public was not asking for him? 'Because it's a good yarn,' Scherick explained to the *New York Times* in an interview the night before the movie aired. 'The epithet "Uncle Tom" as it is understood today is not reflective of the character that Harriet Beecher Stowe created ... I hope when people see this film they will know something more about the original character of Uncle Tom. And I hope they'll understand why this novel had the tremendous social and political impact that it did.'[1]

At the time, Lathan admitted he originally had trepidations about the project; in fact, he had not read the book when he embarked on the film. 'Even [after reading the book], a lot of my friends told me to leave it alone. The Hollywood chapter of the NAACP was apprehensive about it. But when we showed them the finished film, they saw no problem with it,' said Lathan. 'Uncle Tom is an admirable figure ... He is a man of God with a sense of commitment and a strong sense of family. He's a self-made man who taught himself to read. He tries to make the most of his situation, and he is an inspiration to everyone around him.'[2]

Television shows often reflect broader public debates and issues. Yet Lathan's *Uncle Tom's Cabin* was not made to satisfy a public demand for Uncle Tom. Rather, the film's producers and Showtime's executives believed viewers would be drawn in by a story about a self-made man with a strong sense of family who inspires everyone around him. This version also eliminated most of the caricatured distortions of Uncle Tom that had formed between the era of the minstrel Tom shows to the 1927 Hollywood film adaptation. Instead, writes African American studies professor Patricia Turner, 'this strong, virile, middle-aged Tom never scrapes or bows. His English is clear and undistorted. His demeanor is serious ... This is a politically correct Uncle Tom.'[3]

Against the backdrop of the neo-conservative 1980s, this Uncle Tom subtly reminded audiences that the 'good' Black America, where God, faith, and a resolute belief in non-violence had been replaced by a 'bad' Black America. At a time when individualism and meritocratic success were increasingly upheld as new forms of moral citizenship, the film's depiction of 'good' Blackness seemed to be compensating for the lack of positive role models on MTV. In a straightforward depiction of pre–Civil War life, Lathan's Tom could be seen as a counterpoint to the Black male hip-hop artists who validated street life and being 'hard' and who delivered stinging critiques of white institutions and the social politics of Ronald Reagan's America.

Additionally, the *Uncle Tom's Cabin* remake was spurred on by the success and controversy over Steven Spielberg's adaptation of Alice Walker's Pulitzer Prize–winning 1982 novel, *The Color Purple*. 'I liked the challenge [*Uncle Tom's Cabin's*] production presented,' said Lathan in an interview with the *New York Times*, describing the film as 'a black man's interpretation of a white woman's interpretation of black reality – a reverse of "The Color Purple."' John J. O'Connor of the *Times* added, 'Mrs. Stowe, I believe, would have approved.'[4]

In *The Color Purple*, the character of Celie is sexually abused by her stepfather as a child; the film charts her growth from adolescence to old age and the love she finds with other Black women but, most importantly, with herself. The film came at the end of a long line of Hollywood studio productions with all-Black casts and themes, such as *Sounder* (1972), *Claudine* (1974), *Cooley High* (1975), *Sparkle* (1976), and *The Wiz* (1978).

Scherick/Lathan's *Uncle Tom's Cabin* took audiences in a different direction than other Black films up until this point. In fact, before the film aired, producers held advance screenings across America, encouraging audience members to ask questions of the cast and production crew about historical misrepresentation and the implications of Stowe's novel. Many of the attendees were surprised to discover that *Uncle Tom's Cabin*, the original novel, had little in common with the pejorative stereotype of Uncle Tom created over subsequent decades – through minstrel and vaudeville shows, advertising, film, etc.

In the early 1990s, Patricia Turner wrote about asking her students to define what made someone an 'Uncle Tom.' Some pointed to Clarence Thomas as the most obvious example, while others described someone whose identification is with his 'masters/employers' or had contempt for Black people, 'racial self-hate,' or 'was always willing to "sell out" blacks in order to placate whites and improve his personal well being.'[5] An unwavering Christian faith, old age, and a constant (toothy) smile were also some of the Uncle Tom traits noted by the students. What's so fascinating about her anecdote is that it shows how layers of meaning accumulated on Tom's shoulders over a long period of time, up to and including the late 1980s and the TV movie's attempt to tell Stowe's tale.

Lathan's film presents Uncle Tom as a man with a quiet dignity and pious subservience, fighting for freedom with his unwavering belief in God. Like Stowe's Uncle Tom, who invoked concern and sympathy in white readers, Lathan's politically correct Uncle Tom is a character that white audiences could feel for. His kindness, loyalty, and conviction would have appealed to their desire for these qualities in their interactions with African Americans in general.

To a white viewer, Uncle Tom's religiosity and devotion to Little Eva (Jenny Lewis) reinforce his goodness and piety. Through Topsy (Endyia Kinney) and her encounters with Eva and Miss Ophelia (Kate Burton), viewers are asked to empathize with white women without understanding the extent of the deprivation and abuse the Black children in the story experienced at the hands of enslavers. Finally, we see Black loyalty to white authority embodied not only through Uncle Tom, but in Legree's brutal overseers, Quimbo (Albert Hall) and Sambo (Paul Osborne).

Shot in and around Natchez, Mississippi, *Uncle Tom's Cabin* focuses primarily on Tom, interspersed with cross-cuts to the iconic flight scenes with Eliza and George and their escape to freedom in Canada. The nearly two-hour film begins on the Shelby plantation in Kentucky in 1852. When slave trader Haley (Frank Converse) arrives, Shelby agrees to sell Eliza's son and Uncle Tom down the river – a transaction that triggers both Eliza's escape and Tom's grim journey from

Kentucky to Louisiana. In the novel, Shelby tells Haley, 'Tom is an uncommon fellow … steady, honest, capable, manages my farm like a clock.'[6]

The opening scene in the film shows George running through fields, jumping into a river, and swimming to freedom. The slave catchers and their dogs are unable to catch him. At the same time, we are introduced to Uncle Tom. Following the plot of the novel, Tom is sold away from Aunt Chloe (Shirley Jo Finney) and their son. As Tom and Chloe embrace prior to his departure, Tom tells her 'they can't steal [this]' – their love.

When Stowe introduces Tom in chapter four of the novel, she describes him as 'a large, broad-chested, powerfully made man, of a fully glossy black, and face whose truly African features were characterized by an expression of grave and steady good sense, united with much kindliness and benevolence.'[7] This description not only celebrates Uncle Tom as a man, but also reinforces traits like kindness that white readers would welcome.

Throughout the novel, Stowe emphasizes Tom's physical strength but also, paradoxically, his gentleness and passivity. This duality is present in Lathan's adaptation. Just like in the novel, while en route to Louisiana via steamboat, Tom meets Evangeline (Little Eva) St. Clare. While singing on the upper deck, Eva accidentally falls overboard. Tom jumps in the river to save her life. As a result of his bravery, and Eva's insistence, her father, Augustine St. Clare (Bruce Dern), buys Tom. The film reconsiders Stowe's rendering of the little girl as the picture of Christian perfection – a beacon of beauty and innocence in a culture of despair and oppression. On the screen, Eva's curls – which inspired the Shirley Temple films of the 1930s – are an underwhelming dirty blond colour, often hidden under bonnets. There are other important differences. Of the death scene in the novel – one of the best-known in nineteenth-century sentimental literature – Harvard University African American studies professor Robin Bernstein, the author of *Racial Innocence*, writes that it 'occasioned a blizzard of whiteness: everything in Eva's bedroom, from statuettes and pictures, to the bed and bedside table, to the girl's corpse itself, was draped in white; and throughout the room, white flowers drooped in baskets and vases.'[8] As she lies there dying, Eva gives all those assembled around her a lock of her beautiful golden hair, explaining that she wants to leave them with a part of herself. '[W]hen you look at it [the curl],' she says, 'think that I loved you and am gone to heaven, and that I want to see you all there.'[9]

In the film, Stowe's narrative is completely recast. Leading up to Eva's death, Tom appears in one scene with her that does mirror the original text: he carries her in his arms singing the song 'Ready for My Lord.' Audiences watch as Tom touches Eva's face, uttering, 'It's over now,' as if he were her parent. As St. Clare grants Eva's dying wish – to free Tom – he appears to be conceding Tom's role as her devoted father. The film version is all about Tom, not Eva.

Later, when we are introduced to Topsy in the film, it is through St. Clare, who presents the child to his cousin, Miss Ophelia, who is newly arrived on the plantation, to serve as her Mammy. At first, Ophelia, who detests slavery but is still deeply prejudiced against enslaved Black people, refuses the request. But St. Clare convinces her to help Topsy, whom he describes as being beaten every day of her life. Bernstein observes that 'the dehumanized pickaninny [is] contrasted with an angelic white child' to illustrate the 'irreconcilable differences between black and white youth.'[10]

The 1980s saw a string of films and television shows that revisited the image of archetypal white innocence. Films such as *Annie* (1982), the musical comedy based on the Broadway production of the same name, centred on a determined yet delightfully pleasant Annie. Despite being orphaned during the Great Depression and living in an orphanage in New York City, Annie is not characterized as depraved, debased, or degenerate. Her impoverished circumstances, in other words, do not constitute her identity.

One of the by-products of the 1980s drug war was the assumption that all Black working-class mothers were neglectful and derelict. Some of these women, often young single mothers living in poverty, relied on the state to support their children. '[N]ews stories began to cover the huge increase in the number of newborns testing positive for drugs,' observes Black feminist scholar Patricia Hill Collins. 'But coverage was far from sympathetic. Addicted pregnant women became demonized as "crack mothers" whose selfishness and criminality punished their children in the womb.'[11] By extension, Black children were often denied the right of childhood itself. As *Cities and Race: America's New Black Ghetto* author David Wilson opines, 'children and youth were acceptable casualties in this war on supposed laziness and bad morals. Innocent kids, caught up in the disciplining of parents for seemingly inexcusable deeds, could be thrust into material deprivation via the punishing of a parent's "lifestyle" and "chosen life course."'[12]

In the first beating scene of the new *Uncle Tom's Cabin* film, Legree tells Tom he is to become an overseer, and his first task is to flog one of the enslaved women named Lucy. Tom refuses, citing his Bible. 'Nobody can buy my soul,' he says. Legree slaps Tom and then instructs Quimbo and Sambo to break him so that he never forgets. In the second and final flogging, Legree blames Tom for Cassy and Emmeline's abscondment. As instructed, Quimbo and Sambo place Tom on a wooden cross, strapping both arms to the post, and whip him nearly to death. This crucifixion scene culminates with Christopher Shelby arriving at Legree's plantation, demanding to buy Tom and return him to his home in Kentucky. However, it is too late. Uncle Tom is near death. It is at this moment that he speaks of his love for Chloe. And before dying, his last words are, 'I'm free.'

While the film could have ended there, Lathan adds a final scene: Christopher Selby punches Legree, who collapses into a pool of muddy water. Then, instead of helping their master, Quimbo and Sambo abandon the sobbing Legree as Tom's dead body is removed from the plantation and sent back to Kentucky for the last time. Ultimately, the film ends with two white men fighting over a Black man who was no longer present to fight for himself.

In the final frame, the narrator says: 'Uncle Tom was right: only his body died at the hands of Simon Legree. Tom's spirit rose out of the pages of Harriet Beecher Stowe's novel to educate the conscience of a nation, and a war was fought. The black people were legally freed. Today, 120 years later, the battle for true freedom still continues.'

This voice-over aimed to tie the film to the novel, as if they could be easily connected. Stowe's *Uncle Tom's Cabin* tried to convince antebellum readers of the horrors of slavery and to see Tom as a sympathetic hero who died a martyr's – Christian – death. But Scherick/Lathan's *Uncle Tom's Cabin* presents a story about a very distant time in American history, one that would have seemed remote to 1980s audiences. For that reason, their revisionist screenplay recast issues of race and racism as features of African American life that were in the past. Although Lathan aimed for a high degree of fidelity to Stowe's original story, the film still fell into the trap of using tropes of Black passivity that had emerged, ironically, through later versions and distortions of this same story.

꙰

Even though this TV movie is scarcely remembered, unlike *Roots*, its existence attests to the way Stowe's *Uncle Tom's Cabin* has a way of constantly returning to the popular imagination. Just a few years later, in fact, the African American playwright Robert Alexander brought *I Ain't Yo' Uncle: The New Jack Revisionist Uncle Tom's Cabin* to the stage. The musical was performed from the point of view of the Black characters, and in the play's prologue, Topsy, Eliza, George, and Tom proposed to put Stowe on trial for 'creatin' stereotypes.' In 1995, the Hartford Stage Company revived Alexander's work with actress Michele Morgan as Topsy and Byron Utley as Uncle Tom. Tom was endowed with all the defiance, repartee, and determination missing in Stowe's Tom, but Topsy proved to be the most revised of all the characters.

'I'm Topsy Turvy, I'm wicked, I'm black,' Morgan chanted defiantly to a rap beat while two 'homeboy-hip-hop-style' dancers strutted behind her, wrote the *New York Times* theatre reviewer, Ben Brantley.[13] '*I Ain't Yo' Uncle* lets Topsy live on, unredeemed and unrepentant, and gives her a twin on the inner-city streets of today. In the play's stunning climax, as Brantley describes, 'Ms. Morgan returns in contemporary clothes, bristling with an incendiary contempt and hopelessness, to remind the audience that a society that can still produce a Topsy still has much to answer for.'[14] The play aimed to make a statement not about Black life centuries ago, but about the connections between slavery and contemporary social problems in America.

In describing Simon Legree's exit line ('I'm gonna join the LAPD … I hear they're looking for a few good men'), a critic with the *North American Review* noted that the play's incursions into the present were received with ambivalence. 'The reactions to current references accentuate the problems attending the running allusion to Stowe's novel: few people know it well and, relative to present issues, fewer still care much about it except as a museum piece.'[15] People know of Uncle Tom; the issue is how to decipher which Tom appears today.

At the play's end, Topsy walks through the audience, boom box blaring, spewing obscenities and getting in people's faces. She then challenges the audience directly: 'You won't sit next to me on the bus. I see you grab your purse. Who are you looking at? Do you want to leave?'[16] People reportedly did leave, though many audiences applauded the dramatic conceit.

I Ain't Yo' Uncle probably made some white audiences uncomfortable, but that was Alexander's point. The play held 'the institution of slavery and the descendants of slave owners accountable for today's racial dilemmas,' writes Patricia A. Turner. 'Audiences are asked to think of Topsy every time they see a sullen African American adolescent with a boom box.'[17] The question remains: how can performance move audiences from merely thinking about the likes of Topsy to doing something to eradicate the social conditions that continue to create such children?

❧

In 2011, the *New York Times* commemorated Stowe's two hundredth birthday with an op-ed piece. Written by David S. Reynolds, author of *Mightier Than the Sword: 'Uncle Tom's Cabin' and the Battle for America*, the essay offers a brief overview of Tom's evolution, from Stowe's original (a forty-something Black man who is muscular and dignified and dies because he refuses to betray his race) to the later caricature (a stooped, obedient old fool who frequents the stage in post-Reconstruction, pre–civil rights America) and his final incarnation (a physically and spiritually weakened figure whose name has become synonymous with racial betrayal).[18]

Reynolds recounted how Uncle Tom was derided by Black activists in the 1960s and 1970s, a time when mainstream civil rights leaders drew accusations of Uncle Tomism. But, as he wrote, it does not have to be this way. 'Uncle Tom should once again be a positive symbol for African American progress,' Reynolds wrote, arguing that non-violent civil rights protesters were wrongly derided as Uncle Toms because they ultimately 'proved most effective in promoting progress.' Passive resistance, he said, can be seen as an active and strong form of protest.

I disagree. The question is not whether passive non-violence is respectful or useful to advance Black social politics. Rather, the question is whether the Black community has been transformed by such acts of non-violence. As history has shown, the illusion of the civil rights era was that Black integration equalled Black progress. In some respects, it did. But in many other ways, it did not. Rosa Parks and Dr. Martin Luther King Jr., as well as others, might have believed that great change could result from non-violent moral protest. Great change did come by way of legislative change and the court-ordered end to segregation. But even as twenty-first-century America becomes ever more diverse – a place where non-white North Americans will make up the majority in just a few decades – the legacy of racial segregation and class discrimination persists.

As Georgetown University law professor Sheryll Cashin comments in *The Failures of Integration*, 'unless and until we complete the unfinished business of the civil rights movement, meaningfully integrating our public and private realms in a way that gives all Americans, especially those who have been most marginalized, real choices and opportunities, we will not solve the conundrum of race and class inequality in America.'[19]

Uncle Tom remains a highly symbolic figure who, in his various incarnations, has been used as a veil, hiding the reality of Black lives to appease whites about the myth of racial progress in America. Martin A. Berger, in his writing about civil rights photography, notes that 'with great consistency, white media outlets in the North published photographs throughout the 1960s that reduced the complex social dynamics of the civil rights movement to easily digested narratives, prominent among them white-on-Black violence.[20] While Berger is not suggesting that civil rights photographs were staged to meet the needs of whites, his argument is that the images helped to manage whites' anxieties about race as Blacks were perpetually depicted as 'victims' of white violence rather than aggressors pursuing the goal of Black social progress. Uncle Tom has performed a similarly misleading role in white America: he keeps Black men perpetually typecast as 'noble' victims rather than as celebrated, self-emancipating heroes.

21

ADVERTISING BLACK BUDDIES

When Bryant Gumbel was on NBC's *Today Show*, from 1982 to 1997, he was often called an Uncle Tom because of his Standard American English, khakis, and perma-smile. In fact, many believed that while Gumbel hosted the *Today Show*, he wore skin-lightening makeup to appeal to a 'whiter' audience.[1] Even in his private life, since leaving NBC, Gumbel has made public comments that reaffirm why some have also called him an 'Oreo' – Black on the outside, white on the inside.

In 2013, at the 9th Annual UNICEF Snowflake Ball, Barneys' then CEO, Mark Lee, accepted an award for work with the charitable organization. The event came in the wake of allegations by two African American customers of racial discrimination at Barneys. According to news reports, after Lee accepted his award, Gumbel, the night's emcee, said this: 'Like these shoes? I got them at Barneys – nice price, and I was only in the tank two hours.'[2] When the crowd laughed uneasily, he added, 'I ran it by Mark, it's okay, trust me.'

Such overt attempts not only to seek approval by white men in authority but also to abandon Black community members in cases of racial discrimination underscore why, for some critics, 'Uncle Tom' as a label remains a necessity for the policing of Black loyalty. It is a reliable trope called upon during moments when a Black individual is perceived by the Black community as maligning the race in order to win favour with whites and institutions.

The comedy *In Living Color* (1990–94), undoubtedly inspired by Gumbel, created characters known as 'the Brothers Brothers.' These two Toms (both were named Tom), were non-threatening African American comedians meant to evoke their namesakes, Thomas and Richard Smothers, a white folk-singing sibling comedy duo from the 1960s. The Brothers Brothers' music and humour were 'white bread' or Gumbel-like Oreo. They were racially Black, but their dress, speech, and sense of humour were white. While the parody was funny, especially to Black audiences, the representation was significant in the ways that it blurred racial lines. Was it a parody of the Smotherses or Gumbel? Further, sometimes it is difficult to reconcile the gap between offensive and funny. For instance, writing in the *New York Times* in 1989, the literary critic Henry Louis Gates Jr. said he enjoyed screening episodes of *Amos 'n' Andy* for Black friends who thought the series was both socially offensive and politically detrimental. After a few minutes, even the hardliners had difficulty restraining their laughter. 'It's still racist,' one of Gates's guests is said to have remarked, 'but it was funny.'[3]

Today, Black buddies are far less likely to make us laugh. Instead, they are meant to make us feel safe. They are useful only if they are clearly committed to the American way of life, which is to say consumer culture.[4] Marketers used Uncle Remus to sell white childhood innocence, Uncle Ben to sell rice, and Bill Cosby to sell pudding. But beginning in the 1990s, Michael Jordan became the first post-Cosby Black buddy, a star who was used to sell white America not just consumer products, but also a squeaky-clean image of Black masculinity.

※

Chicago Bulls superstar was the first African American celebrity in the post-Cosby era to become America's Black buddy. In 1990, Jordan helped transform Nike into a mega-brand. He not only starred in Nike's 'Air Jordan' ads, he also was on the cover of Wheaties cereal packages and appeared in spots for Coca-Cola, Gatorade, and McDonalds – always wearing a large smile. A clean-cut basketball player, Jordan was kid-friendly – a point reaffirmed in the live-action/animated film *Space Jam* (1996), where Jordan essentially plays himself, alongside Bugs Bunny.

Notably, he was not 'street' compared to other leading Black athletes of the decade. In 1997, for instance, star NBA guard Latrell Sprewell choked P. J. Carlesimo, his coach on the Golden State Warriors. Almost overnight, the then-three-time all-star became a symbol of what many saw as the worst of basketball.[5] Sprewell, as well as other Black basketball players such as the members of the University of Michigan's 1991 'Fab Five,' who were embroiled in a financial scandal, signalled a

Michael Jordan receiving the Presidential Medal of Freedom from President Barack Obama at the White House in Washington, D.C., November 23, 2016.

reworking of historical representations of Black masculinity. 'We were the bad guys,' recalled Jalen Rose, one of the Fab Five, in an interview with the *New York Daily News*. Some of that, he admitted, came from their style: trash-talking, baggy shorts, black socks, a lot of playground swagger.[6] This style was unapologetically Black, urban, and unpolished.

Most notably, cornrow-wearing basketball superstar Allen Iverson was an unapologetic anti-Tom. As Patricia Hill Collins observes, 'By retaining his cornrows and continuing to hang out with his friends from the 'hood, his run-ins with the law provided much bad press.' But, she adds, Iverson was a 'walking reminder that the day of *cultural* crossover, when black stars such as ... Michael Jordan sought and won white acceptance, were over. Iverson was leading a new generation of ballplayers, kids much less interested in acquiescing to white, main-stream taste.'[7] The 1990s hip-hop slogan 'keeping it real' reinforced not only the need to avoid the traps of 'selling out' but also the importance of staying true to one's cultural and community roots. Forgetting where you came from became another measure of Uncle Tomism.

Importantly, the choices that Black players made did not sit well with the custodians of the NBA's corporate image. In 2005, then-commissioner David Stern made the NBA the first major sports league to enforce a dress code. In the post-Jordan era, athletes were required to wear business casual attire to games and a sports coat with dress shoes on the bench. Many felt the move was an attempt to recreate Jordan. According to David J. Leonard, author of *After Artest: The NBA and the Assault on Blackness*, the debates that surrounded the dress code, which frequently evoked Jordan's name, positioned the former NBA player as representing a better moment for the league, and not simply because of his greatness, his turnaround jump shot, or his gravity-defying dunks. As Leonard writes, Jordan 'offered the public a more marketable and palatable inscription of blackness. In the white imagination he was not a thug, a criminal or someone to fear, but … a modern American image.'[8] However, Iverson and the new generation refused to forget or minimize where they came from or whom they associated with. Hence, Jordan remained *the* Black male athlete buddy through the early 1990s – until golfer Tiger Woods arrived to take over the mantle.

Woods's mixed-race background, and his rejection of a 'Black' identity, contributed greatly to his success as a marketable commodity. He earned a large salary but presented a deferential persona, a star who upheld white American values. He was also playing a sport that was not just majority white, but that had also maintained rigid racial lines. While public golf courses began to de-segregate in the 1970s, most private clubs were much slower to this shift. In fact, it was not until 1990 that the Augusta National Gulf Club (home to the Masters) admitted its first African American member – but only after it was forced to do so by the PGA.[9] Against this backdrop, Woods's non-threatening stance made him acceptable for inclusion in a sport that had always been a white man's domain. Since 1997, when Woods became the youngest player ever to win the Masters, he has remained the highest-paid golfer in the world. *Forbes* estimated that Woods earned $63.9 million in 2019. Since turning pro in 1996, in fact, Woods has made $1.5 billion, with less than 10 per cent of those earnings coming from competition prize money.[10]

Alongside his clean-cut image, Woods also refuses to identify as African American. In 1997, he infamously told Oprah Winfrey that he is 'Cablinasian,' a blend of white, Black, Indian, and Asian.[11] His Black identity, however, was imposed on him when Fuzzy Zoeller, a white American golfer, made a racially insensitive comment to Woods after he won the Masters. In keeping with tradition, Woods, as winner of the Masters, was entitled to choose the champions' dinner menu for the following year. 'You pat him on the back and say congratulations and enjoy it and tell him not to serve fried chicken next year,' Zoeller said of 'that little boy.' 'Got it? Or collard greens or whatever the hell they serve.'[12] Woods mostly brushed off the comments. As with Jordan, who never commented publicly on issues related to race and racism in the NBA, Woods remained race-neutral to white fans of the sport.

In 2009, allegations surfaced about an extramarital affair between Woods and New York nightclub manager Rachel Uchitel. At one point, a seemingly drunk Woods rammed his Escalade into a fire hydrant outside his Orlando home. Shortly thereafter, he checked himself into a sex-addiction clinic, and immediately lost lucrative endorsement deals with Accenture, AT&T, Gatorade, and General Motors. When he failed a sobriety test and was subsequently arrested in 2014, he insisted prescription medications to treat pain from back surgery caused his condition. Suddenly, Tiger Woods was no longer an Uncle Tom; the fallout from his seemingly reckless behaviour had mounted. Woods had now become the brute whose sexual appetite for white women conjured up the most destructive and punitive trope of Black masculinity.

In 2019, however, Woods won the Masters, his first PGA title since 2008. The victory partially restored his image, making him a 'comeback kid.' While the days of his squeaky-clean Black buddy image were long gone, Woods's story illustrates how Uncle Tom remains such a burden in the contemporary arena of Black masculinity and popular culture. The public offers no second chances once the veneer of non-threatening servility is stripped away. While the 'bad boy' or Black brute can become 'good' (e.g., Mike Tyson has restored his image from an abusive husband and ear-biter in the 1990s and 2000s to appearing on talk shows as a gentle giant, of sorts), Uncle Tom can never deviate from the stereotype. If he strays from the image of the deferential, loyal, and asexual Black male, he can never make a comeback. What's more, in our cultural construction, no one worries that Black buddies will steal the silverware, converse in Black English, or rape a white woman.[13] Because by committing any of these offences, those men who aspire to fill the role of the Uncle Tom-like Black buddy will see their careers end.

❧

In this century, Black male TV commercial spokesmen – such as Dennis Haysbert as 'the Allstate Guy,' Samuel L. Jackson for Capital One, Laurence Fishburne for Kia, and John Legend for Pampers – have perpetuated the legacy of 'kid-friendly' Black buddies who can be seen as trusted friends. On the surface, these actors are very different people. Yet in the context of these advertisements, they still serve the function of a Black buddy: all but one are depicted as not having families or any type of relationships, sexual or otherwise, that might distract them from their main purpose in life: loyalty to their jobs.

Their screen personas tell a very different story. Few will ever forget Laurence Fishburne as Morpheus in *The Matrix* trilogy – the intense character in a long black trench coat, black sunglasses, and unnerving stare. But these actors ultimately put their strength and virility in the service of social institutions such as the criminal justice system, or they assist white leading characters in their screen roles.[14]

In the case of Jackson, his appearance in Quentin Tarantino's *Django Unchained* (2012) drew comparisons to Stowe's Uncle Tom. In the film, he plays Stephen, the house servant of Calvin Candie, played by Leonardo DiCaprio. Jackson's character is not only loyal to Candie, he is also subservient. Describing Jackson's early scenes, critic Aisha Harris called it your 'run-of-the-mill Uncle Tom stereotype.' But as the film progresses, he seems to redeem himself because he 'uses that loyalty as a kind of personal power,' Harris continues. '[I]n creating Stephen, Tarantino seems to have given real thought to the complicated pain of the "peculiar institution."'[15] So while Black subservience and loyalty to whites has always meant Uncle Tomism, Jackson's portrayal in *Django*, an otherwise revisionist and factually inaccurate film, is somewhat accurate for revealing how Uncle Tom figures are strategic in their loyalty to white authority. As with sleeping car porters and enslaved people before them, they smiled at customers not because they were happy or sought to appease white desires for a contented racial world. Their demeanour indicated a desire to keep their jobs. These men had respect for themselves even though the outside (white) world did not view their position with respect.

In the realm of advertising, by contrast, the servile Uncle Tom is alive and well in the guise of the Black buddy pitchman, in large part because the products they promote do not benefit Black people. These advertising Black buddies are serving the interests of white-owned companies selling products that are predominantly purchased by whites. For example, a 2015 Consumer Federation of America report found that insurance premiums differ greatly by race. The CFA found that even safe drivers living in areas that are predominantly African American are charged significantly higher premiums for auto insurance. The CFA's analysis looked at quotes from the five largest insurers – Allstate being one of them – and found that premiums were on average 70 per cent higher for residents of mostly Black communities, versus mostly white ones.[16] Similarly, visible minorities are less likely to have access to credit than white Americans. In 2013, 20 percent of whites did not have access to a credit card, compared with 47 per cent of African Americans and 30 per cent of Hispanics.[17] Additionally, since women are more likely than men to buy diapers, Legend's appearance in a Pampers campaign conformed to feminine modes of behaviour;[18] Uncle Tom is most recognizable by 'feminine' attributes, such as kindness and deference.

In other words, the advertising Black buddy is an instance of a new form of racism, one in which Black pitchmen are offered as evidence of a colour-blindness that purports to characterize contemporary economic opportunity – a world in which meritocracy has eliminated racial discrimination. The subtext says something else entirely. While that Blackness must be visible in such corporate marketing messages, it also must be contained and stripped of any imagery that may threaten white people.[19]

22

UNCLE BEN AND AUNT JEMIMA 2.0

In March 2007, just a few weeks after Barack Obama, then an Illinois senator, announced his intention to seek the Democratic nomination for president, Mars Inc. launched a rebranding campaign to modernize the image of Uncle Ben, the advertising trademark for its Converted Rice brand. Mars gave Uncle Ben a new look as a business executive with a penchant for sharing what the *New York Times* reported as 'his "grains of wisdom" about rice and life.'[1] This *new* Ben, dressed in a blue suit with bow tie and cufflinks, looked far removed from the plantation. In one crucial respect, however, Uncle Ben's biography remained the same: he was still just Ben, a pitchman without a last name.

Ben's rebranding paralleled a slightly earlier move by the Quaker Oats Company. In 1989, in celebration of the one hundredth anniversary of the Aunt Jemima trademark, the company made extensive alterations to her face and body. Jemima's updated image did not include her familiar headband. Instead, she wore pearl earrings and a lace collar. Her hair was straightened, and she appeared visibly younger.[2] Aunt Jemima had always been a heavy-set, dark-skinned, bandana-wearing Black woman with a broad, toothy smile. But, according to a company spokesperson, the updated version was 'to make her look like a working mother, an image the company claimed was supported by test-marketing of the new logo among blacks and whites.'[3]

Then in 1994, Quaker Oats announced that soul singer Gladys Knight had agreed to represent Aunt Jemima products in a series of television advertisements. Immediately, the singer faced accusations that she was perpetuating a derogatory image of Black women. At the time, however, Knight made a distinction: 'I'm not Aunt Jemima. I'm only a spokesperson. What matters to me is what's inside the box.'[4] Symbolically, a real Black woman with her grandchildren was speaking for an imaginary Black woman. As M. M. Manring, author of *Slave in a Box: The Strange Career of Aunt Jemima*, observed, 'If Aunt Jemima is recognized as anything more today than Gladys Knight is, then it be must owed more to Aunt Jemima's past than to her present – no one is buying the product because it is somehow connected with modern black working grandmothers, or Gladys Knight could do the job without Aunt Jemima.'[5]

All Aunt Jemima products are still successful – even without their image – because of the nostalgic sentimentalism attached to the Black servant narrative. Aunt Jemima and Uncle Tom still haunt African Americans who have achieved celebrity; however, some folks did not see anything wrong with celebrities like Knight singing the praises of Aunt Jemima products. 'Aunt Jemima's critics insult the hardworking women after whom its famous icon was modeled,' wrote Robert J. Brown, in an article for *AdAge* in 1994, adding, 'I remember vividly the women in my community who put food on their tables by working long hours in other people's kitchens. My grandmother, who raised me, was one of them. I can still see her tying on an apron and wrapping her head with a scarf as she prepared to cook. She was strong and wise, a magnificent woman who commanded respect.'[6] That real Black women were being compared to a fictional Black woman spoke to the power of these images to blur the lines.

In an interview with the *New York Times*, Vincent Howell, president of the food division of the Masterfoods USA unit of Mars, said that because consumers described Uncle Ben as having 'a timeless element to him, we didn't want to significantly change him.'[7] 'What's powerful to me is to show an African American icon in a position of prominence and authority,' Howell said. Ben was still elderly, and his outfit maintained the same colour palette, but the marketers' decision to place him inside an executive office and add a wedding band, cufflinks, and a commanding posture meant that we are to read this *new* Ben not as a passive figure but as a 'man in charge.' 'As an African-American,' Howell remarked, 'he makes me feel so proud.'[8] At the time, market research showed that consumers felt a 'positive emotional connection' with both the name 'Uncle Ben' and the image, associating them with 'quality, family, timelessness, and warmth.'[9] 'Because consumers from all walks of life echoed many times through the years that Uncle Ben stood for values similar to their own,' he added, 'we decided to reinforce and build on that existing positive connection through the new campaign.'

Over the past fifty years, Uncle Ben, Aunt Jemima, and Rastus have all been redesigned. Now silent trademark characters, they no longer speak in advertisements and are reduced to headshots, staring mutely from packages.[10] The new millennium has seen the emergence of a new generation of highly successful Black entrepreneurs, moguls, and politicians, such as Oprah Winfrey, Barack Obama, and in advertising, celebrity pitchmen like Dennis Haysbert and Samuel L. Jackson. In various ways, they all signal that the traditional Black consumer trademarks not only needed to be redesigned; they also had to enter the middle-upper class and the boardrooms of America.

All this rebranding, however, has been met with mixed reviews. Luke Visconti, a partner at New Jersey media firm Diversity Inc., told the *Times* that Mars was glossing over years of baggage: 'This is an interesting idea, but for me it still has a very high cringe factor.'[11] Similarly, Marilyn Kern Foxworth, author of *Aunt Jemima, Uncle Ben and Rastus: Blacks in Advertising Yesterday, Today and Tomorrow*, applauded Mars for trying to update the trademark, but felt the decision to retain essential elements of the Uncle Ben portrait showed they were still trying to hold on to something that folks like her are trying so hard to shed. The ads are 'asking us to make the leap from Uncle Ben being someone who looks like a butler to overnight being a chairman of the board,' Kern Foxworth said.[12] 'It does not work for me.' 'Now that you are a big shot, Uncle Ben, you're going to need your own private chef,' quipped Stephen Colbert, then host of Comedy Central's *The Colbert Report*. 'I recommend the Cream of Wheat guy.'[13]

Others were even harsher in their critiques. Carmen Van Kerckhove, co-founder of the firm New Demographic, wrote on her blog, racialicious.com: 'This rebranding campaign is really the epitome of putting lipstick on a pig. Uncle Ben is still grinning and wearing a bow tie. There's nothing Chairman of the Board-esque about that image. Uncle Ben still has no last name. When's the last time you heard a powerful man referred to by his first name? No matter what fantasies you weave about him being the Chairman of the Board, his very name still comes from the culture of slavery.'[14]

Despite these criticisms, the 'new' Ben remained perched atop all Converted Rice products as of early 2020. Ben's Original, without the image, appears in 2021. The irony of this new Ben is that nothing about the Uncle Tom trope is original. Even if his image is removed, Ben – a name now synonymous with service – is still a Tom.

In the digital age, Mars directly tracked consumer interest in the first Uncle Ben rebranding. The interest was undeniable: traffic to the Uncle Ben website soared during the summer of 2007. Unique visits ballooned from 191,000 in the third quarter of 2006 to 3.6 million in the same period of 2007, according to comScore.[15] The image of a servile Black man continued to resonate on a global scale, especially in Britain, where, in 2016, the Uncle Ben's brand claimed a 40 per cent share of the rice market, with sales of £89 million.[16] The tracking results from the 2021 rebranding will be very telling about whether consumer appetites for centuries-long Black stereotypes have changed.

＊

What matters is that other brands took note. The Uncle Ben campaign was followed by another consumer brand modernization: 'Annie,' the spokesperson for Popeyes Louisiana Kitchen, played by the critically acclaimed theatre actor Deidre Henry. A modern iteration of Aunt Jemima and, by extension, the Southern Mammy, Annie first appeared around the same time Ben moved into the C-suite.

Timing is everything. In 2008, the U.S. economy faced the worst financial crisis since the Great Depression. Popeyes Louisiana Kitchen had been founded in 1972 by Al Copeland, who opened his first fried-chicken joint, Chicken on the Run, in a New Orleans suburb. Like Aunt Jemima in the early twentieth century, Popeyes was a brand without an identity. While the chain had over a thousand locations in the U.S. and franchises around the world, including Canada, it enjoyed little brand recognition. By 2008, in fact, the company was struggling to keep afloat. The company hired Cheryl Bachelder, a fast-food-chain veteran, to step in as CEO. Her first move was to change the company's name from Popeyes Chicken & Biscuits to Popeyes Louisiana Kitchen. The change linked the brand to a place that enjoys long-standing significance as the site of authentic Southern cuisine.

Louisiana evokes many other associations besides Southern cooking. New Orleans was formed through a mixture of African, Acadian French (Cajun), Continental French, Spanish, and Native American communities. While each retained its unique culture, language, and style of dress, elements of these groups also combined to form a distinctly New Orleans milieu evident in architecture, culture, and cuisine. Yet in Stowe's novel, Uncle Tom exists at a distance from the social realities of Louisiana. 'The climate … is compared to that of Africa, and the voice of the omniscient narrator reflects on Tom's ancestors,' not on his new locale, observed race historian Thomas F. Gossett.[17]

The image of historical Louisiana is one of sprawling plantations and enslaved African Americans. Contemporary consumer culture has tried to partially distance itself from that past while retaining some of the more palatable elements, especially food. For many years, Popeyes restaurants contained in-store advertisements describing 'The 7 Nations of Louisiana.' The caption read: 'Louisiana was settled by people from seven different nations. Each culture brought products and cooking methods unique to its area. They were then meshed with products of other cultures to give us what is currently known as Louisiana Cajun Cooking.' This narrative helped to rebrand the cuisine as 'authentically' Cajun.

But its new spokesperson, Annie, ensured the growth of Popeyes' presence in the crowded fast-food sector. In each ad, Annie presents herself as not only a cook, but also the inventor of new products, as well as a key figure in Popeyes' strategic plays. She is also there to soothe, help, and care for the chicken-eating public. In one representative ad from 2019, Annie is seated in a white male therapist's office in New Orleans, confiding in him that she's finally created the perfect chicken sandwich. As he bites into the bun, she explains, 'I've been trying to make the perfect chicken sandwich forever.' After he inquires how that makes her feel, she explains her perfectionism in cooking. 'I think we've made a lot of progress here, I feel great,' the therapist says as he continues to devour the sandwich. 'Good talk ... I'm proud of you.' In the voice-over, Annie continues: 'My new chicken sandwich is buttermilk battered and served on toasted brioche – spicy or classic.'[18] The dynamic here is simple. While Black women are there to serve whites, whites are, in return, only required to eat the food, not listen to their problems.

Between 2009 and 2016, the period following Annie's launch, the publicly traded company doubled its earnings per share. The stock price soared, from $4.89 in January 2009 to $59.17 in January 2016. Importantly, this was a strong period of rebound for the U.S. economy, which grew an average of 2.3 per cent per year from 2009 to 2019.[19] While Annie is not the only reason Popeyes had so much success during this period, what can be said is that the chain's brand recognition grew substantially with Annie at the helm.

In 2017, Restaurant Brands International, which at the time owned Burger King and Tim Hortons, the Canadian coffee chain, made an offer to buy Popeyes Louisiana Kitchen. The $1.8 billion deal gave Popeyes shareholders $79 for each share. After the transaction closed, RBI took the company private, meaning Popeyes stock no longer traded. This buyout was more proof that the company's success in the preceding decade had made it attractive to larger players in the sector. Annie had helped Popeyes establish itself as a brand with an identity.

Popeyes' rebranding personified the advertising narrative of 'Southern hospitality' in the image of a Mammy figure updated for the twenty-first century. The company edited out the plantation, the red-checked bandana, and Aunt Jemima's rotund body, and replaced all that with Annie's contemporary homespun wisdom, delivered in a soothingly sonorous voice. Popeyes' recent success, in fact, can be attributed in large part to Annie's appeal as a modern Mammy – dutiful yet always upbeat; in charge, yet only in benefit of others.

Annie's brand positioning parallels the transformation of Uncle Ben in other ways. Like Ben, she has no last name – no lineage, no family, no connection to anyone but the trademark for which she speaks. The 'feisty spokesperson to tell it like it is,' as described by Popeyes' website, is a modernized depiction of Mammy because while she is aggressive in her homespun wisdom, she acknowledges her subordination often through the absurdity of where she appears, as evidenced by one ad, in which she claims to be a professor at Spice University! In another ad, she laments, 'You know what some places' idea is of seafood, don't you? A squished-together fish patty in a bun. Uh-um, not in my kitchen!' After explaining the chain's latest seafood offering, Annie reminds us, 'Now we're talking seafood.'[20] Annie takes ownership over the food to convince viewers that she really is the cook, just as Ben is believed to be the butler.

'When Annie is talking,' Popeyes' chief marketing officer Dick Lynch said in a 2014 interview with *Advertising Age*, 'she is characterizing [Popeyes] as being from Louisiana, so we don't have to spend time convincing people we're different, because Louisiana is differentiation enough.'[21]

What makes Popeyes' invocation of Louisiana both a return and a reimagining is that it is the South without slavery. Annie, we are told, embodies the new South, a region that is quaint and prosperous, apparently unscathed by the 2008 financial crisis. Here, plantations are not sites of enslavement and suffering, but rather form a part of the state's cultural heritage. In her writings about the South's new plantation economy and processes of remembering through forgetting, University of California lecturer Jessica Adams argues that it 'is not only a product of dominant culture's ability to hide things in plain sight … [but also reflects] … denial and disinterest.'[22] Annie represents the ethos of a place where plantations are now promoted in tourism as neutral sites of returning. She may be a frank and outspoken Black woman seemingly in command of the company's strategic decisions, but Annie is still very much a descendant of Aunt Jemima – a figure conjured up by marketers exploiting nostalgia for the South for commercial gain.

At one point in 2014, news spread on social media that Annie had died. In reality, she had been the victim of an Internet hoax. Annie was not dead, nor was Henry, who played her in Popeyes ads.[23] Mainstream media and Popeyes did not comment on Annie's supposed death. The corporate silence recalled the actual death of Nancy Green, the first Black woman to play Aunt Jemima, ninety-one years earlier. In 1923, the Chicago-based *Associated Negro Press* reported that Green had been killed while standing on the sidewalk under an overpass on East 46th Street in Chicago.[24] Quaker Oats remained silent and quietly replaced Green with another Black woman a few years later.

The return of Uncle Ben and Aunt Jemima in the twenty-first century is significant. It not only parallels early-twentieth-century sojourns back into the nineteenth century via cultural products like *Uncle Tom's Cabin*, but it speaks to how constant these Black trademarks are in Western culture. Why are we still clinging to Uncles and Aunties?

꒰꒱

In 2016, I noticed a series of advertisements from the Louisiana Office of Tourism popping up around Toronto. In July of that year, the LOT announced it would launch a multimedia marketing campaign in Canada, as well as Australia, Brazil, China, France, Germany, Japan, Mexico, and the United Kingdom. LOT's top attractions and destinations were plantation homes. In one advertisement, the state's seafood appears in the forefront, and in the background sits Oak Alley plantation, located on the west bank of the Mississippi River, in the community of Vacherie, St. James Parish. 'Come enjoy Louisiana Seafood Gumbo paired with Architecture Aged to Perfection,' the ad read.

Today, plantations are not only tourist destinations for white tourists and wedding parties. They are also sites of return for Black entertainers such as Beyoncé, who, in the 2006 video for 'Déjà Vu,' dances in front of the Oak Alley plantation. In the 2016 video of 'Formation,' she is depicted once more in nine locations across Louisiana, including two plantations (Madewood Plantation House in Napoleonville and the Destrehan Plantation).[25]

Why, in the early decades of the twenty-first century, are we continually returning to sites of slavery through media culture? These representations glorify the architectural lustre of the plantation because they erase the trauma, torture, and brutality of Black enslavement – in 'Formation' we see the hallways and interiors of the plantation, for instance, but we are not shown the slave quarters or the cotton fields. We can also ask how consumer culture's nostalgia for Uncles and Aunts perpetuates past images of indentured Black bodies? If Louisiana, the fictional site of Simon Legree's plantation, where Uncle Tom is eventually beaten to death, is being promoted as a tourist destination and film set, which histories are being erased?

White and Black consumers alike have been drawn to the modern-ization of Uncle Ben and the introduction of Annie. 'Focus groups, one-to-one meetings and other qualitative research uncovered that consumers had a tremendous amount of respect for the Uncle Ben icon and that he represented quality, trust and family,' Bryan Crowley, vice president of marketing and sales for Mars Food U.S., said in 2007 about the Uncle Ben rebranding. The firm's market research identified one particularly enthusiastic target audience: thirty-five- to fifty-four-year-old mothers who were devoted to their home environment, had attended college, and were avid readers interested in health. About 80 per cent were white and most of the remaining 20 per cent were African American, plus a small percentage of Hispanics and Asians.[26]

In 2019, the *New York Times* reported that the return of Popeyes' chicken sandwich struck a chord for many African Americans, especially those who grew up eating soul food. 'Its celebrated sand-wich tastes like something that could have come from a black home kitchen,' observed writer John Eligon.[27] When Annie was first intro-duced as the 'Chicken Queen,' many African Americans found that she evoked Aunt Jemima, Uncle Ben, and the racist trope of the Black servant/cook. However, nearly a decade later, many African

Americans embrace her. 'The location of many Popeyes restaurants in black communities have given many African-Americans a sense of connection with the menu,' says Psyche Williams-Forson, the chairwoman of American studies at the University of Maryland-College Park and the author of *Building Houses Out of Chicken Legs: Black Women, Food and Power*. 'Black communities can say, "This is our own and it tastes like our own,"' she added. 'You've got location. You've got taste. You've got texture. And you've got a food that people enjoy. You have a perfect storm there.'[28] In other words, if Black people do not have a problem with the trademark, are the criticisms much ado about nothing?

⚜

Some marketing experts once believed that, regardless of the criticism, Uncle Ben's image – as an old and servile Black man – was just too valuable to remove. In 2008, for instance, Larry Vincent, group director of strategy for Siegel+Gale, argued that changing the backstory of Uncle Ben would be 'a risky branding move even without the race issue.' He continued: 'It is difficult to reinvent history in a way that is different than what consumers perceive. When a brand pulls an about-face, people subconsciously get the feeling [that] it is trying to pull the wool over their eyes.'[29] But in an article in *AdWeek*, Barbara Lippert disagreed: 'There's a tone problem with the print ... that doesn't seem to match Ben's new executive role. It comes across as less CEO-ey and more throw-back folksy.' While Lippert liked the virtual campaign –online visitors could go through the double mahogany doors for a 'tour' of Ben's office, which included a kitchen-timer graphic (the kind used for rice) so they could take a 360-degree look at this executive inner sanctum – she recognized that Ben, who remained essentially unchanged from previous incarnations, still harkened back to a different time.[30]

This inability, by consumer products giants, marketers, and consumers, to let go of figures like Uncle Ben and Aunt Jemima, and their branded descendants, has real-life implications. These trademarks have become templates for modes of behaviour psychologists now call 'Uncle Tom Syndrome,' as well as 'Mammy-ism,' which refers to the way some Black women feel the need to accommodate white people (women especially) by acquiescing to their demands and assuming an inferior position in the workplace, at school, and in institutional settings.

According to *The Encyclopedia of Multicultural Psychology*, Uncle Tom Syndrome describes 'a ritualized, accommodating, sycophantic style of behavior in African Americans towards [whites]. The African American acts in a docile, non-assertive manner to appear non-threatening to European Americans.'[31] Although derived from *Uncle Tom's Cabin*, the term, as we have seen, has taken on specific cultural meanings beyond the original text. This condition speaks to an internalized belief in sufferers, who are Black, that being eager to please will make them less threatening to white authority. As Uncle Tom's branded successor, the new Ben may appear to be in charge and autonomous, but the reality is that he is nothing more than a modernized Tom.

23

O.J. SIMPSON, A PASSING UNCLE

On June 17, 1994, Orenthal James (O.J.) Simpson, the celebrity football star turned corporate pitchman, hopped into a white Ford Bronco and drove down a Los Angeles interstate, threatening to kill himself. I had just settled in to watch the FIFA World Cup, which was being held in the U.S. for the first time. Simpson, a.k.a. 'the Juice,' was to have turned himself in to LAPD that morning on two counts of murder in the deaths of his ex-wife, Nicole Brown Simpson, and Ron Goldman. Instead, he was in an SUV driven by long-time friend Al Cowlings, speeding down the interstate as Cowlings was on the phone, talking to police. Hundreds of fans cheered the car on from overpasses until it arrived safely at Simpson's Southern California home. That car chase took over network and cable news. Even the World Cup and the NBA finals, between the Houston Rockets and New York Knicks, were interrupted to broadcast the moment. Over 95 million people tuned in to watch as Simpson evaded police.[1]

During the so-called 'trial of the century' that followed – which ran from January 24 to October 3, 1995, and culminated in Simpson's acquittal on both counts – race relations in America was also put on on the stand. Simpson became a surrogate for African American men who had been unjustly accused of crimes they did not commit. Even before the sensational court proceedings, Black America had decided that Simpson was sufficiently African American to merit support, even though he had spent decades steeped in white culture, through his relationships and friendships, endorsement and promotional deals, and his squeaky-clean image. Because he was famous and powerful, his careerism was largely forgiven, as many African Americans who tuned in to the trial believed he could use his celebrity to win some measure of justice for the Black community. What ended up happening, however, is that the trial turned into a symbolic clash between a 'real' Black man on trial for his life and an 'Uncle Tom' Black man representing the state and, by implication, the LAPD.

Simpson's legal team was led by the charismatic defence lawyer Johnnie Cochran, then a high-profile litigator known for defending other African American celebrities, such as Michael Jackson, Tupac Shakur, and Sean Combs, during the latter's trial on gun and bribery charges. Cochran was pitted against L.A. County district attorney Christopher Darden, who would be cast in this legal drama as a servile Uncle Tom, doing the work of the state to destroy the reputation of an apparently wrongfully convicted Black hero. During the drama of the televised trial, Darden emerged as the victimizer, acquiescing to white authority. Meanwhile, Cochran did his best to show that he was not just defending Simpson; he was representing the Black community.

The trial of the century fundamentally changed television culture. As distinguished media and cultural studies professor Douglass Kellner observes, '[T]he year of the Simpson spectacle ... [made] clear that the priorities of corporate journalism [were] infotainment and profits, merging news into entertainment and journalism into business.'[2] TV news also exploited the violent aspects of the case, with re-enactments of the murders featuring actors playing the victims and Simpson. Another television special recreated the murders using a computer-animated figure, depicted as an African American, slashing the throat of another computer-animated figure, white and blond.[3] Simpson was not just a former sports hero who had fallen from grace. His lawyers wanted to show that he represented the fight against anti-Black racism.

Indeed, when his mug shot appeared on the cover of *Time* and *Newsweek*, it affirmed that stereotypes of Black criminality not only lingered in American society, but had the power to shape public opinion about the trial. Where *Newsweek* used the mug shot as provided, *Time* heightened the contrast, thus darkening Simpson's skin tone. The sight of the two magazines sitting side by side on news-stands inflamed public opinion, with *Time*'s decision to doctor the image suggesting the predominantly white magazine had already decided Simpson was guilty. *Time*'s editor claimed that prejudging Simpson was not the intention. 'The photo had been given to an artist who was asked to interpret it,' he told the *New York Times*.[4] However, this decision added racial tension to an already racially charged case.

Race relations in America in the early 1990s had been on fragile ground, especially in L.A. Simpson's trial came just four years after a racially motivated police attack on a Black man that eventually led to widespread rioting in L.A. and other cities. On March 3, 1991, Rodney King was violently beaten by LAPD officers during an arrest. The brutal attack, caught on videotape and subsequently broadcast worldwide, sparked widespread outrage.

The incident brought the decades-long practice of systematic police brutality in L.A. into public view. In the 2017 documentary *Burn Mother-fucker, Burn!*, archival footage from the 1940s and 1950s showed the lives of large groups of African Americans who had moved to California from the Southern states (and elsewhere), in search of better oppor-tunities, more freedom, and less oppression. But as filmmaker Sacha Jenkins showed, the city's fast-growing freeway system and ineffective public transit contributed to the isolation of Black neighbourhoods.[5] The 1965 Watts riots, in turn, were the result of years of intensive police surveillance of these largely segregated Black communities.

Those tensions never disappeared. Almost three decades later, the trial of the four police officers charged in King's assault ended in acquittals on charges of excessive use of force. Within hours of the jury's verdict, the city once again erupted in riots that lasted for almost a week, from April 29 to May 4, 1992. Many wondered when Black people in L.A. would see justice.

Simpson lived in a very different America than Rodney King, at least in part because of the way he presented himself racially. At the

University of Southern California, when the Watts riots were taking place, Simpson made the conscious decision to ignore civil rights politics. Even though he had grown up in San Francisco and lived with his family in the housing projects of the Potrero Hill neighbourhood, he downplayed his racial identity while at USC – a choice that cast him even then as a sellout Uncle Tom. In the 1970s, as he rose to fame playing football with the Buffalo Bills, he surrounded himself with everything white culture had to offer. He left his African American wife Marguerite and began dating white women exclusively, ultimately marrying Nicole Brown. He also became a spokesperson for Hertz, and later, in the 1980s, a sports broadcaster. Like Bill Cosby, he presented himself as America's advertising Black buddy – safe, loyal, non-threatening.[6]

The trial of the century remapped Simpson's story. Revisiting his narrative asks us to consider how it was that a Black man went from being a sellout to a hero. His transformation speaks not only to the legacy of Uncle Tom but also the trope's mutability.

❧

Simpson was one of the most prolific running backs in the history of the National Football League. In 1973, he was named the league's MVP. That year, he surpassed Cleveland Browns running back (and outspoken 1960s civil rights activist) Jim Brown for single-season rushing (1,863 yards), becoming the first running back to top 2,000 yards in a season. Since Simpson's record-breaking career, only six other running backs have joined him in the 2,000-yard club.[7]

On the field in the 1960s and 1970s, first as a star college player and then in the NFL, 'Simpson gracefully juked, dodged, and eluded linebackers as instinctively as he evaded his social responsibility to the civil rights movement,' observed sports commentator Dominique Foxworth.[8] While Brown joined a group of top African American athletes, including NBA stars Bill Russell and Kareem Abdul-Jabbar, to support Muhammad Ali's contentious 1971 decision to reject the draft during the Vietnam War, Simpson remained quiet. Indeed, as far back as 1967, during a meeting of the Negro Industrial and Economic Union in Cleveland, he declared that he would not involve himself in the political and social issues of the time. He was not a Black activist. He was O.J.

After his illustrious football career ended, Simpson became an advertising spokesperson, broadcaster, and actor. His stint as the Hertz Rent-A-Car spokesperson began in 1975, while he was still an all-star running back for the Buffalo Bills. The company was searching for a new way to attract customers. At the time, Hertz's advertising stressed differences between its service and those of its competitors. After polling its best customers, who were overwhelmingly white male businessmen, Hertz found that speed of service was their key concern. Hertz officials decided to develop an ad campaign showing how Hertz could get its customers to the plane or out of the airport quickly. Enter Simpson. Ad agency art director Nick Pappas created a series of storyboards showing an ordinary businessman, dubbed 'Mr. Joe Average,' turning into superstar and 'juking' through an airport – jumping over obstacles and getting out first. His slogan was 'The superstar in rent-a-car.'[9]

At that time, Pappas recalled seeing Simpson on the ABC show *Superstars*, in which well-known athletes competed in various events. After watching outtakes of Simpson, Pappas and his team realized they had found what they were looking for. Not only was Simpson the embodiment of speed; focus-group participants saw him as racially neutral. It was a big deal at the time to turn a Black man into the corporate symbol for what was essentially a white company. But, according to a 1994 interview with the *Washington Post*, one official with the ad agency that created the campaign said Simpson's race was not an issue. 'People thought of O.J. Simpson as O.J. Simpson, not O.J. Simpson, the black athlete.'[10] He was the opposite of the Black men on TV during the decade – George Jefferson, J.J., and Fred Sanford, all of whom spoke critically of white America.

In television and print ads, Simpson was seen rushing through an airport terminal sporting a three-piece business suit and carrying a briefcase instead of a football. By 1977, he was named *Advertising Age*

Star Presenter of the Year. In 1984, he was pegged as the most popular athlete spokesperson by the consumer research firm Video Storyboard Tests.[11] 'People identify with me and I don't think I'm that offensive to anyone,' Simpson told the New York Times.[12] 'People have told me I'm colorless. Everyone likes me. I stay out of politics, I don't try to save people for the Lord and, besides, I don't look that out of character in a suit.'

In other words, Simpson was willing to do whatever his white management asked of him, and he also relished the idea of not being seen as Black. The dream of removing oneself from one's race is another example of how Stowe's Uncle Tom mutated over time, and in this case dates to the Jim Crow era when the practice was called 'racial passing.'

In A Chosen Exile, historian Allyson Hobbs posits that white skin functioned as a cloak in antebellum America: when linked to the appropriate dress, cadences of speech, and proper comportment, she argues, racial ambiguity could mask one's slave status and provide an effective strategy for escape. African Americans who learned to mimic white behaviours and whose skin was light enough to appear white could literally pass into the dominant race.[13]

For African Americans, racial passing was also imbued with socio-political intent. In both the antebellum era and the reconstruction period, some African Americans practised tactical or strategic passing – i.e., passing temporarily with a particular purpose in mind – out of a desire for freedom. In the twentieth century, however, passing allowed racially ambiguous men and women to get jobs ('nine-to-five passing'), to travel without encumbrance, and to attend elite colleges.[14] This form of passing reflected a desire for social mobility.

In 'I'm Through with Passing,' a first-person testimonial that appeared without a byline in the March 1951 issue of Ebony, the editors included a long and descriptive subtitle: 'Negro girl tells of her 12 years of bitterness and frustration while posing as white to get decent job, finally decides to drop mask and return to her people.'[15] The memoir offers a glimpse of how class and racial fluidity worked, or did not, in the era of racial segregation.

Simpson never attempted to pass by altering his physical body, i.e., lightening his skin, straightening his hair, or dressing 'white.' Nevertheless, unlike the Uncle Tomism of Bill Cosby or Clarence Thomas, Simpson created for himself an image of someone who had passed into whiteness, culturally, politically, and socially. He became a passing Uncle Tom.

Historically, racial passing has demarcated both the boundary of freedom (i.e., an enslaved person 'passing as free') and the parameters of social mobility (i.e., a Black person 'passing as white' to gain better employment). But as a passing Uncle Tom, Simpson shifted the metaphoric and literal locus of his identity away from Black community. Though he was born and raised in the projects, he became an emblem of corporate America and the white-owned companies that made him into a household name. He did not present himself as Stowe's pious Uncle Tom, the duplicitous Uncle Toms created during Reconstruction, or the Floyd Patterson Uncle Tom who loved segregation. What's more, Simpson was not just a capitalist Uncle Tom who worshipped corporate America above anything else. Because he wanted to blend in and mingle with wealthy whites, his ability to pass meant that his Blackness never seemed to get in the way of his career.

With his Hertz visibility, Simpson garnered other endorsements for orange juice, Dingo boots, athletic shoes, Foster Grant sunglasses, Schick razors, and Royal Crown cola, among others. He also became a national spokesman for General Motor's Chevrolet division and Wilson Sporting Goods. In addition to all his endorsement deals, Simpson served on corporate boards, including Infinity Broadcasting Corp. And by virtue of his 'affable and well-known image,' NBC hired him as a sportscaster.[16]

By the late 1980s, in fact, Simpson, as president and chief executive of O.J. Simpson Enterprises, owned hotels, restaurants, and real estate. And at the time of his divorce from Nicole Brown in 1992, his assets were estimated to be worth $10 million, while his annual income hovered above $1 million.[17]

❧

If Simpson had unequivocally played the role of an Uncle Tom throughout his career, the tables turned during his trial with the prospect of life imprisonment looming.

During the trial, Marcia Clark, a white woman, served as lead prosecutor, but Christopher Darden served as co-prosecutor, with equal authority in trying the case. Soon after the trial began, some African Americans began to accuse Darden of being an agent of the state, going above and beyond his job as prosecutor to personally trample a Black man's rights. 'He became, and this is an exaggeration, but only a slight exaggeration, a pariah in the black community,' said Reginald Holmes, a former head of the Los Angeles Black bar association in an interview with the *Washington Post* in 1995. Many African Americans, Holmes continued, believed that Darden was letting himself be used by white prosecutors, a belief that was widely held, even among some attorneys.[18]

Critics felt that Darden, who had joined the prosecution late, had been added by the district attorney's office as a racial counterbalance to Cochran and Simpson. As a result, many distrusted his motives. Todd Boyd, professor of critical studies at the University of Southern California School of Cinema-Television, recalled that he felt both Clark and Darden had been 'very arrogant and very condescending [in] the way that they approached the jury.' The jury was not composed of upper-middle-class, well-educated, white people, but rather several Black women who, Boyd argued, were 'probably … not attuned to the same theories of feminism that Marcia Clark was using to make [… her] argument.'[19] The composition of the jury was just as much a part of the trial's racial undercurrent as Simpson, Cochran, and Darden.

In his article about racial stereotypes and Black jurors, legal scholar Richard Boswell writes that 'the perception that a jury including African Americans would be unable to find a Black defendant guilty (should the evidence be sufficient) is particularly telling' in that it demonstrated how stereotypes of race that impact decision-making are 'applied only to African Americans and not to whites serving on juries or appearing as witnesses.'[20] Implicit bias in the legal system often presumes that white juries are 'impartial' while African American juries are not. At the same time, many whites have perceived that race relations in America are not all that bad, while African Americans feel very differently. As journalist Ta-Nehisi Coates wrote in the *Atlantic*, 'the Simpson story turned out to be intimately enmeshed with the story of black Los Angeles and its relationship with the police. This was the community the Simpson jury was drawn from, and ultimately the one that held his life in the balance.'[21] According to one of the jurors, Carrie Bess, 'the beating of Reginald Denny [a white construction worker attacked by a group of Black men during the 1991 riots in L.A.] was vengeance for the beating of Rodney King. And vengeance for King played a role in Simpson's acquittal.'[22]

❧

The image of a Black lawyer prosecuting a Black sports hero followed Darden around for years, although some of his critics said he had been defending the racism of the LAPD long before Simpson appeared in court. In 1997, he appeared on *The Oprah Winfrey Show*. During the interview, Winfrey read from a letter, dated October 4, 1995, penned by one of Darden's many Black detractors: 'You have been a disgrace to the black community … How could you be such an Uncle Tom? You sold out your black people for publicity and kissed the white man's a– … You are not wanted as a black person, Uncle Tom. Good riddance.' 'I thought … I was performing an important service for my community,' he replied. 'I thought I was doing the right thing.'[23]

His detractors did not see it that way. In one pretrial hearing, Simpson's defence attorneys had sought to include evidence demonstrating that LAPD investigator Mark Furhman was a racist. Testifying during the preliminary hearing, the defence drew on files from a 1981 disability compensation lawsuit in which Fuhrman was quoted as using racial slurs.[24] The implication was that the racist detective had planted the infamous black glove at the crime scene to implicate Simpson. On the tape, Fuhrman bragged about, among other things, beating Black suspects, whom he identified as 'niggers.' He explained how he ignored their constitutional rights. 'You don't need probable cause,' Fuhrman said. 'You're God.'[25]

'If you allow Mr. [Johnnie] Cochran to use the race card,' Darden argued to Judge Lance Ito, 'the entire complexion of this case changes. It is not an issue of guilt or innocence; it's an issue of color. Who's the blackest man up here? The jury will forget about the evidence. All they'll think of is "frame-up."'[26]

Visibly angered, Cochran dismissed Darden's remarks as 'demeaning to Afro-Americans,' who, he added, live daily with offensive words, looks, and actions by whites.[27] Cochran went on to imply that while Darden was 'Black,' he was not 'O.J. Black.' What's more, Cochran described Darden as someone less loyal to African Americans than to the institutions that have historically disenfranchised Black people.

At the same time, according to Ezra Edelman's award-winning documentary, *O.J.: Made in America*, Simpson's defence team worked hard to make him more Black, for example redecorating his house with the works of Black artists and pictures of Black friends and family. Cochran hoodwinked both the jury and the viewing public into seeing Simpson as a Black man framed by a racist police force and justice system, when the reality was that O.J. had literally and figuratively spent his career running away from any sense of duty to give back to the African American community.

Reflecting on Darden's role in the Simpson trial, Brando Simeo Starkey, author of *In Defense of Uncle Tom*, argues that he became a lightning rod from the moment he was named to the prosecution team. 'The state wanted his black skin, so goes the theory, to send a message to black jurors: Darden, a black watchdog, ensures nothing nefarious transpires behind the curtains. A popular opinion held that Darden, therefore, should have declined the opportunity that his white bosses never would have extended but for him being black.' Darden's Uncle Tomism was attributed to the fact that as a Black man, he had allowed whites to use him. He should have declined the job, Starkey wrote, 'not because *he* didn't want it, but because *whites* wanted him to have it.'[28] His extreme loyalty and devotional service to the criminal justice system responsible for decades of brutality, including the assault on Rodney King just a few years earlier, is what transformed Darden into an Uncle Tom 'just doing his job' to thwart L.A.'s Black community.

Simpson, in turn, had long ignored that same community until, as an accused person in the context of a racially charged trial, he became an unlikely surrogate for social justice.

After the verdict in 1995, Darden left the district attorney's office, becoming a defence lawyer. He worked as a legal commentator on television and, in 1996, published a book, *In Contempt*. Darden 'suffered personal consequences from Mr. Cochran's manipulation of the race issue,' wrote *New York Times* reviewer Michiko Kakutani. 'The defense lawyer's suggestion that Mr. Darden was a token black recruited by the prosecution team for the color of his skin led to accusations, on the street, that he was "an Uncle Tom, a sellout, a house Negro," Mr. Darden says. He writes that he received death threats and was spat upon, and that his family, too, was harassed.'[29]

Since the trial, many observers have expressed sympathy for the way Darden was characterized. 'It is unfortunate and regrettable that so many African Americans hated him for doing his job,' commented African American Harvard Law professor Charles J. Ogletree Jr. 'That's just wrong. Just as Johnnie Cochran had an obligation to defend O.J. Simpson with every legal means available to him, Chris Darden had an obligation with every legal means available to him to convict him.'[30] These comments further reveal that while there is no monolithic Black point of view, an accusation of Uncle Tomism still has the power to divide the Black community. (In 2019, Darden was again in the public spotlight as defence attorney for Eric Ronald Holder Jr. the Black man charged with killing Nipsey Hussle, a rapper and advocate for Black communities in South Los Angeles.)

It is also worth noting that when Simpson was arrested in 1994, Hertz issued a short statement saying the company was 'shocked and saddened by this development' and then dropped him as a spokesperson.[31] That outcome did not come as a surprise – a lesson Tiger Woods learned years later. Throughout Uncle Tom's tumultuous evolution from fictional character to racial epithet, the one unifying outcome of his eventual death – be it real or symbolic – is that white authority *always* moves on without remorse.

In 2008, thirteen years to the date of his acquittal, Simpson stood trial for robbery in Nevada, where an all-white jury found him guilty of all charges. In 2017, Simpson was released from prison, after serving nine years. But this time, America, the media, and the Black community had all moved on. Whether or not O.J. will reappear in the public spotlight remains to be seen. But the real question is, what was the legacy of his passing Uncle Tomism?

24

BARACK OBAMA AND THE
PARADOX OF BLACK POLITICAL POWER

Whenever African Americans have reached the highest echelons of American political life, accusations of being Uncle Toms and Aunt Jemimas have followed them. Even in the first years of this new millennium, the issue of racial loyalty hovered around those Blacks who entered positions of authority and institutions that have, historically, not been inhabited by African Americans.

In 2000, Condoleezza Rice, a former member of George H. W. Bush's foreign policy team and advisor on George W. Bush's political campaign, gave a speech at the Republican National Convention in support of Bush Jr.'s nomination. 'The first Republican that I knew was my father, John Rice,' she said, 'And he is still the Republican that I admire most. My father joined our party because the Democrats in Jim Crow Alabama of 1952 would not register him to vote. The Republicans did.'[1]

Rice, who was born in Birmingham, Alabama, in 1954, became a Republican shortly after the Soviet Union invaded Afghanistan in 1979. Only three years earlier, she had registered as a Democrat to cast her first presidential vote for President Jimmy Carter. But with the invasion of Afghanistan, Rice, whose doctoral dissertation centred on Soviet military policy and politics, regarded Carter's response to the crisis as weak and naive.[2] In 1980, she voted for Ronald Reagan; by 1982, she had changed her registration from Democrat to Republican.

'The biggest challenge right now for African Americans is to understand the particular witches' brew of racism and poverty when it's linked,' Rice said in an interview with *Washington Post* in 2000. 'If you focus on those people and you ask about opportunities for those people, you have to ask if the orthodoxy of the Democratic Party has done anything in 30 years to help the situation in those poor inner-city high schools.'[3]

Only a few years later, of course, another African American with impressive educational credentials took up residence in the White House, representing the party Rice had so sharply dismissed. On November 4, 2008, Barack Obama made history as the first African American to be elected president of the United States. As the forty-fourth person to hold that office, he broke the most impenetrable colour barrier of them all. As an estimated 240,000 people packed into Grant Park in Chicago, and millions more watched on television, the first Black President-elect delivered his victory speech. Many believed that *we* had overcome.

Obama's win ended the Bush era, and that administration's racial indifference. 'George Bush [didn't] care about Black people,' Kanye West said in 2005 during a telethon to support the victims of Hurricane Katrina.[4] After Obama spoke and roused the crowd with cheers of 'Yes we can! Yes we can!' his remarks felt like more than just another political speech; he was the person who would finally care about Black people. The crowd in Grant Park was euphoric, with many experiencing a sense of hope they had never felt before.

'Yes We Can,' the slogan attached to his presidential campaign, also became a single for the Black Eyed Peas frontman will.i.am. The 2008 hit imagined a united America, while the slogan winked knowingly at Black America. An unprecedented amount of political capital now was possible, Obama seemed to be saying, and his catchphrase suggested that he identified with the 'we' of Black America. It was an important message. Because of his biracial parentage – his mother was white; his father, Kenyan – and the fact that he was not born or raised in Black community, but rather in multi-ethnic Hawaii, Obama had to *become* African American during his campaign. In fact, while Donald Trump and other conservatives questioned his birth certificate, there were also prominent African Americans who questioned his Blackness.

In the 1980s, Obama had been a community organizer in Chicago's South Side, where his wife, Michelle, was born and raised. He attended a historical Black church, Trinity United Church of Christ, and with two African American daughters, Sasha and Malia, Obama checked every box as far as an authentic African American identity was concerned. Yet his loyalty to Black community was questioned right from the start, when media reports surfaced in the middle of the 2008 presidential race, quoting Trinity Church's African American pastor, Jeremiah Wright using inflammatory racial language. 'The government,' he preached, 'gives them [African Americans] the drugs, builds bigger prisons, passes a three-strike law and then wants us to sing "God Bless America." No, no, no, God damn America.' In a sermon after the terrorist attacks on September 11, 2001, Wright had said the U.S. had brought on al Qaeda's attacks because of its own terrorism: 'America's chickens were coming home to roost.'[5] Obama did not distance himself when the remarks were made public. Instead, he gave a speech entitled 'A More Perfect Union.'

Obama sought to put Wright's comments into a broader historical context, denouncing what the pastor had said, but not him as a person. Obama condemned Wright's contention that America supported state terrorism against Palestinians and Black South Africans. He called Wright's sermons divisive and 'racially charged at a time when we need[ed] to come together.' But he credited Wright for mentoring him as a Christian and preaching about the importance of community. Yet, Obama added,

> Like other predominantly black churches across the country, Trinity embodies the black community in its entirety – the doctor and the welfare mom, the model student and the former gang-banger. Like other black churches, Trinity's services are full of raucous laughter and sometimes bawdy humor. They are full of dancing, clapping, screaming and shouting that may seem jarring to the untrained ear. The church contains in full the kindness and cruelty, the fierce

intelligence and the shocking ignorance, the struggles and successes, the love and yes, the bitterness and bias that make up the black experience in America.[6]

While Obama left the church within months of the controversy, he also took care not to cast aspersions on the whole institution. 'I'm not denouncing the church, and I'm not interested in people who want me to denounce the church.'[7]

Such observations showed that Barack Obama was not just a Black man running for the highest office in the world; he was also part of, and on the side of, the Black community, its lineage, its narrative of struggle and triumph over segregation and discrimination, of civil rights and social justice, and of hope and resolve, that was bigger than him as an individual. Obama was not a cultural interloper. Through years of effort and outreach to the pillars of Blackness in America – the church, the community, and Black women – he had *become* an African American.

⚓

For the integrationist-era civil rights leader Rev. Jesse Jackson, Obama was not exactly the change and hope he had sought. During the campaign, Jackson had been forced to apologize for critical and, to some, crude remarks he made about Obama. In his comments, recorded on a live microphone prior to an interview with a *Fox News* anchor, Jackson criticized Obama for how he talked down to African Americans, the implication being that he was not one.

Jackson especially took issue with how Obama, in his speeches, often singled out Black men for failing to uphold their responsibilities as fathers.[8] During the campaign, Obama spoke to one Black church about the high percentage of African American men failing to be fathers to their children. Soon after, he found himself facing accusations of Uncle Tomism from Jackson, who had been a presidential candidate in 1988. In *Muzzled: The Assault on Honest Debate*, journalist Juan Williams described Jackson's TV faux pas. 'Acting as the enforcer of politically correct speech for liberal politicians,' he writes, 'Jackson damned [Obama] for talking down to Black people.' 'I want to cut his nuts out,' an infuriated Jackson was caught on microphone telling another guest about Obama.[9]

In an essay in the *Wall Street Journal*, Shelby Steele, a senior fellow at the Hoover Institution, sought to examine why folks like Jackson appeared to hate Obama. He offered several arguments.[10] First, he observed that for decades Jackson had been considered the mouthpiece for African American socio-political justice. Part of Dr. Martin Luther King Jr.'s inner circle, Jackson was at the Lorraine Motel in Memphis, Tennessee, on April 4, 1968, when the civil rights leader was assassinated. Steele described Jackson as a profoundly American archetype: 'the self-invented man who comes from nothing and, out of sheer force of personality, imposes himself on the American consciousness. If he never reached the greatness to which he aspired, he nevertheless did honor to the enduring American tradition of bold and unapologetic opportunism.'[11]

Jackson was also a fervent challenger of white racism. 'He confronted American institutions (especially wealthy corporations) with the shame of America's racist past and demanded redress,' wrote Steele, adding that while he could have taken up King's mantle, he and the rest of the civil rights establishment opted instead to '[pursue] equality through the manipulation of white guilt.' In other words, folks like Jackson kept white America 'on the hook' for injustices, and never took their foot off the pedal until they felt justice had been served. King, by contrast, argued for equality out of a faith in the imagination, which he believed could drive his own people forward.[12]

In a 1986 illustration of Jackson's outspokenness, he called on African Americans to boycott Revlon's beauty products until the company agreed to pull 'its business out of South Africa and develop better relations with black America.' According to Jackson (and others), Revlon was 'stealing business away from black companies.'

During the civil rights era, Uncle Tom was a race traitor, a sellout, and, most of all, someone who did not put the interests of the Black community ahead of his own. From Jackson's point of view, Uncle Tom in the new millennium had evolved into something more than a harsh judgment on a self-interested Black man. This new Uncle Tom did not pressure white leaders to atone for past wrongdoings toward Black people, such as policies of mass incarceration, defunding social programs, etc. Obama became a viable Black presidential candidate because he did the one thing that Jackson could not do: he set aside his moral leverage over whites.[13] Either out of conviction or political expediency, Obama refused to shame white America for its racism. But in Jackson's eyes, that showed Obama was an Uncle Tom, someone willing to work within the frame built and maintained by white America rather than assign blame squarely on white Americans for causing many of the problems faced by the Black community.

 ❧

Does being a leader from a different generation, and someone who disagreed with Jackson and others' approach to the cause of Black progress, make Obama an Uncle Tom?

Obama was not anti-Black as president, nor did he wilfully neglect the Black community for the sake of his own political ends. But what he did do while president was avoid inflaming racial tensions by forcing white America to confront systemic racism.

He also made statements that, at times, came across as unfair critiques of the Democratic Party's Black base – the very people who got him elected. In a speech to the Congressional Black Caucus (CBC) in 2011, for example, he ran down a list of his administration's accomplishments (e.g., pushing for the passage of his jobs bill). But Obama concluded his speech by saying: 'I expect all of you to march with me and press on. Take off your bedroom slippers, put on your marching shoes. Shake it off. Stop complaining, stop grumbling, stop crying. We are going to press on. We've got work to do, CBC.'[14] In a blog post not long afterwards, activist Yvette Carnell, a controversial figure who has played a formidable role in the American Descendants of Slavery reparations movement, was dismissive of Obama's comments:

President Obama isn't speaking to us, but about us – to conservative leaning independents. He's speaking to the stereotype that they hold, that African Americans are lazy critters who aren't capable of self-actualization. And it was remarkable to hear Obama bark patronizingly at an African American crowd, then watch the crowd answer in applause. In a word, heartbreaking.[15]

According to Mark Halperin and John Heilemann's *Double Down: Game Change 2012*, a behind-the-scenes look at the 2012 election, 'Obama had little patience for the "professional left," and vanishingly close to zero for what one of his senior African American aides, Michael Strautmanis, referred to as "professional blacks" (as opposed to black professionals).' They added: 'Apart from Georgia congressman John Lewis and Jim Clyburn of South Carolina [civil rights integrationists], Obama had nearly as much contempt for the CBC as he did for the Tea Party Caucus.' 'Jesse Jackson Sr.,' they wrote, 'was effectively banned from the White House.'[16]

Obama's supposed comments garnered sharp attacks from prominent Black figures, including sociologist Michael Eric Dyson, former talk show host Tavis Smiley, and even Bill Cosby. Perhaps the harshest words came from Harvard University professor Cornel West, one of Obama's most pointed critics – someone who called out America's first Black president for failing Black America:

> … Obama said not a mumbling word about the dead Palestinian children but he did call Baltimore black youth 'criminals and thugs' … In addition, Obama's education policy unleashed more market forces that closed hundreds of public schools for charter ones. The top 1% got nearly two-thirds of the income growth in eight years even as child poverty, especially black child poverty, remained astronomical.[17]

Many people would agree with West's list of grievances against Obama. But it is reasonable to ask if African American political leaders, especially Black Democrats, do not go far enough to change, challenge, and address historical injustices, are they then 'selling out'? Does an unwillingness to act decisively look like Uncle Tomism?

Journalist and lawyer Sophia A. Nelson, a contributor to the progressive African American digital news site *The Root*, argues that

Black folks should not have their 'Black card' revoked just because they do not share the mainstream political views of the Black community. 'There is a troubling trend emerging in the black community relative to our freedom of speech and the right to dissent,' she writes. 'I have been attacked and vilified, marginalized by some because I call for lower taxes and less government spending, and God forbid I try to talk about a strong national defense or disagree with President Obama's handling of any particular issues. The smears come in a flood.'[18]

⚜

The debate over how Black men with differing political viewpoints ought to deal with one another stretches back to the beginning of the last century. At the time, two prominent African American men – the 'conservative' Booker T. Washington and the 'radical' W. E. B. Du Bois – had very public disagreements about their vision for African Americans post-Reconstruction. Jamaican-born Marcus Garvey, founder of the Universal Negro Improvement Association (UNIA) and the most vocal proponent of the pan-Africanist movement, also publicly challenged Du Bois about race and Black identity.

Born in Massachusetts shortly after the end of the Civil War, Du Bois, a sociologist, was the first African American to earn a doctorate (from Harvard). His 1903 book, *The Souls of Black Folks*, was and remains a seminal text for understanding the African American experience at the turn of the twentieth century. In another work also published that year, *The Negro Problem*, Du Bois coined the phrase 'talented tenth.' The concept, at its core, recommended that higher education develop the leadership capacity among the most able 10 per cent of African Americans. Du Bois, in effect, was arguing for not just African American educational advancement, but also the creation of an elite intelligentsia and leadership class.

He also felt that educated African Americans were obligated to sacrifice their personal interests and endeavours in favour of community activities designed to improve the social, economic, and political condition of the entire race.[19] Du Bois was one of several

Black intellectuals who believed that industrial training as the only viable career choice would confine African Americans to the ranks of second-class citizenship.

This stance was in direct opposition to Washington's *Up from Slavery* (1901) and his belief in racial accommodation. Born into slavery, Washington believed that former slaves and their immediate descendants needed financial independence most of all. He asserted that Black communities could prosper only by running their own businesses, and argued that if African Americans stayed in their own lane – i.e., accepted discrimination for the time being, and focused on working with their hands – they could attain economic stability and perhaps even prosper without interference from Southern whites, who vehemently (and violently) sought to preserve segregation and the Jim Crow laws.[20]

'Much has been discussed ... of the notion that Washington was an "Uncle Tom,"' writes critic Rebecca Carroll in her introduction to *Uncle Tom or New Negro?: African Americans Reflect on Booker T. Washington*, published in 2006. 'It is a curious notion, as the Uncle Tom stereotype has become primarily qualified by a passive nature, if also by an eagerness to please white people. Booker T. Washington ... was not passive.'[21] Most notably, Washington founded the Tuskegee Institute in Tuskegee, Alabama, which became one of the largest landowners in the county and by 1895 had more students than any other institution of higher learning in that state. Yet Washington also endorsed Southern segregation of the races – 'In all things that are purely social,' he said in 1895, Blacks and whites are 'as separate as the fingers' – and therefore stood accused of racial disloyalty.[22]

Although Du Bois was very clear and precise about the role of the 'talented tenth,' Washington charged him with being an elitist who was able to understand only theories and ideas.[23] In 1905, in an effort to strategize about ending racial segregation while working to oppose Washington's calls for conciliation and large-scale industrial training for African Americans, Du Bois established the Niagara Movement. It was the precursor to the NAACP, which he co-founded in 1909. The group convened its first meeting near Fort Erie, Ontario.

What's important to recognize in a discussion of Washington's legacy is that historical examinations of his life and contemporary retrospectives both reveal how challenging it is to arrive at a consensus on the influence of Uncle Tom after Stowe's novel.

Washington was one of the first to loudly declare that the twentieth century was 'a new century, for a new Negro' in his acclaimed book of the same name, published in 1900. But in *Uncle Tom: From Martyr to Traitor*, author Adena Springarn argues that Washington was frequently cast as an Uncle Tom in the Black press of the day. In a 1905 critique of Washington in the St. Louis (Missouri) *Advance*, for example, he was described as 'the apostle of servility and submission.' The Negro newspaper noted that the 'Haitian revolutionary Toussaint L'Ouverture, with his bold resistance, provided a far better model for the race.'[24]

Uncle Tom stood for a variety of traits at the turn of the century. As Springarn writes, Tom represented 'an attitude (acceptance and even encouragement of the spread of Southern racial practices such as segregation to the North), an image (perpetuation of a submissive version of modern black manhood), a strategy (submission to a racial injustice rather than vigorous contestation), and a performance (an act knowingly affected in order to get ahead).'[25] Many of these attributes have morphed and mutated, attaching to Black actors, activists, politicians, and public figures at various moments during the twentieth century.

In his defence of Washington, philosopher Bill E. Lawson explains that 'Washington never said, as many have claimed, that black people should get only an industrial education. He never said that black people shouldn't participate in the political process.' But, Lawson added, Washington also understood how some Black people saw him. In 1903, for example, Washington wrote: 'When a people are smarting under the wrongs of injustices inflicted from many quarters, it is but natural that they should look about for some individual in whom to lay the blame for their seemly misfortunes. In this case, I seem to be the one.'[26]

As award-winning journalist Cora Daniels observes, 'The Uncle Tom status [of Washington] is given … from us looking back.' She continues: 'If you go back to some of the things he was saying, it was all about how earning "a dollar in a factory is worth infinitely more than the opportunity to spend a dollar in an opera house." Or "No race can prosper till it learns that there is as much dignity in tilling a field as in writing a poem." These are old-fashioned work ethic basics that we have all heard and nodded our heads to at some point in our lives.'[27]

In the context of the post-Reconstruction era, Washington's outlook was rooted in the prevailing Protestant ethic of hard work and thrift, while many of Du Bois's ideas were deeply informed by the notion of racial uplift based on the extraordinary advantages afforded to those African Americans who were not only born of privilege (like him), but were also light-skinned, educated, and socially mobile.

Marcus Garvey, in turn, saw Du Bois as a member of America's (white) elite class. He came from a pedigreed, financially stable family – 'purely and simply,' Garvey said, 'a white man's nigger.'[28] As an intellectual, Du Bois sought institutional progress for Black America, whereas Garvey, a Jamaican immigrant, wanted self-empowerment. He also believed that Black people should support Black-owned businesses and services, and avoid contact with whites, whom he considered injurious to a healthy Black psyche.[29] Du Bois, on the other hand, once said of Garvey, '[He] is, without doubt, the most dangerous enemy of the Negro race in America and in the world. He is either a lunatic or a traitor.'[30]

The tension between these two thinkers was not just about ideology; it also stemmed from their physical appearances: Garvey was dark-skinned and Du Bois was light-skinned. At the turn of the twentieth century, many light-skinned Blacks – men and women who had built America's Black churches and schools, and who began to live together in segregated communities for 'mulatto elites,' as they were called – could be found in virtually every major urban centre across America. When Du Bois dismissed Garvey as 'a little, fat black man; ugly, but with intelligent eyes and a big head,'[31] he was equating his rival with an antiquated Blackness. But Du Bois was also reaffirming that for members of America's Black elite class, social progress required lighter skin – shaking off the past of enslavement.

While the ghost of Uncle Tom followed Du Bois and Washington, Garvey was the first public figure to use 'Uncle Tom' as a pejorative term. According to scholar Stephen Railton, who examined his speeches and other UNIA publications and public events, Garvey gave wide circulation to the term to stigmatize Blacks who betrayed the cause of their race. 'Uncle Tom dead and buried,' proclaimed protest signs at the parade that opened the UNIA's first convention in 1920 in New York. According to a *Negro World* report on an address to the convention, Rev. George Alexander McGuire declared that 'the Uncle Tom nigger has got to go and his place must be taken by the new leader of the Negro race … not a black man with a white heart, but a black man with a black heart.'[32] In a 1921 speech, directed specifically at Du Bois and his followers, Garvey said, '[They] are not such fools as we think they are; they are simply playing foolish to be wise – to get some cheap money. They are allowing themselves to be used even as Uncle Tom and his bunch were used for hundreds of years.'[33] Nearly a century later, public squabbles between African American leaders continue to play out in the shadow of Uncle Tom.

❧

Obama's second term marked a period when unarmed Black men and women were shot and killed by police: Trayvon Martin, Michael Brown, Eric Garner, Freddie Gray, Tamir Rice, Sandra Bland, Oscar Grant, Laquan McDonald, to name a few. It is difficult to not attach some blame to Obama and his administration for their inaction on police reform and social justice legislation. But, as activist and scholar Angela Davis has observed, 'People like to point to Obama as an individual and hold him responsible for the madness that has happened. Of course, there are things that Obama as an individual might have done better – he might have insisted more on the closing of Guantánamo – but people who invested their hopes in him were approaching the issue of political futures in the wrong way to begin with … it's always a collective process to change the world.'[34] Davis was not disappointed in the failure of the first African American president to speak out about police violence against Black people. She saw other ways of advancing those agendas. 'Why,' she asked, 'have we not created the kind of movement that would put more pressure on Obama and force the Obama Administration to deal with these issues?'

Ultimately, racial loyalty is not just about one's racial identification. It is also about perception. Black political leaders must measure their own actions against the Black community's perception about what they do and do not do. Black men who are seen as aligning with institutions, white authority, or corporations, or those who are viewed as actively hindering Black progress and participation, run the risk of being labelled Uncle Toms, even as they remain culturally and/or socially tied to their roots. It is an impossible quandary to resolve.

Obama did not solve all the ills of the Black community. In some instances, he missed opportunities to effect real change that would have benefited African Americans. This was especially apparent in his comments about reparations. In 2008, Obama said he feared that reparations would 'be an excuse for some to say "we've paid our debt" and to avoid the much harder work of enforcing our anti-discrimination laws in employment and housing.'[35] Later that year, when asked in a CNN interview what approach he would take toward reparations – i.e., either apologizing for slavery or offering reparations to various groups – he responded, 'I have said in the past – and I'll repeat again – that the best reparations we can provide are good schools in the inner city and jobs for people who are unemployed.'[36] The topic of reparations returned again in a 2016 interview with journalist Ta-Nehisi Coates following the publication in the *Atlantic* of his feature 'The Case for Reparations.' Obama told Coates that his dream for his children is that they will 'be sensitive to and extra thoughtful about the plight of people who have been oppressed in the past, [or] are oppressed currently.'[37] But he skirted any direct comments on the matter of reparations.

In 2019, Coates testified before the House Judiciary Subcommittee on the Constitution on the issue of reparations. He outlined the history of slavery and its continued impact on the African American community and laid out some hard truths about structural inequalities that have uniquely impeded Black progress. 'The typical black family in this country has one-tenth the wealth of the typical white family,' he said. 'Black women die in childbirth at four times the rate of white women. And there is, of course, the shame of this land of the free boasting the largest prison population on the planet, of which the descendants of the enslaved make up the largest share.'[38]

So here is the paradox. Obama, arguably the most influential Black man in America, remained unwilling to address a topic that, while controversial, was embraced by several candidates during the 2020 Democratic primaries, including then-California senator Kamala Harris.[39] Why was Obama so reluctant to do so?

In a 2019 interview with *New York Magazine*, Coates, though a frequent critic, acknowledged Obama's importance as the first Black president:

> There's a politics of him, and there's Obama as a mythical figure, the symbolic aspect of what he is ... Symbols open people's minds to what's possible. It actually was quietly really important that while Barack Obama never disguised the fact that he was biracial, he identified as a black man ... I think that was really inspiring to a lot of black people and a lot of white people. I don't think it was everything. I don't think it was enough, but I think one should not underestimate the power of Obama as a symbol of the first black president.[40]

I agree with Coates. Symbolic victories matter. Obama did not fix the problems of past administrations as far as the African American community is concerned, but nor did he lose sight of who he was, and how he had to fit into Washington's inner circle of wealthy white men. His lack of commitment to reparations raised doubts about his racial loyalty, but his two terms in office ultimately left us with an important question: is it the sole responsibility of Black politicians to change policies, structures, and institutions that have, historically, hindered Black progress, or does the responsibility lie with the Black community to lobby political leaders to enact policies that directly benefit them? The answer remains theoretical, however, because Obama's presidency never made overt strides to address them.

CONCLUSION

THE IMMORTAL UNCLE TOM

There has never been a moment in my life when I have not been aware of Uncle Tom. Like Mammy, Uncle Tom is more than a literary character or racial epithet. He exists beyond labels and justifications. Uncle Tom transcends boundary, border, literary pages, film scripts, and TV screens. Like language itself, Uncle Tom encircles the globe.

In 2020, following the tragic killing of George Floyd, as well as Breonna Taylor and Ahmaud Arbery, an anti-Black-racism movement went global. People did not care that we were in the grip of a pandemic. For the first time since the civil rights movement, the desire for change rippled through every facet of society, from the media to universities to justice and law enforcement systems, where demands to 'defund the police,' while decades old, were finally heard.

Suddenly, the nation (and the world) began to ask, what is the rightful place for Black people in our society? When will we be free? When will they see us? These questions were not new. But under the light of a pandemic, people were hearing what lay beneath these questions: Black fatigue about the persistence and perniciousness of anti-Black racism.

I finished writing this book during this historical moment, which was bracketed by the arrival of Black Lives Matter into the zeitgeist and the exit of Donald Trump from the White House. With these events as backdrop, I felt the weight of trying to sum up not only why Uncle Tom is still present, but how we can make sense of him in a post-Trump America that is rife with contradictions. During his time in office, Trump repeatedly claimed he had done more for Black people than Abraham Lincoln, even as he simultaneously disparaged attempts, such as the *New York Times'* 1619 project, to place the enslavement of African Americans at the centre of America's origin story. His presidency was, in a word, topsy-turvy.

⅌

If you think about it, Uncle Tom is quite possibly the most resilient figure in American history. He has survived pandemics, lived through thirty-three presidents (including Joe Biden), and remains the most recognizable Black character in history. We hate him, but it seems we cannot live without him. The insatiable appetite for a docile, symbolically emasculated Black male archetype speaks profoundly to how monumentally resistant to change this character has been.

I can see parallels between Uncle Tom's death by beating in Chapter 41 of the novel and the brutality of Floyd's murder by Minneapolis police in the summer of 2020. Just as the latter spawned a global anti-Black-racism response, this scene in Stowe's novel fundamentally changed people's attitudes about slavery. Almost overnight, the language used to describe Black enslavement shifted from the 'peculiar institution' to a cruel, immoral, and unjust system that needed to end. Social change in the nineteenth century took the form of abolitionists and a transatlantic anti-slavery movement. Today, social change happens on the streets and across the internet. People will spend decades debating whether George Floyd was a martyr or a hero. But if we can take anything away from Stowe's Uncle Tom, it is that the line separating martyrdom and heroism is very thin.

The reality is that Floyd was a real Black man who died tragically, and who was given an internationally televised funeral worthy of a statesman. Uncle Tom, on the other hand, has never been figuratively buried. But what if he were put to rest once and for all? What if we held a funeral for him, and then never heard from him again? Why can he not just fade from memory, as have so many other characters from other mid-nineteenth-century novels?

Over many generations, prominent figures, from Duke Ellington to Langston Hughes, have tried to imagine a world without Uncle Tom. In the early 1940s, Ellington's musical revue, *Jump for Joy,* was a celebration of Uncle Tom's death.[1] A few years later, the writer Brion Gysin, who is white, published an essay entitled 'To Master, A Long Goodnight.' As he writes, 'It will be a great day when we can shout together, "Uncle Tom is dead."'[2]

Langston Hughes's poem 'Epitaph' also imagined Uncle Tom posthumously. The poem is about Uncle Tom's service to white people, and ends with 'Now, thank God, Uncle Tom Is dead.'[3]

More than three generations later, Hughes's words remain as poignant as they were when he wrote them. 'Uncle Tom is a burning wish,' writes poet Harmony Holiday in *A Jazz Funeral for Uncle Tom,* published in 2019. '[H]e is a wish that burns eternal. He is a songbook purged through rehearsal, one who must be practiced to be destroyed, loved into uselessness, and then at last, gone.'[4]

Uncle Tom Syndrome is also highly recognizable among contemporary Black public figures who have been accused of Uncle Tomism like Supreme Court Justice Clarence Thomas, Dr. Ben Carson, and more recently, Kentucky's Attorney General Daniel Cameron. These non-threatening contemporary African American males carry the same historical baggage as the fictional Uncle Tom did. Are Toms there to serve the interests of white authority and institutions? And do they thwart Black progress? These are the questions that surround contemporary Black men in positions of not only authority but also power and prestige, and who are either in service to white institutions or become the public spokespersons for white companies.

Uncle Tom Syndrome did not just appear because of Stowe's novel; the likes of Uncle Ben and others have contributed to this psychological phenomenon. At the same time, today's Uncle Tom is often misdiagnosed, mislabelled, and misidentified due to shifts in media culture, and, more broadly, the condition of the Black community in contemporary America.

It seems to me that the paradox of Uncle Tom is that we can find utility in him at the same time as we must hate him. These two desires can never be reconciled. We have been trying to kill off someone who, ironically, we are unable to live without.

Is accusing a Black man of Uncle Tomism justified? Sometimes it is, and sometimes it is not. What is most important is that Black people pay attention to the circumstances under which his name is uttered. I believe that one of the reasons Uncle Tom has never faded away is that his presence is, strangely, necessary. Stowe may have created this character to support the abolition of slavery. However, through constant reinvention and reproduction, Uncle Tom, the archetype, has kept Black people mentally enslaved. And he will continue to do so if the Black community remains divided on how to live within a capitalist system built on slave labour. Yet this figure also reminds us to look deeper and to ask difficult questions about how we choose to relate to white society and its institutions.

Uncle Tom is our collective whisper.

NOTES

CHAPTER 1

1. Quissell, *Sentimental and Utopian Novels*, 19.
2. Hochman, *Uncle Tom's Cabin and the Reading Revolution*, 2.
3. Beckert, *Empire of Cotton*, 245.
4. Pickering, *Blackface Minstrelsy in Britain*, 23.
5. Bernstein, *Racial Innocence*, 15.
6. Morgan, *Uncle Tom's Cabin as Visual Culture*, 55.
7. Hirsch, 'Uncle Tomitudes,' 316–18.

CHAPTER 2

1. Wood, *Blind Memory*, 173.
2. Morgan, 31.
3. Ibid., 190.
4. Hirsch, 311.
5. Bernstein, *Racial Innocence*, 6.

CHAPTER 3

1. Lott, *Love and Theft*, 3.
2. Jones Jr., *Captive Stage*, 56.
3. Ibid., 55.
4. Toll, *Blacking Up*, 31.
5. Nathan, 'Performance of the Virginia Minstrels,' 36.
6. Mahar, *Behind the Burnt Cork Mask*, 227.
7. Hochman, *Uncle Tom's Cabin and the Reading Revolution*, 3.
8. Morgan, 49.
9. Moynagh, 'African-Canadian Theatre,' viii.
10. Springhall, *Genesis of Mass Culture*, 70.
11. Meer, *Uncle Tom Mania*, 53.
12. Springhall, 70.
13. Glazer and Key, 'Carry Me Back,' 8–9.
14. Nowatzki, *Representing African Americans*, 12.
15. Morgan, 80.

16. Southern, 'The Georgia Minstrels,' 164.
17. Taylor and Austen, *Darkest America*, 50.
18. Springhall, 71.

CHAPTER 4

1. *Hamilton Spectator*, December 12, 1893, 8.
2. 'Cleveland Minstrels,' *Globe*, July 31, 1893, 8.
3. Archer-Straw, *Negrophilia*, 41.
4. Taylor and Austen, 72.
5. Russell, *Loew's Yonge Street*, 2.
6. Glenn, *Female Spectacle*, 50.
7. Taylor and Austen, 75.
9. Toll, 245.
10. Ibid., 257, 259.

CHAPTER 5

1. Hochman, *Uncle Tom's Cabin and the Reading Revolution*, 148.
2. Wallace-Sanders, *Mammy*, 61.
3. Manring, *Slave in a Box*, 75.

CHAPTER 6

1. As quoted in 'How Rastus Gets His Turkey,' AFI Catalog of Feature Films, https://catalog.afi.com/Catalog/MovieDetails/39165.
2. Pilgrim, *Understanding Jim Crow*, 85.
3. A. Moore, '12 Racist Logos You Didn't Know Were Used by Popular Brands,' *Atlanta Black Star*, May 7, 2014, https://atlantablackstar.com/2014/05/07/12-racists-logos-you-didnt-know-were-used-by-popular-brands/4/.
4. Pilgrim, 84.
5. Kern-Foxworth, *Aunt Jemima, Uncle Ben, and Rastus*, 45.
6. Pilgrim, 85–6.
7. Cream of Wheat Advertisement, 'Goin' Prospectin,' *Chatelaine*,

February 1938, 23.

8. Cream of Wheat Advertisement, *Chatelaine*, October 1939, 82.

9. Cream of Wheat Advertisement, *Chatelaine*, November 1939, 67.

10. Cream of Wheat Advertisement, *Chatelaine*, February 1958, 7.

11. Gordon Brown Scheibell's Uncle Eben Cartoon, *Toronto Daily Star*, October 3, 1929, 20.

CHAPTER 7

1. Kwate, *Burgers in Blackface*, 28.

2. Shackel, 'Heyward Shepherd,' 138.

3. Laura Martin Rose, *The Ku Klux Klan or Invisible empire*, 31-32. Retrieved from: https://archive.org/details/cu31924083530117/page/32/mode/2up.

4. Tony Horwitz, 'The Mammy Washington Almost Had,' *The Atlantic*, May 31, 2013, retrieved at: https://www.theatlantic.com/national/archive/2013/ 05/the-mammy-washington-almost-had/276431/.

5. United Daughters of the Confederacy, 'Statement from the President General,' retrieved at: https://hqudc.org.

6. Shackel, 146.

7. Starkey, *In Defense of Uncle Tom*, 133.

8. Horwitz, 'The Mammy Washington Almost Had.'

9. Frick, *Uncle Tom's Cabin on the American Stage*, 6.

10. Savage, *Standing Soldiers*, 77.

11. Hochman, *Uncle Tom's Cabin and the Reading Revolution*, 139-40.

12. Taylor and Austen, 57.

13. McClintock, *Imperial Leather*, 213.

14. Hartman, *Scenes of Subjection*, 28.

15. Hine, *Total Package*, 88.

CHAPTER 8

1. Kwate, 70–72.

2. 'The Story of Lil Sambo's Restaurant,' Lil Sambo's Restaurant, retrieved at: https://lilsambos.com/about-us/.

3. Strausbaugh, *Black Like You*, 279.

4. Boskin, *Sambo*, 58.

5. Kern-Foxworth, 30.

6. See Henry Pidding, 'Massa Out. "Sambo Werry Dry."' Paper messotint etching, 1828. London. The British Museum, #1935,0522.3.195.

7. See George Cruikshank, 'George Cruikshank's Omnibus' (Frank Heartwell). Paper etching, 1842. London: Charles Tilt. The British Museum, #1978,U,2569.

8. Kern-Foxworth, 46.

9. Kibler, *Rank Ladies*, 119.

10. Wernick, *Promotional Culture*, 22.

11. Kwate, 50.

12. Bernstein, *Racial Innocence*, 11.

13. Bogle, *Toms, Coons, Mulattoes, Mammies & Bucks*, 7.

14. Olson, *Black Children in Hollywood Cinema*, 42.

15. Meer, 38.

16. Morgan, 6.

17. Gates, *Signifying Monkey*, 190.

18. Bernstein, *Racial Innocence*, 6.

19. Strausbaugh, 276.

CHAPTER 9

1. Adams, *Wounds of Returning*, 5.

2. Starkey, 29.

3. Ibid., 30.

4. Pilgrim, 44.

5. Mathieu, *North of the Color*, 101.

6. Pilgrim, 47.

7. Ibid., 48.

8. Ibid., 84.

9. Elliott, 'Uncle Ben, Board Chairman,' *New York Times*, March 30, 2007, accessed July 30, 2018, https:// www.nytimes.com/2007/03/30/business/media/30adco.html.

CHAPTER 10

1. Stowe, *Uncle Tom's Cabin*, 258.

2. Wood, 172–3.

3. Sánchez-Eppler, *Touching Liberty*, 133.

4. Turner, *Ceramic Uncles & Celluloid Mammies*, 15.

5. David Porter, 'Black Rag Dolls Meant to Be Abused Are Pulled from Stores,' Associated Press, July 26, 2019, https://apnews.com/9a9dad 8649c3445ea7c206dbc3bdd05d.

6. Strausbaugh, 276.

7. See Ibid.; Meer, 1–2.

8. Kern-Foxworth, 75.

9. Sánchez-Eppler, 133.

10. Wallace-Sanders, 34.

11. Bernstein, *Racial Innocence*, 215.

12. Bernstein, 'Children's Books,' 164.

13. Ibid., 165.

14. Belisle, *Retail Nation*, 67.

15. Topsy Advertisement, *Chatelaine*, September 1937, 57.

16. Lisa Wade, 'Theories of the First Topsy-Turvy Doll,' *Pacific Standard*, https://psmag.com/social-justice/ theories-first-topsy-turvy-doll-95322. See also, National Black Dolls Museum of History & Culture, https://nbdmhc.org.

17. See Julian K. Jarboe, 'The Racial Symbolism of the Topsy-Turvy Doll,' *Atlantic*, November 20, 2015, https:// www.theatlantic.com/technology/ archive/2015/11/the-racial-symbolism-of-the-topsy-turvy-doll/416985/.

18. Stephen Railton, *Topsy & Eva*, http://utc.iath.virginia.edu/onstage/ films/duncmovhp.html.

19. Noble Johnson Biography, IMDB, https://www.imdb.com/name/ nm0425903/bio.

20. Wallace-Sanders, *Mammy*, 35.

21. Bogle, *Toms, Coons, Mulattoes, Mammies*, 47.

22. Hilhorst and Hermes, '"We Have Given Up So Much,"' 219.

23. Ibid., 220.

24. Daniel Pollack-Pelzner, '"Mary Poppins," and a Nanny's Shameful Flirting With Blackface,' *New York Times*, January 28, 2019, https://www. nytimes.com/2019/01/28/movies/mary-poppins- returns-blackface.html.

25. Ibid.

26. Ibid.

27. Hilhorst and Hermes, 'We Have Given Up So Much,' 223.

28. Bianca Collins, 'The Preservation of History: Alison Saar,' *Journal of National Academy of Design*, March 5, 2019, https://www.nadnowjournal. org/ reviews/a-preservation-of-history-alison-saar/.

CHAPTER 11

1. Frick, 186.

2. The vitascope premiered at Koster and Bail's vaudeville theatre on 23rd Street in New York. See Ibid., 187.

3. Bogle, 5–6.

4. Starkey, 34.

5. 'The First *Uncle Tom's Cabin* Film: Edison-Porter's Slavery Days (1903),' a Multi-Media Archive, accessed June 15, 2019, http://utc.iath.virginia.edu/ onstage/films/mv03hp.html.

6. Pilgrim, 'Tom Caricature.'

7. Staples, *Male-Female Comedy Teams*, 92.

8. Morgan, 59.

9. Starkey, 34.

10. 'Universal Super Jewel Production (1927), *Uncle Tom's Cabin* and American Culture,' a Multi-Media Archive, accessed June 15, 2019, http://utc.iath.virginia.edu/onstage/ films/mv27hp.html.

11. Frick, 67.

12. Bogle, 41.

13. Pilgrim, 83.

14. Bogle, 176.

15. Frick, 219.

CHAPTER 12

1. Cox, *Dreaming of Dixie*, 58.
2. Mel Watkins, 'What Was It About "Amos 'n' Andy"?' *New York Times*, July 7, 1991, https://www.nytimes.com/1991/07/07/books/what-was-it-about-amos-n-andy.html.
3. Ibid.
4. Ibid.
5. Barlow, *Voice Over*, 334.
6. Cox, 58.
7. Amos 'n' Andy Advertisement, *Chatelaine*, August 1930, 43; 41; 37.
8. See 'Jack Benny in the 1940s: The 1933-1934 Season,' https://sites.google.com/site/jackbennyinthe1940s/jack-benny-in-the-1930-s/1933-1934-season.

CHAPTER 13

1. Bogle, 135.
2. Snead, *White Screens*, 93–94.
3. Teresa Jusino, 'Whoopi Goldberg Encourages Disney to Stop Hiding Song of the South, Along with Our History,' *The Mary Sue*, July 17, 2017, accessed June 16, 2019, https://www.themarysue.com/whoopi-goldberg-encourage-disneys-to-not-hide-song-of-the-south/.
4. As quoted in John Lingan, 'Bristling Dixie,' *Slate*, January 4, 2013, accessed June 16, 2019, https://slate.com/culture/2013/01/song-of-the-south-disneys-most-notorious-film-by-jason-sperb-reviewed.html.
5. Turner, 112–113.
6. Dave Tompkins: Music Database, accessed at https://www.cs.ubc.ca/~davet/music/list/Best1.html.
7. Xan Brooks, 'Is *Song of the South* Too Racist to Screen?' *Guardian UK*, March 28, 2007, accessed June 16, 2019, https://www.theguardian.com/film/filmblog/2007/mar/28/therearetwodisneyfilms.

8. Dirk Libbey, 'Disney Is Bringing Its Entire Vault to Streaming Service Disney+,' *Cinema Blend*, accessed June 16, 2019, https://www.cinemablend.com/news/2468063/disney-is-bringing-its-entire-vault-to-streaming-service-disney.
9. Matt Singer, 'Just How Racist is 'Song of the South,' Disney's Most Notorious Movie?' *Screen Crush*, March 4, 2016, accessed June 16, 2019, https://screencrush.com/song-of-the-south-racism/.
10. Higginbotham, *Righteous Discontent*, 189.
11. Starkey, 17.
12. Guerrero, *Framing Blackness*, 27.
13. Feagin, *White Racial Frame*, 129.
14. Sperb, *Disney's Most Notorious Film*, 63.
15. Ibid., 64.
16. As quoted in Ibid.
17. Korkis, *Who's Afraid of Song of the South?*, 27–34.
18. Wynn, *African American Experience During World War II*, 41.
19. Brode, *Multiculturalism and the Mouse*, 53.
20. Sperb, 64.
21. Brode, *Multiculturalism and the Mouse*, 54.
22. Ibid., 54.
23. As quoted in Cohen, *Forbidden Animation*, 60–61.
24. 'Movie Maids,' *Ebony*, August 1948, 56–58.
25. See Singer, 'Just How Racist.'
26. Cohen, 61.

CHAPTER 14

1. As quoted in Miller, 'What Does It Mean to Be an American?,' 53.
2. Tracy Jan. 'Redlining Was Banned 50 Years Ago. It's Still Hurting Minorities Today,' *Washington Post*, March 28,

2018, retrieved from: https://www. washingtonpost.com/news/wonk/wp /2018/03/28/redlining-was-banned-50-years-ago-its-still-hurting-minorities-today/.

3. Blackwelder, *Styling Jim Crow*, 144.

4. Moritz Kuhn, Moritz Schularick, and Ulrike I. Steins. 'Income and Wealth Inequality in America, 1949–2016.' *Institute Working Paper* 9, June 14, 2018. Retrieved from: https:// www.minneapolisfed.org/research/ institute-working-papers/income-and-wealth-inequality-in-america-1949-2016.

5. As quoted in Bruce C. T. Wright, 'Little Rock Nine Photos, Videos And Quotes On 60th Anniversary of Desegregation Milestone,' *News One*, September 25, 2017. Retrieved from: https://newsone. com/3749349/little-rock-nine-anniversary-photos-video-quotes-central-high-desegregation/.

6. Berger, *Seeing Through Race*, 27–28.

7. Turner, 54.

8. McElya, *Clinging to Mammy*, 242–243.

9. Bogle, 100.

10. Whitlatch, 'The House Committee on Un-American Activities,' 238.

11. Starkey, 195.

12. Pilgrim, 86.

13. Starkey, 48–49.

14. Ibid., 101.

CHAPTER 15

1. Bogle, 169.

2. As quoted in Collier-Thomas and Franklin, *My Soul Is a Witness*, 55.

3. Amanda Petrusich, 'Harry Belafonte and the Social Power of Song,' *New Yorker*, February 22, 2017, retrieved at: https://www.newyorker.com/ culture/ cultural-comment/harry-belafonte-and-the-social-power-of-song.

4. Charles Blow, 'Harry and Sidney: Soul Brothers,' *New York Times*, February 20, 2017, retrieved at: https://www.nytimes.com/2017/02/ 20/opinion/harry-and-sidney-soul-brothers.html.

5. Russell and Wilson, et al., *Color Complex*, 149.

6. Van Deburg, *New Day in Babylon*, 195.

7. Witt, *Black Hunger*, 6.

8. Miller, *Soul Food*, 63-4.

9. As quoted in Starkey, 226.

10. Pilgrim, 84.

11. Clifford Mason, 'Why Does White America Love Sidney Poitier So?' *New York Times*, September 10, 1967, 21.

12. As quoted in *I Am Not Your Negro*, dir. Raoul Peck, Velvet Film: 2017.

CHAPTER 16

1. Haley, *Autobiography of Malcolm X*, 465.

2. Davis, *Women, Race & Class*, 13.

3. As quoted in Crenshaw, 'Mapping the Margin,' 1254, note. 42.

4. Kain, 'Housing Segregation,' 183; 196.

5. As quoted in Carl Rowan, 'Crisis in Civil Rights Leadership,' *Ebony*, November 1966, 29.

6. Rooks, *Ladies' Pages*, 131.

7. Durant and Louden, 'Black Middle Class in America,' 255–56.

8. Collins, 'Making of the Black Middle Class,' 369.

9. Tye, 194.

10. Ibid., 197.

11. Baldwin, 'Letters from a Region in my Mind,' *New Yorker*, November 17, 1962, https://www.newyorker.com/ magazine/1962/11/17/letter-from-a-region-in-my-mind.

12. As quoted in Tye, 413.

13. Rowan, 'Crisis in Civil Rights Leadership,' 30.

14. Michael Beschloss, 'Jackie Robinson and Nixon: Life and Death of a Political Friendship,' *New York Times*, June 6, 2014, https://www.nytimes.com/2014/06/07/upshot/jackie-robinson-and-nixon-life-and-death-of-a-political-friendship.html.

15. As quoted in Jonah Goldberg, 'Politics & Pugilists,' *Commentary Magazine*, June 1997, retrieved at: https://www.commentarymagazine.com/articles/jonah-goldberg/politics-pugilists/.

16. As quoted in Tex Maule, 'Cruel Ali with All the Skills,' February 13, 1976, retrieved at: https://vault.si.com/vault/1967/02/13/cruel-ali-with-all-the-skills.

17. As quoted in Sean Gregory, 'Why Muhammad Ali Matters to Everyone,' *Time*, June 4, 2016, retrieved at: https://time.com/3646214/muhammad-ali-dead-obituary/.

18. Starkey, 10.

19. *Life*, November 1968. See also Douglas Hartmann, *Race, Culture, and the Revolt of the Black Athlete: The 1968 Olympic Protests and Their Aftermath*. Chicago: University of Chicago Press, 2003, 298, note 85.

20. Berger, 33.

21. Ibid., 34.

22. Louis Moore, 'Jesse Owens Ran the Wrong Race: Athletes, Activism, and the 1960s,' *Sport in American History*, July 28, 2016, retrieved at: https://ussporthistory.com/2016/07/28/8552/.

23. As quoted in Ibid.

24. Ibid.

25. Ahiza Garcia, 'Why Pepsi Made "Uncle Drew" Into a Movie,' *CNN Money*, June 29 2018, retrieved at: https://money.cnn.com/2018/06/29/news/companies/pepsi-uncle-drew-movie/index.html.

26. Dunn, *'Baad Bitches' and Sassy Supermamas*, 1.

CHAPTER 17

1. Gray, *Television*, 288.

2. Kara Kovalchik, '10 Things You Might Not Know About Good Times'. Mental Floss, May 16, 2018, https://www.mentalfloss.com/article/544598/10-things-you-might-not-know-about-good-times.

3. Turner, 131.

4. 'John Amos discusses why he stopped doing Good Times,' *Foundation Interviews*, March 15, 2015, YouTube, https://www.youtube.com/ watch?v=Jm36gRGe5bo&feature=youtu.be.

5. Louie Robinson, 'Bad Times on the *Good Times* Set,' *Ebony*, September 1975, 34.

6. Ibid.

7. Ibid., 35–6.

8. Kovalchik, '10 Things You Might Not Know About *Good Times*.'

9. Turner, 53.

10. hooks, 120.

11. Von Schilling, *Magic Window*, 260.

12. Brian Lowry, 'Protests After KNX Considers "Amos 'n' Andy,"' *Los Angeles Times*, Dec. 29, 2000, https://www. latimes.com/archives/la-xpm-2000-dec-29-ca-5892-story.html.

13. Aisha Harris, 'How Amos 'n' Andy Paved the Way for Black Stars on TV,' *Slate*, September 13, 2016, https://slate.com/culture/2016/09/how-amos-n-andy-paved-the-way-for-black-stars-on-tv.html.

14. Ibid.

CHAPTER 18

1. Terence McArdle, 'MLK Was Dead.

Cities Were Burning. Could James Brown Keep Boston From Erupting, Too?' *Washington Post*, April 5, 2008, https://www.washingtonpost.com/news/retropolis/wp/2018/04/05/mlk-was-dead-cities-were-burning-could-james-brown-keep-boston-from-erupting-too/.

2. 'James Brown & His Fans at the Boston Garden (Live),' YouTube, June 19, 2013, https://www.youtube.com/watch?v=CZ2PEJGeNHw.

3. Echols, 'The Land of Somewhere Else,' 28.

4. 'Black Supporters of President Under Fire,' *New York Times*, October 17, 1972, 29.

5. Ibid.

6. Weems, 12.

7. Ibid.

8. 'Negro Spokesmen Bitter on Goldwater Nomination, Saying It Will Aid Racists; Dr. King Assails Senator's Views,' *New York Times*, July 17, 1964, 12.

9. Mehrsa Baradaran, 'The Real Roots of "Black Capitalism,"' *New York Times*, March 31, 2019, https://www.nytimes.com/2019/03/31/opinion/nixon-capitalism-blacks.html.

10. Lieberman, 'Legislative Success and Failure,' Note 32.

11. As quoted in Kotlowski, 'Black Power Nixon-Style,' 411.

12. Ibid.

13. Baradaran, *Color of Money*, 164.

14. Kotlowski, 441.

15. '1968, Nixon - The First Civil Right - political ad - closed captioned,' YouTube, February 19, 2015, https://www.youtube.com/watch?v=swyFqRB3dxY&feature=youtu.be.

16. Richard Nixon, *Statement on Establishing the Office for Drug Abuse Law Enforcement*. Online by Gerhard Peters and John T. Woolley, The American Presidency Project, https://www.presidency.ucsb.edu/node/25# 4830.

17. Baradaran, 214.

18. Lauren-Brooke Eisen and Inimai Chettiar, '39% of Prisoners Should Not Be in Prison,' *Time*, December 9, 2016, https://time.com/4596081/incarceration-report/.

19. Banner-Haley, *From du Bois to Obama*, 70.

20. Massey and Tannen, 'Suburbanization and Segregation,' 1595.

21. Vincent Canby, 'Cheers for 'Claudine',' *New York Times*, May 5, 1974, 1.

22. Banner-Haley, 66.

23. Danzy Senna, 'George Schuyler: An Afrofuturist Before His Time,' *New York Review of Books*, https://www.nybooks.com/daily/2018/01/19/george-schuyler-an-afrofuturist-before-his-time/.

24. Banner-Haley, 68.

25 Ondaatje, 61.

26. Ibid., 1.

27. See interview of Thomas Sowell, 'Black and Right,' *Salon*, November 10, 1999, https://www.salon.com/1999/11/10/sowell_2/.

28. Banner-Haley, 69.

29. Ondaatje, 16.

30. West, *Race Matters*, 52.

31. Office of Equal Opportunity and Diversity, 'A Brief History of Affirmative Action,' http://www.oeod.uci.edu/policies/aa_history.php.

32. Gabbard, 'Eddie Murphy,' 130.

33. Bogle, 285.

34. Ibid., 267.

35. Ondaatje, 12.

36. Banner-Haley, 82.

37. Robin, *Enigma of Clarence Thomas*, 3.

38. Starkey, 275.

39. 'The Thomas Nomination,' *New York Times*, October 13, 1999, 28.

40. 'Flashback – Clarence Thomas:

'It's a High-Tech Lynching for Uppity Blacks,' CNS News, September 17, 2018, https://www. cnsnews.com/news/article/cnsnewscom-staff/flashback-clarence-thomas-denies-anita-hill-allegations-calls-senate.

41. Pilgrim, 87.

42. 'Radio Host Calls Rice "Aunt Jemima,"' Associated Press, November 19, 2004, accessed January 7, 2020, https://www.foxnews.com/story/radio-host-calls-rice-an-aunt-jemima.

43. Quoted in Leonard Pitts, 'Daring to challenge groupthink rules,' *Chicago Tribune*, October 22, 2002, accessed January 8, 2020, https:// www.chicagotribune.com/news/ct-xpm-2002-10-22-0210220312-story.html.

44. 'Clinton's 'plantation' remark draws fire, CNN, January 18, 2006, accessed January 7, 2020, http://www.cnn.com/2006/POLITICS/01/17/clinton.plantation/.

45. As quoted in Ibid.

46. 'Uncle Thomas: Handkerchief Head Negro,' *Emerge*, November 1993.

47. D'Souza, *End of Racism*, 496–80.

48. As quoted in Gerber, *First Principles*, 31

49. Starkey, 274.

50. Jack E. White, 'Uncle Tom Justice,' *Time*, June 24, 2001, accessed 23 June 2019, http://content.time.com/time/magazine/article/0,9171,983080,00.html.

51. Ibid.

52. 'Dem: Yes, Clarence Thomas Is 'Uncle Tom,' *Daily Beast*, April 14, 2017, accessed June 23, 2019, https://www.thedailybeast.com/dem-yes-clarence-thomas-is-uncle-tom.

53. Reneegede, 'Why Black America Calls SCOTUS Justice Clarence Thomas "Uncle Tom"-ish,' *Urban Intellectuals*, https://urbanintellectuals.com/scotus-thomas/.

54. Dahleen Glanton, 'Justice Thomas' Story Deserves More In-depth Telling at African-American Museum,' *Chicago Tribune*, October 16, 2016, https://www.chicagotribune.com/columns/dahleen-glanton/ct-clarence-thomas-history-glanton-20161009-column.html.

CHAPTER 19

1. Danziger and Haveman, 'Reagan Administration's Budget,' 13.

2. Ronald Reagan, 'Statement on United States Immigration and Refugee Policy Online by Gerhard Peters and John T. Woolley,' The American Presidency Project, https://www.presidency.ucsb.edu/node/246714.

3. Troy, *Morning in America*, 10.

4. Ronald Reagan, 'The President's News Conference Online by Gerhard Peters and John T. Woolley,' The American Presidency Project, https:// www.presidency.ucsb.edu/node/259821.

5. Ondaatje, 6.

6. Ronald Reagan, 'Remarks in Denver, Colorado, at the Annual Convention of the National Association for the Advancement of Colored People Online by Gerhard Peters and John T. Woolley,' The American Presidency Project, https://www.presidency.ucsb.edu/node/247463.

7. Bill Kauffman, 'Freedom Now II: Interview with Clarence Thomas,' *Reason Magazine*, November 1987, https://reason.com/1987/11/01/clarence-thomas/.

8. Troy, 188.

9. Gray, 292.

10. Turner, 133.

11. '*The Cosby Show*: Cast & Details,' TV Guide, CBS Interactive Inc. Retrieved at: https://www.tvguide.com/tvshows/cosby/cast/100456/.

12. 'TV Guide's 50 Greatest TV Dads of All Time,' TV *Week*, Retrieved at: https://www.tvweek.com/in-depth/2014/01/tv-guides-50-greatest-tv-dads/.

13. John Leonard, 'Leave It to Cosby,' *New York*, October 22, 1984, p. 154.

14. Troy, 188.

15. William Raspberry, 'Cosby Show: Black or White?,' *Washington Post*, November 5, 1984, https://www.washingtonpost.com/archive/politics/1984/11/05/cosby-show-black-or-white/4ad8e415-b493-4970-b888-c35811288515/.

16. Hill Collins, *Black Sexual Politics*, 166–67.

17. Troy, 188.

18. Leonard, 'Leave It to Cosby,' 154.

19. Troy, 176.

20. Hill Collins, 131.

21. Henry Louis Gates Jr., 'TV's Black World Turns – But Stays Unreal,' *New York Times*, November 12, 1989, https://www.nytimes.com/1989/11/12/arts/tv-s-black-world-turns-but-stays-unreal.html?pagewanted=4.

22. Alexander, *New Jim Crow*, 5.

23. Ibid., 6.

24. Alexander, 98. See also Jeremy Travis, *But They All Come Back: Facing the Challenges of Prisoner Reentry* (Washington, DC: Urban Institute, 2002), 32, citing Bureau of Justice Statistics.

25. Guerrero, 163.

26. Magill, 'Celebrity Culture,' 126; 129.

27. Frank Dexter Brown, 'The 1990 Census: Will Blacks Be Counted Out?' *Black Enterprise*, February 1990, 196.

CHAPTER 20

1. Stephen Farber, 'Cable Service Dusts Off "Uncle Tom's Cabin" For TV,' *New York Times*, June 13, 1987, https://www.nytimes.com/1987/06/13/arts/cable-service-dusts-off-uncle-tom-s-cabin-for-tv.html.

2. Ibid.

3. Turner, 85.

4. John J. O'Connor, 'Uncle Tom's Cabin,' *New York Times*, June 12, 1987, accessed on May 6, 2018, https://www.nytimes.com/1987/06/12/arts/uncle-tom-s-cabin.html.

5. Turner, 69.

6. Stowe, 42.

7. Ibid., 68.

8. Bernstein, *Racial Innocence*, 5.

9. Stowe, 196.

10. Bernstein, *Racial Innocence*, 15.

11. Hill Collins, 131.

12. Wilson, *Cities and Race*, 115.

13. Ben Brantley, 'Theater Review; Topsy Returns to Confront Another Century's Legacy,' *New York Times*, November 25, 1995, 13.

14. Ibid.

15. King, 'Eastern Regionals,' 46.

16. Ibid.

17. Turner, 88.

18. David Reynolds, 'Rescuing the Real Uncle Tom,' *New York Times*, June 13, 2011, https://www.nytimes.com/2011/06/14/opinion/14Reynolds.html.

19. Sheryll Cashin, 'The Failures of Integration,' Center for American Progress, June 15, 2005, https://www.americanprogress.org/issues/courts/news/2005/06/15/1497/the-failures-of-integration/.

20. Berger, 4.

CHAPTER 21

1. Wallace Mathews, 'The Slight of the Century,' *New York Post*, August 6, 2000, https://nypost.com/2000/08/06/the-slight-of-the-century/.

2. Jenni Avins, 'Bryant Gumbel Jokes About Being Arrested at

Barneys, in Front of Barneys CEO,'
New York, Dececember 13, 2013,
http://nymag.com/intelligencer/2013/
12/bryant-gumbel-barneys-race-joke-
ceo-shoes-tank.html.

3. Henry Louis Gates Jr., 'TV's Black
World Turns – But Stays Unreal.'

4. Hill Collins, 167.

5. Ibid., 152.

6. David Hinckley, 'Untold Tale of
Legendary Fab Five Charts Controversial Group that Changed College
Basketball,' *Daily News*, March 10, 2011,
https://www.nydailynews.com/enter-
tainment/tv-movies/untold-tale-
legendary-fab-charts-controversial-
group-changed-college-basketball-
article-1.118046#ixzz2PTSfotbP.

7. Hill Collins, 155-56.

8. Leonard, *After Artest*, 146.

9. Schmid, *Golf as Meaningful Play*, 114.

10. See 'The World's Highest-Paid
Athlete,' *Forbes*, https://www.forbes.
com/athletes/list/#tab:overall and
https://www.forbes.com/profile/tiger-
woods/?list=athletes#75905fed2593.

11. 'Tiger Woods describes himself
as "Cablinasian,"' Associated Press,
April 22, 1997.

12. 'Golfer says comments about
Woods "misconstrued,"' CNN, April
21, 1997, accessed June 29, 2019, http://
www.cnn.com/US/9704/21/fuzzy/.

13. Hill Collins, 168.

14. Ibid., 170.

15. Aisha Harris, 'Why Samuel L.
Jackson's "Uncle Tom" Is Tarantino's
Best Character Yet,' *Slate*, January 8,
2013, https://slate.com/culture/2013/
01/samuel-l-jackson-in-django-
unchained-deserves-an-oscar-as-
stephen-quentin-tarantinos-best-
character-yet.html.

16. Bourree Lam, 'How To Get
Cheaper Car Insurance: Be White,' *The
Atlantic*, November 20, 2015, accessed
June 22, 2019, https://www.theatlan-
tic.com/business/archive/2015/11/
auto-insurance-race-discrimination/
416988/.

17. 'Report on the Economic Well-
Being of U.S. Households in 2013,'
Board of Governors of the Federal
Reserve System, August 15, 2014.
https://www.federalreserve.gov/econ-
resdata/2014-economic-well-being-
of-us-households-in-2013-household-
credit-behavior.htm#subsection-184-
B14E9ACA.

18. Bridget Brennan, 'The Real
Reason Women Shop More Than
Men,' *Forbes*, March 16 2013, accessed
June 22, 2019, https://www.forbes.
com/sites/bridgetbrennan/2013/03/06
/the-real-reason-women-shop-more-
than-men/#190344a374b9.

19. Hill Collins, 178.

CHAPTER 22

1. Stuart Elliott, 'Uncle Ben, Board
Chairman,' *New York Times*, March 20,
2007, https://www.nytimes.com/2007/
03/30/business/media/30adco.html.

2. 'Aunt Jemima's Historical Time-
line,' Quaker Oats Company, accessed
September 26, 2012, http://www.aunt-
jemima.com/aj_history/.

3. Manring, 172.

4. Witt, 40.

5. Manring, 178.

6. Robert J. Brown, 'Aunt Jemima
No Program for Gladys Knight,'
AdAge, October 24, 1994, accessed
January 7, 2020, https://adage.com/
article/news/aunt-jemima-problem-
gladys-knight/89595.

7. Elliott, 'Uncle Ben, Board Chairman.'

8. Ibid.

9. Andrew Clark, 'Uncle Ben
Promoted to the Board,' *The Guardian*,

March 30 2007, accessed June 20, 2019, https://www.theguardian.com/media/2007/mar/30/marketing-andpr.race.

10. Elliott, 'Uncle Ben, Board Chairman.'

11. Clark, ' Uncle Ben Promoted to the Board.'

12. As quoted in Elliott, 'Uncle Ben, Board Chairman.'

13. Joan Voight, 'Say Uncle,' *Media Post*, April 1, 2008, accessed June 20, 2019, https://www.mediapost.com/publications/article/79730/say-uncle.html.

14. As quoted in Ibid.

15. Ibid.

16. Clark, ' Uncle Ben Promoted to the Board.'

17. Gossett, *Uncle Tom's Cabin and American Culture*, 141.

18. Popeyes Chicken Sandwich TV Commercial, 'Therapist', August 17, 2019, https://www.ispot.tv/ad/dhly/popeyes-chicken-sandwich-therapist.

19. 'Chart Book: Tracking the Post-Great Recession Economy,' Center on Budget and Policy Priorities, April 29, 2020, https://www.cbpp.org/research/economy/chart-book-tracking-the-post-great-recession-economy.

20. 'Popeyes "Annie/Butterfly Shrimp Tackle Box,"' c. 2010, https://vimeo.com/10013592.

21. Maureen Morrison, 'How Annie Helped Popeyes Find Its Brand Identity – Louisiana,' June 24, 2014, accessed December 12, 2015, https://adage. com/article/cmo-strategy/annie-helped-popeyes-find-brand-identity-louisiana/293818.

22. Adams, 68.

23. Katie McFadden, 'Popeyes Lady Died? Commercial Actress Deidrie Henry Becomes Victim of Internet Death Hoax,' February 27, 2014, https://www.travelerstoday.com/articles/8966/20140227/popeyes-lady-died-commercial-actress-deidrie-henry-becomes-victim-of-internet-death-hoax-dead-die.htm.

24. 'Original "Aunt Jemima" Gone,' Reprint from Associated Negro Press in *The Dawn of Tomorrow*, September 15, 1923, 1.

25. Lauren LaBorde, 'Mapping the Louisiana Locations in Beyonce's "Lemonade," *Curbed New Orleans*, June 2, 2016, accessed January 5, 2020, https://nola.curbed.com/maps/beyonce-lemonade-louisiana-filming-locations.

26. Quoted in Joan Voight, 'Say Uncle.'

27. John Eligon, Popeyes Sandwich Strikes a Chord for African-Americans,' *New York Times*, November 5, 2019, accessed January 5, 2020, https://www.nytimes.com/2019/11/05/dining/popeyes-chicken-sand-wiches.html.

28. Ibid.

29. Joan Voight, 'Say Uncle.'

30. Barbara Lippert, 'Barbara Lippert's Critique: Uncle Ben's Problem,' *Adweek*, April 9 2007, accessed June 16, 2019, https://www.adweek.com/brand-marketing/barbara-lipperts-critique-uncle-bens-problem-88563/.

31. Priester, *Encyclopedia of Multicultural Psychology*, 461.

CHAPTER 23

1. '95 Million Watched the Chase,' *New York Times*, June 22, 1994, accessed June 29, 2019, https://www.nytimes.com/1994/06/22/us/95-million-watched-the-chase.html.

2. Kellner, *Media Spectacle*, 100–1.

3. Thussu, *News as Entertainment*, 28.

4. Deirdre Carmody, 'Time Responds to Criticism Over Simpson Cover,' *New York Times*, June 25, 1994, 8.

5. Sheila O'Malley, 'Burn Motherfucker, Burn!' *RogerEbert.com*, April 21, 2017, accessed January 8, 2020, https://www.rogerebert.com/reviews/burn-motherfucker-burn-2017.

6. *O.J. Made in America*. Dir. Erza Edelman. ESPN, 2016. Film.

7. Domonique Foxworth, 'O.J.'s 1973 Season is Best of Any Running Back – Ever,' *The Undefeated*, June 13, 2016, accessed January 8, 2020, https://theundefeated.com/features/o-j-s-1973-season-is-best-of-any-running-back-ever/.

8. Ibid.

9. Kara Swisher, 'O.J. and Hertz: The Rise and Fall of A Rent-A-Star,' *Washington Post*, July 10, 1994, accessed January 9, 2020, https://www.washingtonpost.com/archive/politics/1994/07/10/oj-and-hertz-the-rise-and-fall-of-a-rent-a-star/fcee117c-d7c1-442c-a46a-da3f3e797488/.

10. Ibid.

11. Ibid.

12. Rona Cherry, 'Hertz Is Renting O. J. Simpson And They Both Stand to Gain,' *New York Times*, November 22, 1976, accessed January 8, 2020, https://www.nytimes.com/1976/11/22/archives/hertz-is-renting-oj-simpson-and-they-both-stand-to-gain-hertz-rents.html.

13. Hobbs, *Chosen Exile*, 29.

14. Ibid.

15. Wald, *Crossing the Line*, 131.

16. Swisher, 'O.J. and Hertz.'

17. Ibid.

18. William Booth, 'Simpson Prosecutor Christopher Darden has Become the Odd Man Out,' *Washington Post*, October 6, 1995, https:// www.washingtonpost.com/archive/politics/1995/10/06/simpson-prosecutor-christopher-darden-has-become-the-odd-man-out/60379b4c-32bf-432c-9138-1e5fc1fe8222/.

19. 'Evaluating the Prosecution's Case: The O.J. Verdict,' *PBS: Frontline*, October 4, 2005, https://www.pbs.org/wgbh/pages/frontline/oj/themes/prosecution.html.

20. Boswell, 'Crossing the Racial Divide,' 238.

21. Ta-Nehisi Coates, 'What O.J. Simpson Means to Me,' *The Atlantic*, October 2016, https://www.theatlantic.com/magazine/archive/2016/10/what-o-j-simpson-means-to-me/497570/.

22. As quoted in Ibid.

23. Brando Simeo Starkey, 'Maybe Chris Darden was just doing his job,' *The Undefeated*, June 15, 2016, accessed June 23, 2019, https://theundefeated.com/features/was-chris-darden-a-race-traitor/.

24. William Claiborne, 'Issue of Racism Emerges at O.J. Simpson Hearing,' *Washington Post*, January 14, 1995, https://www.washingtonpost.com/archive/politics/1995/01/14/issue-of-racism-emerges-at-oj-simpson-hearing/6440aad1-c7a7-4f30-ab61-30c8a437f83a/.

25. Coates, 'What O.J. Simpson Means to Me.'

26. Claiborne, 'Issue of Racism Emerges at O.J. Simpson Hearing.'

27. Ibid.

28. Starkey, 'Maybe Chris Darden.'

29. Michiko Kakutani, 'A Simpson Prosecutor's View of Life and the Trial,' *New York Times*, March 26, 1996, 18.

30. 'Evaluating the Prosecution's Case: The O.J. Verdict.'

31. Christy Fisher, 'The Nightmare:

O.J. Had it All, then …' *AdAge*, June 20, 1994 https://adage.com/node/2015511/printable/print

CHAPTER 24

1. 'Condoleezza Rice at the Republican National Convention,' *Washington Post*, August 1, 2000, https://www.washingtonpost.com/wp-srv/onpolitics/elections/ricetext080100.htm.

2. Dan Balz, 'The Republicans Showcase a Rising Star,' *Washington Post*, August 1, 2000, https://www.washingtonpost.com/archive/politics/2000/08/01/the-republicans-showcase-a-rising-star/430295bb-7c08-4c39-b7ab-36a0a3de8c57/.

3. Ibid.

4. Christopher Rosen, 'Kanye West 'Spoke A Truth' About Hurricane Katrina, Says Mike Myers,' *Huffington Post*, May 21 2014, accessed January 10, 2020, https://www.huffingtonpost.ca/entry/kanye-west-mike-myers-hurrican-katrina_n_5362017?ri18n=true.

5. Walker and Smithers, *Preacher and the Politician*, 13–4.

6. 'Barack Obama's Speech on Race,' *New York Times*, March 18, 2008, accessed January 9, 2020, https://www.nytimes.com/2008/03/18/us/politics/18text-obama.html.

7. Michael Powell, 'Following Months of Criticism, Obama Quits His Church,' *New York Times*, June 1, 2008, https://www.nytimes.com/2008/06/01/us/politics/01obama.html.

8. Jeff Zeleny, 'Jesse Jackson Apologizes for Remarks on Obama,' *New York Times*, July 10, 2008, https://www.nytimes.com/2008/07/10/us/politics/10jackson.html.

9. Williams, *Muzzled*, 60.

10. Shelby Steele, 'Why Jesse Jackson Hates Obama,' *Wall Street Journal*, July 22, 2008, accessed 22 June 2019, https://www.wsj.com/articles/SB121668579909472083.

11. Ibid.

12. Ibid.

13. Ibid.

14. Frank James, 'Obama's "Stop Complaining" Order To Black Caucus Causes Stir,' NPR, September 26, 2011, https://www.npr.org/sections/itsallpolitics/2011/09/26/140802831/obama-stop-complaining-order-to-cbc-fires-up-some-folks.

15. Quoted in Ibid.

16. Michiko Kakutani, 'Playing the Game Again, With an Insider's Look at the Players,' *New York Times*, November 4, 2013, https://www.nytimes.com/2013/11/05/books/double-down-by-mark-halperin-and-john-heilemann.html.

17. Cornel West, 'Pity the sad legacy of Barack Obama,' *The Guardian*, January 9, 2017, accessed June 23, 2019, https://www.theguardian.com/commentisfree/2017/jan/09/barack-obama-legacy-presidency.

18. Sophie A. Nelson, 'Who You Callin' Uncle Tom?' *The Root*, October 30, 2009, accessed June 23, 2019, https://www.theroot.com/who-you-callin-uncle-tom-1790873576.

19. Battle and Wright, 'W. E. B. Du Bois' Talented,' 655.

20. Karen Grigsby Bates, 'A History Of Beef Between Black Writers, Artists, and Intellectuals,' NPR, April 22, 2015, accessed June 29, 2019, https://www.npr.org/sections/codeswitch/2015/04/22/401021823/a-history-of-beef-between-black-writers-artists-and-intellectuals.

21. Carroll, *Uncle Tom or New Negro?*, 3.

22. Blair L.M. Kelley, 'Rethinking Booker T. Washington,' *Ebony*, January

18, 2012, accessed June 23, 2019, https://www.ebony.com/news/rethinking-booker-t-washington/.

23. Battle and Wright, 'W. E. B. Du Bois' Talented,' 656.

24. Springarn, *Uncle Tom*, 146.

25. Ibid., 147.26. See Carroll, 10.

27. Ibid., 104–5.

28. As quoted in Pilgrim, 'Tom Caricature.'

29. Bates, 'History of Beef.'

30. 'W. E. B. Du Bois,' *The Crisis*, May 1924, 8–9.

31. Bates, 'History of Beef.'

32. '"Uncle Tom" in the Twentieth Century' in *Uncle Tom's Cabin and American Culture*, ed. Stephen Railton, http://utc.iath.virginia.edu/africam/afin20c.html.

33. 'Mr. Garvey's Speech,' *Negro World*, September 17, 1921, in *Uncle Tom's Cabin and American Culture*, ed. Stephen Railton, http://utc.iath.virginia.edu/africam/afar94at.html.

34. Stuart Jeffries, 'Angela Davis: "There is an unbroken line of police violence in the US that takes us all the way back to the days of slavery,"' *The Guardian*, December 14, 2014, accessed January 8, 2020, https://www.theguardian.com/global/2014/dec/14/angela-davis-there-is-an-unbroken-line-of-police-violence-in-the-us-that-takes-us-all-the-way-back-to-the-days-of-slavery.

35. Eugene Scott, 'What Obama Actually Said in His Rejection of Reparations,' *Washington Post*, July 9, 2019, https://www.washingtonpost.com/politics/2019/07/09/what-obama-actually-said-his-rejection-reparations/.

36. 'Interview With John McCain; Q&A With Barack Obama,' CNN *Late Edition with Wolf Blitzer*, July 27, 2008, http://edition.cnn.com/TRANSCRIPTS/0807/27/le.01.html.

37. See Ta-Nehisi Coates, '"Better Is Good": Obama on Reparations, Civil Rights, and the Art of the Possible,' *Atlantic*, December 21, 2016, https://www.theatlantic.com/politics/archive/2016/12/ta-nehisi-coates-obama-transcript-ii/511133/.

38. 'Here's What Ta-Nehisi Coates Told Congress About Reparations,' *New York Times*, June 19, 2019, https://www.nytimes.com/2019/06/19/us/ta-nehisi-coates-reparations.html.

39. '2020 Dems Back Idea of Reparations for Descendants of Slaves,' PBS *News Hour*, February 25, 2019, https://www.pbs.org/newshour/politics/2020-dems-back-idea-of-reparations-for-descendants-of-slaves.

40. Zak Cheney-Rice, 'In the 2010s, White America Was Finally Shown Itself: Ta-Nehisi Coates on "Obama's decade," reparations, and Kaepernick,' *New York*, November 25, 2019, https://nymag.com/intelligencer/2019/11/ta-nehisi-coates-on-obama-reparations-kaepernick.html.

CONCLUSION

1. See Springarn, 189.

2. See Parfait, *Publishing History*, 182. See also Bryon Gysin, *To Master – A Long Goodnight: The Story of Uncle Tom, A Historical Narrative*. New York: Creative Age Press, 1946, 199.

3. 'Epitaph [2],' in *The Collected Poems of Langston Hughes*, ed. Arnold Rampersad. New York: Knopf, 1994; originally published in *Amsterdam News*, October 8, 1941, 8.

4. Holiday, *Jazz Funeral for Uncle Tom*, 56.

SELECTED BIBLIOGRAPHY

Adams, Jessica. *Wounds of Returning: Race, Mimicry, and Property on the Postslavery Plantation*. Chapel Hill: The University of North Carolina Press, 2007.

Alexander, Michelle. *The New Jim Crow: Mass Incarceration in the Age of Colorblindness*. New York: The New Press, 2010.

Archer-Straw, Petrine. *Negrophilia: Avant-Garde Paris and Black Culture in the 1920s*. New York: Thames & Hudson, 2000.

Banner-Haley, Charles Pete. *From du Bois to Obama: African American Intellectuals in the Public Forum*. Carbondale, Illinois: Southern Illinois University Press, 2010.

Baradaran, Mehrsa. *The Color of Money: Black Banks and the Racial Wealth Gap*. Cambridge, MA: Harvard University Press, 2017.

Barlow, William. *Voice Over: The Making of Black Radio*. Philadelphia: Temple University Press, 1998.

Battle, Juan, and Earl Wright II. 'W.E.B. Du Bois's Talented Tenth: A Quantitative Assessment.' *Journal of Black Studies* 32.6 (July 2002): 654-72.

Beckert, Sven. *Empire of Cotton: A Global Industry*. New York: Alfred A. Knopf, 2014.

Belisle, Donica. *Retail Nation: Department Stores and the Making of Modern Canada*. Vancouver: UBC Press, 2011.

Berger, Martin A. *Seeing Through Race: A Reinterpretation of Civil Rights Photography*. Berkeley: University of California Press, 2011.

Bernstein, Robin. *Racial Innocence: Performing American Childhood from Slavery to Civil Rights*. New York: New York University Press, 2011.

_____. 'Children's Books, Dolls, and the Performance of Race; or, The Possibility of Children's Literature.' *PMLA* 126.1 (January 2011): 160-69.

Blackwelder, Julia K. *Styling Jim Crow: African American Beauty Training during Segregation*. College Station, TX: Texas A&M University Press, 2003.

Bogle, Donald. *Toms, Coons, Mulattoes, Mammies, & Bucks: An Interpretive History of Blacks in American Films*. 3rd ed. New York: Continuum, 2000.

Boskin, Joseph. *Sambo: The Rise and Demise of an American Jester*. New York and Oxford: Oxford University Press, 1986.

Boswell, Richard A. 'Crossing the Racial Divide: Challenging Stereotypes About Black Jurors.' *Hastings Women's Law Journal* 6 (1995): 233-40.

Brockhouse, Robert. *The Royal Alexandra Theatre: A Celebration of 100 Years*. Toronto: McArthur and Company, 2007.

Brode, Douglas. *Multiculturalism and the Mouse*. Austin: University of Texas Press, 2005.

Brody, Jennifer DeVere. *Impossible Purities: Blackness, Femininity, and Victorian Culture*. Durham and London: Duke University Press, 1998.

Carlin, Bob. *The Birth of the Banjo: Joel Walker Sweeney and Early Minstrelsy*. North Carolina and London: McFarland & Company, 2007.

Carroll, Rebecca. *Uncle Tom or New Negro?: African Americans Reflect on Booker T. Washington*, ed. Rebecca Carroll. New York: Broadway Books, 2006.

Collier-Thomas, Bettye, and V. P. Franklin. *My Soul Is a Witness: A Chronology of the Civil Rights Era, 1954-1965.* New York: Henry Holt and Co., 2000.

Collins, Bianca. 'The Preservation of History: Alison Saar,' *Journal of National Academy of Design,* March 5, 2019, https://www.nadnowjournal.org/reviews/a-preservation-of-history-alison-saar/.

Collins, Sharon M. 'The Making of the Black Middle Class.' *Social Problems* 30.4 (April 1983): 369-82.

Cohen, Carl F. *Forbidden Animation: Censored Cartoons and Blacklisted Animators in America.* Jefferson, North Carolina: McFarland Publishing, 2004 [1997].

Cox, Karen L. *Dreaming of Dixie: How the South Was Created in American Popular Culture.* Chapel Hill: The University of North Carolina Press, 2011.

Crenshaw, Kimberlé. 'Mapping the Margins: Intersectionality, Identity Politics, and Violence against Women of Color.' *Stanford Law Review* 43.6 (1991): 1241-99.

Danziger, Sheldon, and Robert Haveman. 'The Reagan Administration's Budget Cuts: Their Impact on the Poor.' *Challenge* 24 (May–June 1981): 5-13.

Davis, Angela. *Women, Race & Class.* New York: Vintage Books, 1983.

Delaney, David. 'The Space That Race Makes.' *The Professional Geographer* 54.1 (2002): 6-14.

D'Souza, Dinesh, *The End of Racism.* New York: Free Press, 1996.

Dubois, Laurent. *The Banjo: America's African Instrument.* Cambridge: Harvard University Press, 2016.

Dunn, Stephane. *'Baad Bitches' and Sassy Supermamas: Black Power Action Films.* Champaign, Illinois: The University of Illinois Press, 2008.

Durant Jr., Thomas J., and Joyce S. Louden. 'The Black Middle Class in America: Historical and Contemporary Perspectives.' *Phylon* 47.4 (4th Qtr., 1986): 253-63.

Echols, Alice. 'The Land of Somewhere Else: Refiguring James Brown in Seventies Disco.' *Criticism* 50.1 (Winter 2008): 19-41.

Ellison, Ralph. *Invisible Man.* New York: Vintage Books, [1952] 1995.

Feagin, Joe R. *The White Racial Frame: Centuries of Racial Framing and Counter-Framing.* New York: Routledge, 2010.

Foster, Cecil. *They Call Me George: The Untold Story of the Black Train Porters.* Windsor: Biblioasis Press, 2019.

'The First *Uncle Tom's Cabin* Film: Edison-Porter's Slavery Days (1903),' a Multi-Media Archive, accessed June 15, 2019, http://utc.iath.virginia.edu/onstage/films/mvo3hp.html.

Frick, John W. *Uncle Tom's Cabin on the American Stage and Screen.* New York: Palgrave Macmillan, 2012.

Gabbard, Krin. 'Eddie Murphy: The Rise and Fall of the Golden Child.' In *Acting for America: Movie Stars of the 1980s,* edited by Robert Eberwein, 120-38. New Brunswick, NJ and London: Rutgers University Press, 2010.

Gates Jr., Henry Louis. *The Signifying Monkey: A Theory of African American Literary Criticism.* New York: Oxford University Press, 1989.

Gerber, Scott Douglas. *First Principles: The Jurisprudence of Clarence Thomas.* New York: NYU Press, 1999.

Glazer, Lee, and Susan Key. 'Carry Me Back: Nostalgia for the Old South in Nineteenth-Century Popular Culture.' *Journal of American Studies* 30.1 (1996): 1-24.

Glenn, Susan A. *Female Spectacle: The Theatrical Roots of Modern Feminism.* Cambridge, MA: Harvard University Press, 2000.

Gossett, Thomas F. *Uncle Tom's Cabin and American Culture.* Dallas: Southern Methodist University Press, 1985.

Gray, Herman. *Television: The Critical View*, ed. Horace Newcomb. London: Oxford University Press, 2000.

Guerrero, Ed. *Framing Blackness: The African American Image in Film.* Philadelphia: Temple University Press, 1993.

Haley, Alex. *The Autobiography of Malcolm X.* New York: Ballantine Books, 1965.

Harrison-Kahan, Lori. *The White Negress: Literature, Minstrelsy, and the Black-Jewish Imaginary.* New Brunswick, NJ: Rutgers University Press, 2011.

Hartman, Saidiya, *Scenes of Subjection: Terror, Slavery, and Self-Making in Nineteenth-Century America.* New York: Oxford University Press, 1997.

Higginbotham, Evelyn Brooks. *Righteous Discontent: The Women's Movement in the Black Baptist Church 1880-1920.* Cambridge, MA: Harvard University Press, 1993.

Hill Collins, Patricia. *Black Sexual Politics: African Americans, Gender, and the New Racism.* New York: Routledge, 2004.

Hilhorst, Sacha, and Joke Hermes. 'We Have Given Up So Much': Passion and Denial in the Dutch Zwarte Piet (Black Pete) Controversy.' *European Journal of Cultural Studies* 19.3 (2016): 218-33.

Hine, Thomas. *The Total Package: The Evolution and Secret Meanings of Boxes, Bottles, Cans, and Tubes.* Boston: Little, Brown and Company, 1995.

Hirsch, Stephen. 'Uncle Tomitudes: The Popular Reaction to *Uncle Tom's Cabin*.' *American Studies in the Renaissance* (1978): 303–30.

Hobbs, Allyson. *A Chosen Exile: A History of Racial Passing in American Life.* Cambridge, MA: Harvard University Press, 2014.

Hochman, Barbara. *Uncle Tom's Cabin and the Reading Revolution: Race, Literacy, Child-hood, and Fiction, 1851-1911.* Amherst and Boston: University of Massachusetts Press, 2011.

———. '*Uncle Tom's Cabin* at the World's Columbian Exposition.' *Libraries & Culture* 41.1 (Winter 2006): 82-108.

Holiday, Harmony. *A Jazz Funeral for Uncle Tom.* Austin, TX: Birds, LLC, 2019.

hooks, bell. *Black Looks: Race and Representation.* Boston: South End Press, 1992.

Horwitz, Tony. 'The Mammy Washington Almost Had,' *The Atlantic*, May 31, 2013. https://www.theatlantic.com/national/archive/2013/05/the-mammy-washington-almost-had/276431/

Jeffords, Susan. *The Remasculinization of America: Gender and the Vietnam War (Theories of Contemporary Culture).* Bloomington: Indiana University Press, 1989.

Johnson, Stephen. 'Uncle Tom and the Minstrels: Seeing Black and White on Stage in Canada West prior to the American Civil War.' In *(Post)Colonial Stages: Critical & Creative Views on Drama, Theatre & Performance*, edited by Helen Gilbert, 55-63. West Yorkshire, UK: Dangaroo Press, 1999.

Jones Jr., Douglas A. *The Captive Stage: Performance and the Proslavery Imagination of the Antebellum North.* Ann Arbor: The University of Michigan Press, 2014.

Kain, John F. 'Housing Segregation, Negro Employment, and Metropolitan Decentralization.' *The Quarterly Journal of Economics* 82.2 (May, 1968): 175-97.

Kellner, Douglas. *Media Spectacle*. London and New York: Routledge, 2003.

Kern-Foxworth, Marilyn. *Aunt Jemima, Uncle Ben, and Rastus: Blacks in Advertising, Yesterday, Today, and Tomorrow*. Westport, CT: Greenwood Press, 1994.

Kibler, Alison M. *Rank Ladies: Gender and Cultural Hierarchy in American Vaudeville*. Chapel Hill and London: The University of North Carolina Press, 1999.

King, Robert L. 'Eastern Regionals.' *The North American Review* 281.2 (Mar.–Apr. 1996): 44-48.

Korkis, Jim. *Who's Afraid of the Song of the South? And Other Forbidden Disney Stories*. Orlando, FL: Theme Park Press, 2012.

Kotlowski, Dean. 'Black Power – Nixon Style: The Nixon Administration and Minority Business Enterprise.' *The Business History Review* 72.3 (Autumn 1998): 409-445.

Kwate, Naa Oyo A. *Burgers in Blackface: Anti-Black Restaurants Then and Now*. Minneapolis: University of Minnesota Press, 2019.

Lenton-Young, Gerald. 'Variety Theatre.' In *Early Stages: Theatre in Ontario 1800-1914*, edited by Ann Saddlemyer, 166-213. Toronto: University of Toronto Press, 1990.

Leonard, David J. *After Artest: The NBA and the Assault on Blackness*. New York: SUNY Press, 2012.

Lieberman, Carl. 'Legislative Success and Failure: The Social Welfare Policies of the Nixon Administration.' In *Richard M. Nixon: Politician, President, Administrator*, edited by Leon Friedman and William F. Levantrosser, 107-30. New York: Greenwood Press, 1991.

Lott, Eric. *Love and Theft: Blackface Minstrelsy and the American Working Class*. New York and Oxford: Oxford University Press, 1993.

Magill, David. 'Celebrity Culture and Racial Masculinities: The Case of Will Smith.' In *Pimps, Wimps, Studs, Thugs and Gentlemen: Essays on Media Images of Masculinity*, edited by Elwood Watson, 126-137. Jefferson, NC: McFarland & Company, 2009.

Mahar, William J. *Behind the Burnt Cork Mask: Early Blackface Minstrelsy and Antebellum American Popular Culture*. Chicago: University of Illinois Press, 1999.

Manring, M.M. *Slave in a Box: The Strange Career of Aunt Jemima*. Charlottesville: University Press of Virginia, 1998.

Massey, Douglas S. and Jonathan Tannen. 'Suburbanization and segregation in the United States: 1970–2010.' *Ethnic and Racial Studies* 41.9 (2018): 1594–1611.

Mathieu, Sarah-Jane. *North of the Color Line: Migration and Black Resistance in Canada, 1870-1955*. Chapel Hill: The University of North Carolina Press, 2010.

McClintock, Anne. *Imperial Leather: Race, Gender and Sexuality in the Colonial Conquest*. New York and London: Routledge, 1995.

McElya, Micki. *Clinging to Mammy: The Faithful Slave in Twentieth-Century America*. Cambridge, MA: Harvard University Press, 2007.

Meer, Sarah. *Uncle Tom Mania: Slavery, Minstrelsy & Transatlantic Culture in the 1850s*. Athens, GA: University of Georgia Press, 2005.

Miller, Adrian. *Soul Food: The Surprising Story of an American Cuisine One Plate at a Time*. Chapel Hill: University of North Carolina Press, 2017.

Miller, James. 'What Does It Mean to Be an American? The Dialectics of Self-Discovery in Baldwin's "Paris Essays" (1950–1961).' *Journal of American Studies*, 42.1 (2008): 51–66.

Miller, Monica. *Slaves to Fashion: Black Dandyism and the Styling of Black Diasporic Identity*. Durham: Duke University Press, 2009.

Morgan, Jo-Ann. *Uncle Tom's Cabin as Visual Culture*. Columbia and London: University of Missouri Press, 2007.

Moynagh, Maureen. 'African-Canadian Theatre: An Introduction.' In *African-Canadian Theatre: Critical Perspectives on Canadian Theatre in English*, edited by Maureen Moynagh. vol. 2, vii-xxii. Toronto: Playwrights Canada Press, 2005.

Nathan, Hans. 'The Performance of the Virginia Minstrels.' In *Inside the Minstrel Mask: Readings in Nineteenth-Century Blackface Minstrelsy*, edited by Annemarie Bean, James V. Hatch, and Brooks McNamara, 35-42. Hanover and London: Wesleyan University Press, 1996.

Nowatzki, Robert. *Representing African Americans in Transatlantic Abolitionism and Blackface Minstrelsy*. Louisiana: Louisiana State Press, 2010.

Ondaatje, Michael L. *Black Conservative Intellectuals in Modern America*. Philadelphia: University of Pennsylvania Press, 2012.

Olson, Debbie. *Black Children in Hollywood Cinema: Cast in Shadow*. London: Palgrave Macmillan, 2017.

Parfait, Claire. *The Publishing History of Uncle Tom's Cabin*. London and New York: Routledge, 2007.

Peabody, Rebecca. 'Strategies of Visual Intervention: Langston Hughes and 'Uncle Tom's Cabin.' *Comparative Literature* 64.2 (Spring 2012): 169-91.

Pickering, Michael. *Blackface Minstrelsy in Britain*. Hampshire, England: Ashgate Publishing, 2008.

Pickles, Katie. *Female Imperialism and National Identity: Imperial Order Daughters of the Empire*. Manchester: Manchester University Press, 2002.

Pilgrim, David. *Understanding Jim Crow: Using Racist Memorabilia to Teach Tolerance and Promote Social Justice*. Oakland: PM Press, 2015.

Priester, Paul. 'Uncle Tom Syndrome.' In *Encyclopedia of Multicultural Psychology*, ed. Yo Jackson, 461-2. Thousand Oaks, California: SAGE, 2006.

Quissell, Barbara Carolyn. *The Sentimental and Utopian Novels of Nineteenth Century America: Romance and Social Issues.'* PhD diss., University of Utah, 1973.

Railton, Stephen. *Topsy & Eva: The Movie*. http://utc.iath.virginia.edu/onstage/films/duncmovhp.html.

Reid, Mandy. 'Racial Profiling: Visualizing Racial Science on the Covers of *Uncle Tom's Cabin*, 1852–1928.' *Nineteenth-Century Contexts* 30.4 (December 2008): 369–387.

Riss, Arthur. *Race, Slavery, and Liberalism in Nineteenth-Century American Literature*. New York: Cambridge University Press, 2006.

Robin, Corey. *The Enigma of Clarence Thomas*. New York: Macmillan Publishers, 2019.

Roediger, David R. *The Wages of Whiteness: Race and the Making of the American Working Class*. London and New York: Verso, 2007.

Rooks, Noliwe. *Ladies' Pages: African American Women's Magazines and the Culture that Made Them*. New Brunswick, NJ: Rutgers University Press, 2004.

Russell, Hilary. *Loew's Yonge Street and Winter Garden Theatres: A Structural, Architectural and Social History*. Toronto: Historical Research Division, Canadian Parks Service, 1990.

Russell, Kathy and Midge Wilson, et al. *The Color Complex: The Politics of Skin Color Among African Americans*. New York: Anchor Books, 1992.

Sammond, Nicholas. *Birth of an Industry: Blackface Minstrelsy and the Rise of American Animation*. Durham, NC: Duke University Press, 2015.

Sánchez-Eppler, Karen. *Touching Liberty: Abolition, Feminism, and The Politics of the Body*. Berkeley: University of California Press, 1993.

Savage, Kirk. *Standing Soldiers, Kneeling Slaves: Race, War, and Monument in Nineteenth-Century America*. Princeton, NJ: Princeton University Press, 1999.

Schmid, Walter Thomas. *Golf as Meaningful Play: A Philosophical Guide*. Lanham, MD: Lexington Books, 2017.

Sedgwick, John. 'Product Differentiation at the Movies: Hollywood, 1946 to 1965.' *The Journal of Economic History* 62.3 (Sept. 2002): 676-705.

Shackel, Paul A. 'Heyward Shephard: The Faithful Slave Memorial.' *Historical Archaeology* 37.3 (2003): 138-48.

Smith, Shawn Michelle. *American Archives: Gender, Race, and Class in Visual Culture*. Princeton, NJ: Princeton University Press, 1999.

Snead, James. *White Screens, Black Images: Hollywood from the Dark Side*, edited by Colin MacCabe and Cornel West. New York: Routledge, 1994.

Southern, Eileen. 'The Georgia Minstrels: The Early Years.' In *Inside the Minstrel Mask: Readings in Nineteenth-Century Blackface Minstrelsy*, edited by Annemarie Bean, James V. Hatch, and Brooks McNamara, 163-175. Hanover and London: Wesleyan University Press, 1996.

Sperb, Jason. *Disney's Most Notorious Film: Race, Convergence, and the Hidden Histories of Song of the South*. Austin: University of Texas Press, 2013.

Sperling, Joy. 'Multiples and Reproductions: Prints and Photographs in Nineteenth-Century England – Visual Communities, Cultures, and Class.' In *A History of Visual Culture: Western Civilization from the 18th to the 21st Century*, edited by Jane Kromm and Susan Benforado Bakewell, 296-308. New York: Berg, 2010.

Spitzer, Nick. 'Monde Créole: The Cultural World of French Louisiana Creoles and the Creolization of World Cultures.' In *Creolization as Cultural Creativity*, edited by Robert Baron and Ana C. Cara, 32-67. Jackson: University Press of Mississippi, 2011.

Spingarn, Adena. *Uncle Tom: From Martyr to Traitor*. Palo Alto, CA: Stanford University Press, 2018.

Springhall, John. *The Genesis of Mass Culture: Show Business Live in America, 1840 to 1940*. New York: Palgrave Macmillan, 2008.

Staples, Shirley. *Male-Female Comedy Teams in American Vaudeville 1865-1932*. Ann Arbor: UMI Research Press, 1984.

Starkey, Brando Simeo. *In Defense of Uncle Tom: Why Blacks Must Police Racial Loyalty*. New York: Cambridge University Press, 2015.

Stowe, Harriet Beecher. *Uncle Tom's Cabin or, Life Among the Lowly*, edited by Ann Douglas. New York: Penguin Books, [1851] 1981.

Strausbaugh, John. *Black Like You: Blackface, Whiteface, Insult & Imitation in American Popular Culture*. London: Penguin Books, 2006.

Taylor, Yuval and Jake Austen. *Darkest America: Black Minstrelsy from Slavery to Hip-Hop*. New York: W.W. Norton & Company, 2012.

Thussu, Daya Kishan. *News as Entertainment: The Rise of Global Infotainment*. London: Sage Publications, 2007.

Thompson, Cheryl. *Beauty in a Box: Detangling the Roots of Canada's Black Beauty Culture*. Waterloo, ON: Wilfrid Laurier Press, 2019.

_____. '"I'se in Town, Honey": Reading Aunt Jemima Advertising in Canadian Print Media, 1919 to 1962.' *Journal of Canadian Studies* 49.1 (2015): 1-33.

Toll, Robert C. *Blacking Up: The Minstrel Show in Nineteenth-Century America*. New York: Oxford University Press, 1974.

Travis, Steve. 'The Rise and Fall of the Theatrical Syndicate.' *Educational Theatre Journal* 10.1 (Mar., 1958): 35-40.

Troy, Gil. *Morning in America: How Ronald Reagan Invented the 1980's*. Princeton: Princeton University Press, 2005

Turner, Patricia A. *Ceramic Uncles & Celluloid Mammies: Black Images & Their Influence on Culture*. Charlottesville and London: University of Virginia Press, 1994.

Tye, Larry. *Bobby Kennedy: The Making of a Liberal Icon*. New York: Random House, 2017.

Van Deburg, William L. *New Day in Babylon: The Black Power Movement and American Culture, 1965-1975*. Chicago: The University of Chicago Press, 1992.

Von Schilling, Jim. *The Magic Window: American Television ,1939-1953*. New York: Routledge, 2002.

Wald, Gayle. *Crossing the Line: Racial Passing in Twentieth-Century U.S. Literature and Culture*. Durham and London: Duke University Press, 2000.

Walker, Clarence E. and Gregory D. Smithers. *The Preacher and the Politician: Jeremiah Wright, Barack Obama, and Race in America*. Charlottesville and London: University of Virginia Press, 2009.

Wallace-Sanders, Kimberly. *Mammy: A Century of Race, Gender, and Southern Memory*. Ann Arbor: University of Michigan Press, 2008.

Weems, Robert E. *Business in Black and White: American Presidents and Black Entrepreneurs in the Twentieth Century*. New York: NYU Press, 2009.

Wernick, Andrew. *Promotional Culture: Advertising, Ideology and Symbolic Expression*. Newbury Park: Sage, 1991.

West, Cornel. *Race Matters*. New York: Vintage, 1994.

Williams, Juan. *Muzzled: The Assault on Honest Debate*. New York: Broadway Paperbacks, 2011.

Wilson, David. *Cities and Race: America's New Black Ghetto*. New York and London: Routledge, 2006.

Witt, Doris. *Black Hunger: Food and the Politics of U.S. Identity.* New York and Oxford: Oxford University Press, 1999.

Wood, Marcus. *Blind Memory: Visual Representations of Slavery in England and America, 1780-1865.* Manchester: Manchester University Press, 2000.

Wynn, Neil A. *African American Experience During World War II.* Lanham, Maryland: Rowman & Littlefield Publishers, 2010.

Whitlach, Michael D. 'The House Committee on Un-American Activities Entertainment Hearings and Their Effects on Performing Arts Careers.' PhD diss., Bowling Green State University, 1977.

IMAGE CREDITS

p. 6. Billings, Hammatt. *Title-page illustration by Hammatt Billings for Uncle Tom's Cabin [First Edition].* Illustration. Boston: John P. Jewett & Company, 1852. Public Domain.

p. 8. H. B. Stowe. *From the original painting by Chappel.* Print. New York: Johnson, Fry & Co., 1872. From Library of Congress: LC-USZ62-10476.

p. 17. *Full-page illustration by Hammatt Billings for Uncle Tom's Cabin [First Edition].* Illustration. Boston: John P. Jewett & Company, 1852. Public Domain.

p. 19. Shelton, William Henry. *Discovery of Nat Turner.* Engraving. 1831. Public domain.

p.20. *Simon Legree and Uncle Tom: A scene from the abolitionist novel, Uncle Tom's Cabin.* Illustration. 1885. Public domain.

p.24. Billings, Hammat. *Little Eva reading the Bible to Uncle Tom in the arbor.* Illustration. Boston: John P. Jewett & Company, 1852. Purchased from Alamy Stock Photo (ID: F15JCP).

p.25. Billings, Hammatt. *Tailpiece illustration by Hammat Billings for Uncle Tom's Cabin.* Illustration. Boston: John P. Jewett and Company, 1853. Public domain.

p. 33. 'Josiah Henson.' Photograph. c. 1883. Public domain.

p. 34. Clay, Edward Williams. *Cover to early edition of Jump Jim Crow sheet music.* Lithograph. New York City: E. Riley at 29 Chatham Street, 1832. Public domain.

p. 35. Sarony, Napoleon and Henry B. Major. *Christy Minstrels. Lithograph.* Boston: Oliver Ditson, 1847. From the Boston Public Library.

p. 37. *Group of men, two holding whips, pointing at two men and a woman on snow-covered bridge.* Photographic Print. 1901. From Library of Congress: LC-USZ62-56614.

p. 38. 'The Original and Only Colored Minstrel Troupe.' Advertisement. n.d. Public domain.

p. 47. Aunt Jemima Co. '1923 newspaper ad for Aunt Jemima'; *South New Berlin bee.* Advertisement. South New Berlin, Chenango County: South New Berlin Bee: 1923. Public domain.

p. 52. 'Advertisement for Cream of Wheat, featuring Rastus.' Advertisement. Used between 1901 and 1925. Public domain.

p. 53. 'Goin' Prospectin'.' Advertisement. *Chatelaine,* 1938.

p. 60. 'To Build a Monument to 'Ol' Black Mammy.' Newspaper. Chicago: Chicago Tribune, 1910. Public Domain.

p. 61. 'A scene from the movie *The Birth of a Nation* (1915).' Still. David W. Griffith Corp, 1915. Public domain.

p. 75. Delano, Jack. *Pullman porter making up an upper berth aboard the Capitol Limited, bound for Chicago, Illinois.* Photograph. From Library of Congress: LC-USW38-000050-D.

p. 99. Gould, J.J. '1930 drawing of Amos 'n' Andy for *New Movie* magazine.' Illustration. *New Movie,* 1930. Public domain.

p. 118. Parks, Gordon. *Washington, D.C. Paul Robeson, baritone.* Photograph. 1942. From Library of Congress: LC-USF34-013362-C.

p. 124. Scherman, Rowland. *Civil Rights March on Washington, D.C. [Actors Sidney Poitier, Harry Belafonte, and Charlton Heston.]*. 1963. From National Archives Catalogue (306-SSM-4D-99-22).

p. 132. Scherman, Rowland. *Civil Rights March on Washington, D.C. [Actor Ossie Davis.]*. Photograph. 1963. From National Archives Catalogue (306-SSM-4C-53-7).

p.136. Van Vechten, Carl. Portrait of James Baldwin. Photograph. 1955. From Library of Congress: LC-USZ62-42481.

p. 155. Knudsen, Robert L. *Nixon meeting with Sammy Davis Jr*. Photograph. 1973. From National Archives Catalogue (NLRN-WHPO-E0376-03A).

p. 197. Souza, Pete. *Michael Jordan receiving the Presidential Medal of Freedom from President Barack Obama at the White House in Washington D.C.* Photograph. 2016. Public domain.

ABOUT THE AUTHOR

Cheryl Thompson is an Assistant Professor at Ryerson University in the School of Creative Industries. She is the author of *Beauty in a Box: Detangling the Roots of Canada's Black Beauty Culture*. She previously held a Banting postdoctoral fellowship at the University of Toronto. Thompson is currently researching the history of blackface in Canada. In addition to her academic writing, she has published articles in the *New York Times*, *The Conversation*, *Toronto Star*, *Spacing*, *Maclean's*, and *Zoomer*. She was born and raised in Toronto, where she currently resides. She has also lived in the United States.

Typeset in Albertina and Bourton

Printed at the Coach House on bpNichol Lane in Toronto, Ontario, on Lynx Cream paper, which was manufactured, acid-free, in Saint-Jérôme, Quebec, and it was printed with vegetable-based ink on a 1973 Heidelberg KORD offset litho press. Its pages were folded on a Baumfolder, gathered by hand, bound on a Sulby Auto-Minabinda and trimmed on a Polar single-knife cutter.

Edited by John Lorinc
Designed by Crystal Sikma
Cover design by Lara Minja, Lime Design
Author photo by Calla Evans

Coach House Books
80 bpNichol Lane
Toronto ON M5S 3J4
Canada

416 979 2217
800 367 6360

mail@chbooks.com
www.chbooks.com